IMAGES
of America

KEY WEST'S DUVAL STREET

On the Cover: Don Pinder, longtime photographer for the *Key West Citizen*, took this photograph of a small parade of cars heading up Duval Street around 1960. Two young women laugh as they are swept along on the hood of the second car. On the left is the street's most famous bar, Sloppy Joe's. (Courtesy of Monroe County Library, Key West.)

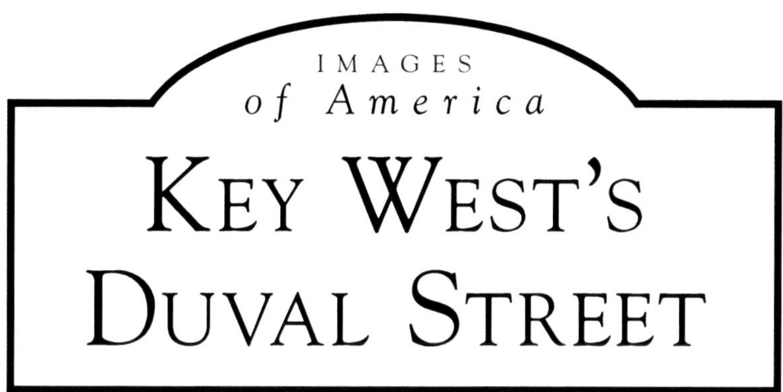

Laura Albritton and Jerry Wilkinson
Foreword by Tom Hambright

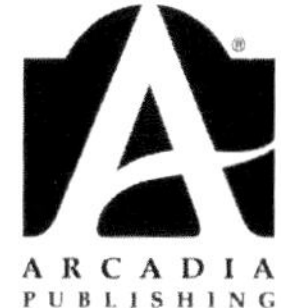

ISBN 978-1-4671-2685-4

Published by Arcadia Publishing
Charleston, South Carolina

Printed in the United States of America

Library of Congress Control Number: 2017933421

For all general information, please contact Arcadia Publishing:
Telephone 843-853-2070
Fax 843-853-0044
E-mail sales@arcadiapublishing.com
For customer service and orders:
Toll-Free 1-888-313-2665

Visit us on the Internet at www.arcadiapublishing.com

For my father, Dallas Albritton, who passed on his love of travel, writing, and Ernest Hemingway.

—L.A.

To my wife, Mary Lou Wilkinson, for her lifelong support.

—J.W.

Contents

Foreword

Duval Street grew with Key West, from its humble beginning as a footbridge across a salt pond to one of the world's most famous streets. After the hurricane of 1846, the city ordered the salt pond filled and Duval Street was able to expand. With the addition of the Russell Hotel, the first hotel on the island, Duval Street became the center of the city's commercial district.

Because Key West remained loyal to the Union during the Civil War, it became the largest city in Florida. With both naval headquarters (located at the harbor end of Duval Street) and Army headquarters (on Front Street near Duval Street), Key West became the center of military power for South Florida and the Caribbean.

Refugees fleeing the revolution in Cuba turned Key West into the center of the hand-rolled Cuban cigar industry, a leading local employer until the late 1920s. The San Carlos Institute on Duval Street was the center of Cuban entertainment and education.

The Great Fire of 1886 touched Duval in several places, but the booming economy allowed the city to rebuild in record time. The commercial district continued to grow, especially around the San Carlos, while the affluent built homes on the 300 and 400 blocks of Duval Street.

The world and Key West changed with the Spanish-American War in 1898. Duval Street flourished with the naval station's expansion and Henry Flagler's decision to build a railroad to the city. The construction of the Southernmost House at the ocean end of Duval Street completed the street from sea to sea.

World War I also saw a Navy training base at the harbor end of Duval, but later, the hurricane of 1919 led to the closing of the naval air station. Americans began smoking cigarettes, and the cigar industry faltered. Along with the rest of the nation, the city slipped into the Great Depression, which left the city and county governments bankrupt.

As World War II revived Key West, Duval Street became the center of business and entertainment for the 10,000 newly-arrived Navy men and women. This boom would last until the late 1960s, when businesses began moving to new shopping centers on the eastern end of the island. In a major military cutback, the naval station closed in 1974 and about half the people and jobs left the Lower Keys. Duval Street was then littered with closed or failing stores, bars, and businesses. Ultimately, tourism saved the economy, and Duval became internationally famous as the "Longest Street that Runs from the Atlantic Ocean to the Gulf of Mexico."

—Tom Hambright
Monroe County historian

Acknowledgments

We would like to express our gratitude to Tom Hambright, Monroe County historian and archivist at the Monroe County Library at Key West, for his invaluable help and cooperation in writing this book. We would like to thank the library and its staff for making historical images from its collections (including those of Wright Langley, Don Pinder, Ray Blazevic, Scott DeWolfe, Jeff Broadhead, and the Heritage House) accessible to researchers and the public. Our thanks also extend to Dr. Diane Silvia, executive director of the Historic Florida Keys Foundation; the State Archives of Florida; photographer Zickie Allgrove; organizer extraordinaire Mary Lou Wilkinson; and the Vassar College Libraries. Last but certainly not least, we wish to thank everyone at Arcadia Publishing who has made this book possible, including Mike Kinsella, Liz Gurley, Jonny Foster, Jim Kempert, and Crystal Murray.

Introduction

Duval Street, the very heart and soul of historic Key West, is one of the most legendary thoroughfares in the United States. Stretching one-and-a-quarter miles through Old Town, from the Atlantic Ocean to the Gulf of Mexico, this iconic avenue has seen everyone from Mark Twain and Ulysses S. Grant to Ernest Hemingway. The oldest house that survives in Key West—now a museum—is situated right here. Key West's oldest church, St. Paul's, rose up here, as did America's "Southernmost House," a gloriously imposing Queen Anne–style mansion. A movement for Cuban independence gained steam inside the San Carlos Hall, located on Duval Street. A famous theater, the Strand, flourished in an ornate building that still stands. Buildings that would soon become Key West landmarks, like the red-and-yellow brick First National Bank and La Concha hotel, appeared on the street as the city grew.

During Prohibition, Duval Street's speakeasies supplied patrons with smuggled rum and whiskey. After Prohibition's repeal in the 1930s, writer Ernest Hemingway made its bar Sloppy Joe's nationally famous. That fabled watering hole, along with others like the Cabaña Cocktail Lounge, turned Duval into a destination where alcoholic libations were consumed with near-religious fervor. Nevertheless, in the 1940s and 1950s, the avenue was hardly a one-dimensional party street: private homes, many of them beautifully constructed and ornamented, still existed, as did regular shops where residents could buy groceries or get a haircut. Yet it is undeniable that Duval became synonymous with rollicking good times. In more recent decades, Duval Street has hosted the floats and revelers of Fantasy Fest, an exuberant celebration that could only take place on this offbeat tropical island.

In the classic 1942 film *Casablanca*, Captain Renault remarks that "everybody comes to Rick's," but in Key West, on the other hand, everybody seems to wind up on Duval Street. The question of how and why Duval Street came to occupy such an outsized place in so many people's affections will be explored through archival images and accompanying captions in this book.

Despite its fame today, Duval Street had relatively modest beginnings. In 1829, a young William Whitehead laid out a grid of streets in Key West and assigned them names. He named Duval for William Pope Duval, then Florida's territorial governor and one of the most influential men in the region. Due to Key West's geography at that time, Duval Street was not the long, impressive avenue that it is today. In fact, a good portion of Duval that exists now (the southern section that extends to the Southernmost House) had not been cleared. Only the northern portion could be considered a "street."

From the 1820s through the 1840s, a tidal pond submerged part of present-day Duval Street. Stretching along Duval Street south of Front Street to Caroline Street, this pond only reached a depth of about 18 inches, making it much too shallow to bring in a boat and just deep enough to be an annoyance to local citizens. The body of water was connected to a larger lagoon, and depending on the tide, the pond's depth fluctuated. According to Key West native Jefferson Browne, the solution townspeople found to this obstacle was to build a wooden footbridge over the water "made of piles and covered with planks," which "commenced within about 100 feet of the corner of Duval and Front Streets." Thus, much of the original Duval Street was in fact a pedestrian footbridge. In 1838, William Whitehead, the original surveyor, drew a sketch that clearly shows the Duval bridge rising just above the water and an uncleared expanse of land to the south.

In 1846, a powerful hurricane swept across Key West as it drowned citizens, uprooted graves, destroyed homes, and carried in quantities of sand. When the storm subsided, the tidal pond, which still covered Duval Street, had been cut off from its source of seawater. Now, Duval Street had to contend with a body of water that was not flushed out regularly by the sea, which made it a perfect breeding ground for mosquitoes.

Around 1853, the city decided to get rid of this watery nuisance; Duval Street residents filled in the remaining pond so that the street could run unimpeded through the heart of the town. The footbridge disappeared, and newly-created dry land meant that there was more room on Duval Street for both private homes and businesses. This development marked a turning point in Duval Street's history.

Before William Whitehead's 1829 survey, Whitehead Street had been known locally as "Main Street," yet now, Duval Street gradually became Key West's de facto main street. Millionaires built their mansions here, while thriving retail stores advertised sales and high-quality goods, from harnesses for horses to corsets and everything in between. At the northern end, a busy harbor saw the importation of freight and the arrival of visitors (an event sometimes heralded in the local newspaper). Although Duval Street boasted saloons from its early days, two of Key West's most distinguished churches, the Episcopal St. Paul's and the Catholic St. Mary's Star of the Sea, could be found here as well.

In the second half of the 19th century, schoolchildren attended lessons at the island's first school inside the Patterson-Baldwin house on Duval Street. Cuban immigrants who fled their own island and Spanish imperialism founded a Cuban cultural center, the San Carlos Hall (later Institute), on Duval, where members strategized about how to win independence. Duval Street was additionally home to one of Key West's first hotels, the Russell House, and later, the imposing Jefferson Hotel. After the turn of the 20th century, Duval Street's theaters hosted plays and musical nights, and eventually, that sensational new phenomenon, silent films.

The people who lived and did business on the street were as varied and complex as the street's history: Bahamian seafarers, New England matrons, Southerners whose loyalty remained firmly with the Confederacy during the Civil War, British barkeeps, and Cuban cigar factory owners. According to South Florida developer George Merrick, local Conchs (descendants of Bahamians) even had their own way of pronouncing the avenue's name: because they transposed or reversed "v's to w's," Duval Street sounded like "Duwal."

The hurricane of 1846 was hardly the only act of nature to alter Duval Street. The Great Fire of 1886 obliterated sections of the avenue and left large gaps in the cityscape. But determined Key Westers rebuilt; soon, a new St. Paul's church and a new San Carlos rose from the ashes. In 1909, another hurricane brutalized the island and wrecked establishments along Duval, as did yet another in 1919. Duval Street's beautiful wooden buildings have been threatened by fire for just short of two centuries, and many landmarks, such as the Jefferson Hotel and the Caroline Lowe house, have fallen victim to conflagrations.

When the Overseas Railroad's first train pulled into Key West in January 1912, thereby connecting Key West with the mainland for the first time and greatly reducing the island's isolation, a grand parade processed down Duval Street. Key Westers also turned out in numbers to watch military personnel march on Duval during World Wars I and II. History was both made and commemorated on Key West's central avenue.

The street proved irresistible, not only to the sailors and soldiers stationed in Key West, but also to the literary crowd. One of the first well-known writers to be recorded on Duval was American novelist and humorist Mark Twain, who attended services at St. Paul's Episcopal. Decades later, Ernest Hemingway befriended Joe Russell when Sloppy Joe's bar was still on Greene Street, then loyally transferred his custom to the new location on Duval in 1937. Hemingway brought along his "mob" of friends, including writer John Dos Passos. When Hemingway departed Key West in 1939 after separating from his wife, Pauline Pfeiffer, he left several of his belongings in a storage room at Sloppy Joe's.

American playwright Tennessee Williams was another writer who indulged in nights out at Sloppy Joe's; he even mentions the bar in a letter to a friend. Williams also enjoyed himself at Casa Cayo Hueso, a nightclub housed for a time in the Southernmost House. Williams's connections to Duval Street go even deeper: it was in a La Concha hotel guestroom that he completed his brilliant play *A Streetcar Named Desire*. When another of his plays, *The Rose Tattoo*, was being filmed, scenes were shot inside the louche Mardi Gras nightclub at 92 Duval Street.

Pulitzer Prize–winning poet Elizabeth Bishop regularly danced the rumba at Sloppy Joe's on Duval Street with her partner, Louise Crane. In an era when it was dangerous for gay men and women like Williams and Bishop to express their sexual orientation openly, Duval Street and Key West offered something of a refuge, albeit an imperfect one. Later on, in 1978, the Key West Business Guild, a gay-oriented chamber of commerce, began promoting tourism and played a role in the economic recovery of Duval Street. Additionally, discos, drag shows, and cabarets brought a new sparkle to the street's nightlife.

Music and musicians have long been a vital ingredient of the street's allure, from jazz bands trumpeting the end of Prohibition to disco stars singing pop anthems to packed nightclubs. Jimmy Buffett played his first Key West gigs inside Duval Street's Chart Room bar at the Pier House; the same bar also witnessed performances by reggae legend Bob Marley. Today, at watering holes like Buffet's Margaritaville, Irish Kevin's, the Bull and Whistle, Sloppy Joe's, and Rick's, the music never seems to stop.

Almost every kind of human drama has played out on Duval Street: births, deaths, baptisms, graduations, romances, artistic expression, protests, politicking, hard partying, religious worship, preparations for war, and celebrations of peace. Over 180 years after Duval Street first appeared on a map, the street's architecture remains elegant, and its spirit irrepressible. This one-and-a-quarter mile stretch of asphalt, extending from ocean to gulf, continues to be cherished as an oasis for escape artists, history lovers, and dreamers.

One

EARLY DAYS

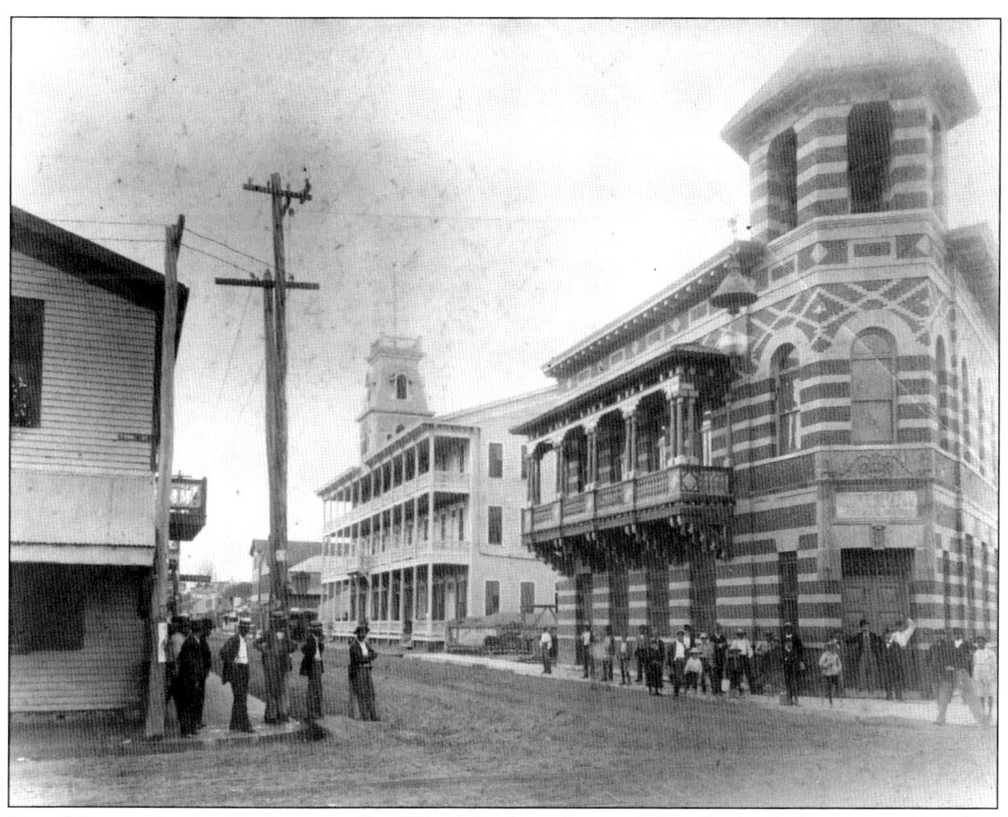

Duval Street, destined to become Key West's liveliest thoroughfare, had a fairly quiet and modest beginning in the first half of the 19th century. By the 1890s, however, businesses proliferated and grand establishments rose up on Duval's southern and northern ends. (Courtesy of Monroe County Library, Key West.)

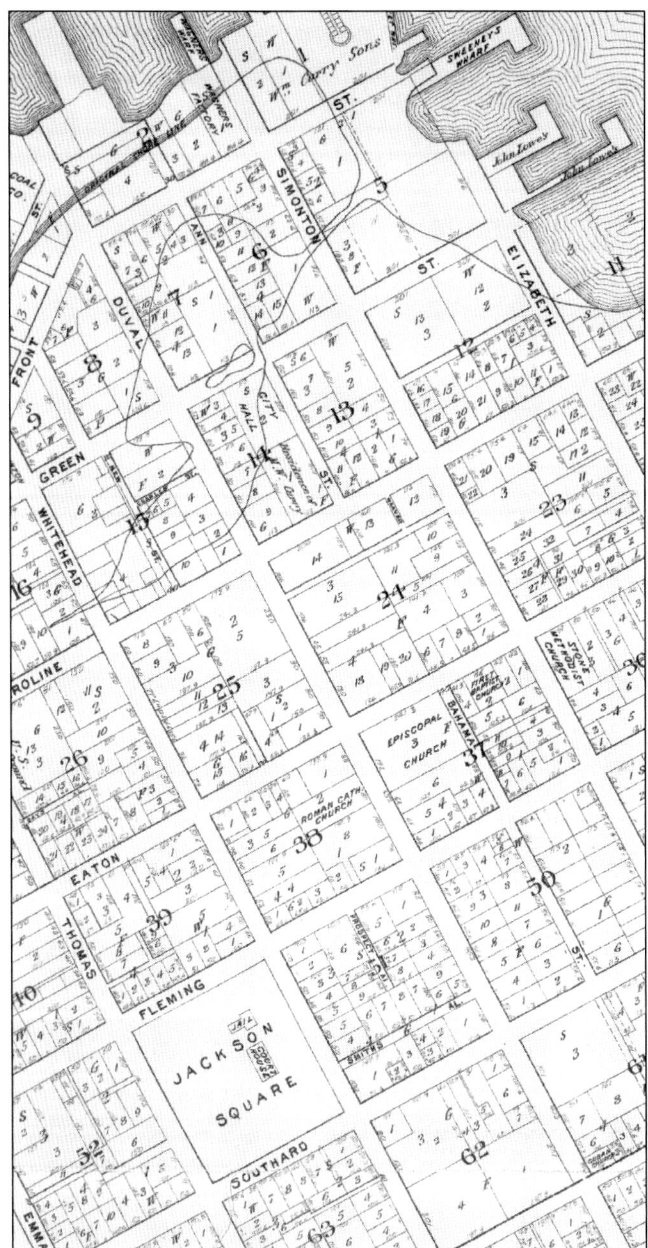

In 1829, a young man named William Whitehead, brother of early Key West pioneer John Whitehead, was given a daunting task. With little to no experience, he had to create a network of city streets around a collection of already-existent buildings. As William laid streets out in a thoughtful grid, some were named after his family (Caroline, William, Thomas, Margaret, Emma, and Whitehead), while others were named after Key West property owners (Simonton, Greene, and Fleming). Still other streets were named for well-known public figures. Duval Street (shown here on a map adapted from Whitehead's initial survey) was named for William Pope Duval, the first civilian governor of the Florida Territory. The detail from this later map shows Duval Street with two churches between Eaton and Fleming Streets: the Roman Catholic church and the Episcopal church. (Courtesy of the Library of Congress.)

This photograph shows an older William Whitehead, who gave Duval Street its name. Key West's first surveyor would go on to serve as the collector of customs and also as mayor, but resigned after townspeople objected to a new tax. In 1838, he left Key West for New York. (Courtesy of the Monroe County Library, Key West.)

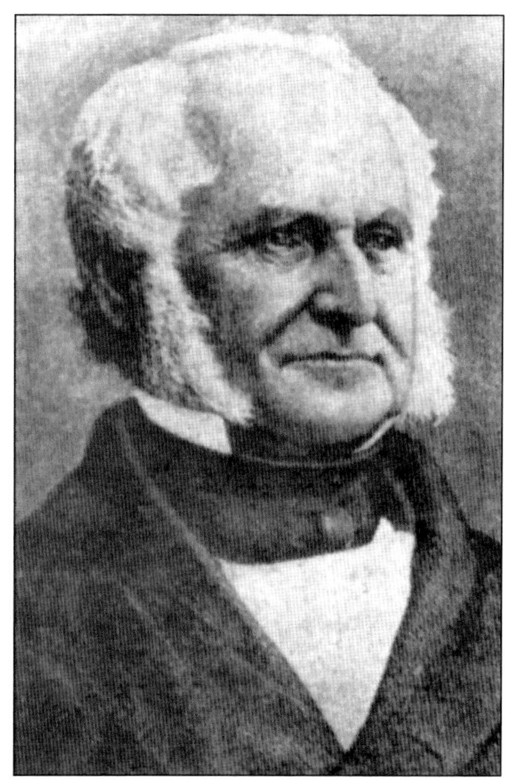

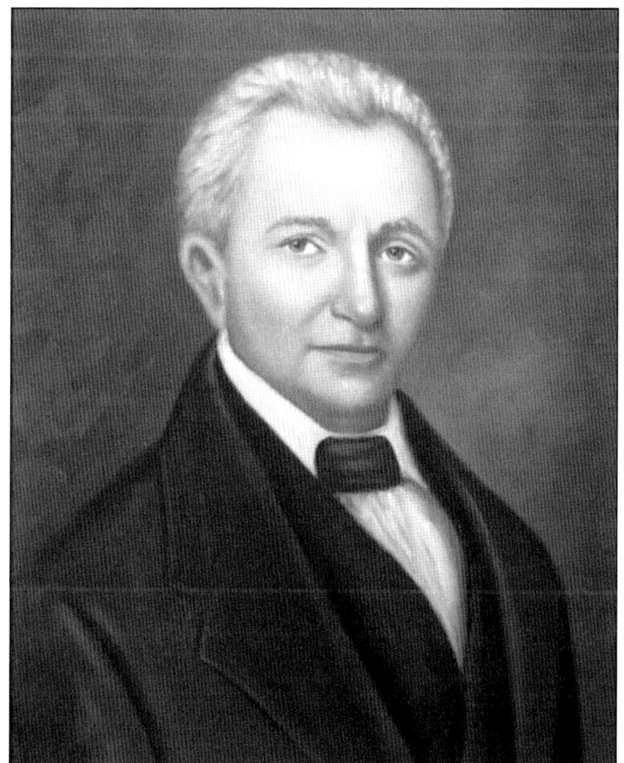

William Pope Duval, the man Duval Street was named for, had quite a career. Born in Virginia, Duval studied law in Kentucky and won election as a Kentuckian representative to the 13th US Congress in 1812. In 1822, Pres. James Madison appointed him governor of the newly acquired Florida Territory. Governor Duval selected Tallahassee as the capital and served in office until 1834. (Courtesy of the State Archives of Florida.)

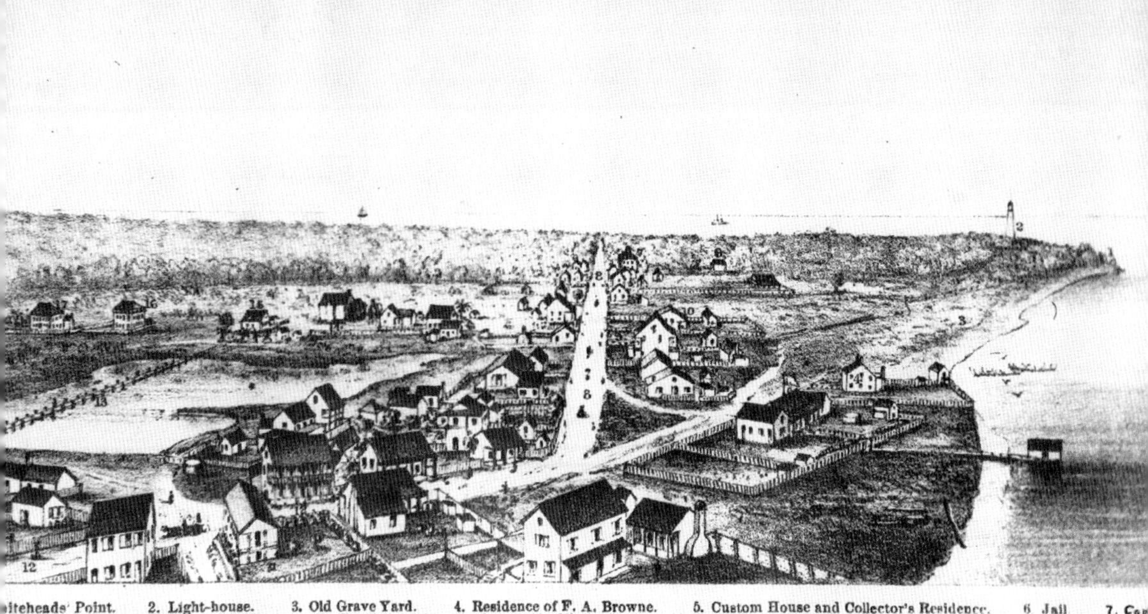

In 1838, nine years after his original survey, William Whitehead sketched a town that had grown considerably. From the cupola of Asa Tift's warehouse, he had an excellent view of the houses and streets that comprised Key West. Visible on the far left is the footbridge that crossed a shallow tidal pond covering part of Duval Street. The footbridge stretched along Duval from Front Street to about Caroline Street, or approximately two city blocks. According to Jefferson B. Browne's *Key West: The Old and the New*, "The depth of water varied with the ebb and flow of the tide, but it was generally about twelve to eighteen inches deep." Browne also notes that "Duval street was only cleared about half way between Eaton and Fleming street as late as 1836." In 1846, a hurricane carried mounds of sand to this part of the island, which blocked off the tidal pond from a large lagoon. As a result, townspeople filled in those watery sections of Duval; the footbridge, no longer needed, was removed. (Courtesy of Monroe County Library, Key West.)

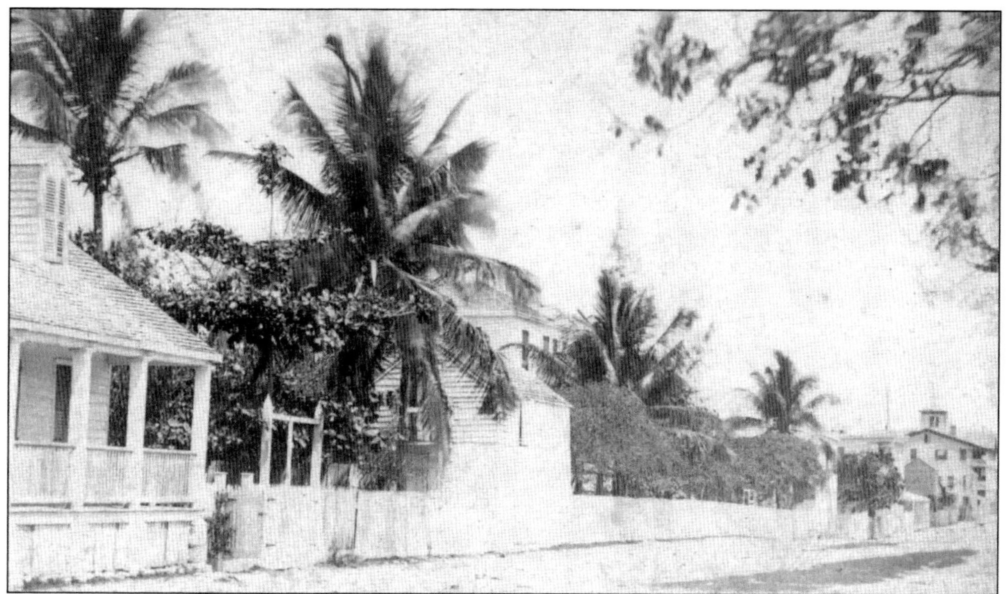

In 1829, Bahamian settler Richard Cussans constructed this home (far left) of Cuban cedar on Whitehead Street. By 1836, the house had been moved on timber rollers to Duval Street. William Wall and then Nicholas Herder owned the home, until in 1869 it was deeded to the Watlingtons. It has survived fires and hurricanes to become Key West's "Oldest House." (Courtesy of Monroe County Library, Key West.)

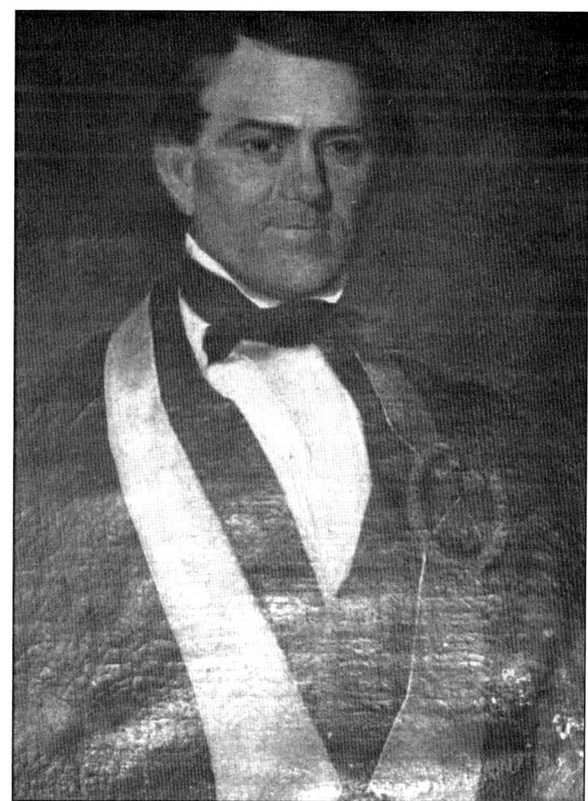

In the 19th century, sea captain and harbor master Francis Watlington lived at 322 Duval Street with his wife, Emeline, and their daughters. The Watlingtons' daughter Lily lived in Key West's Oldest House until she died in 1936. Today, the house has been restored and operates as a museum. (Courtesy of Monroe County Library, Key West.)

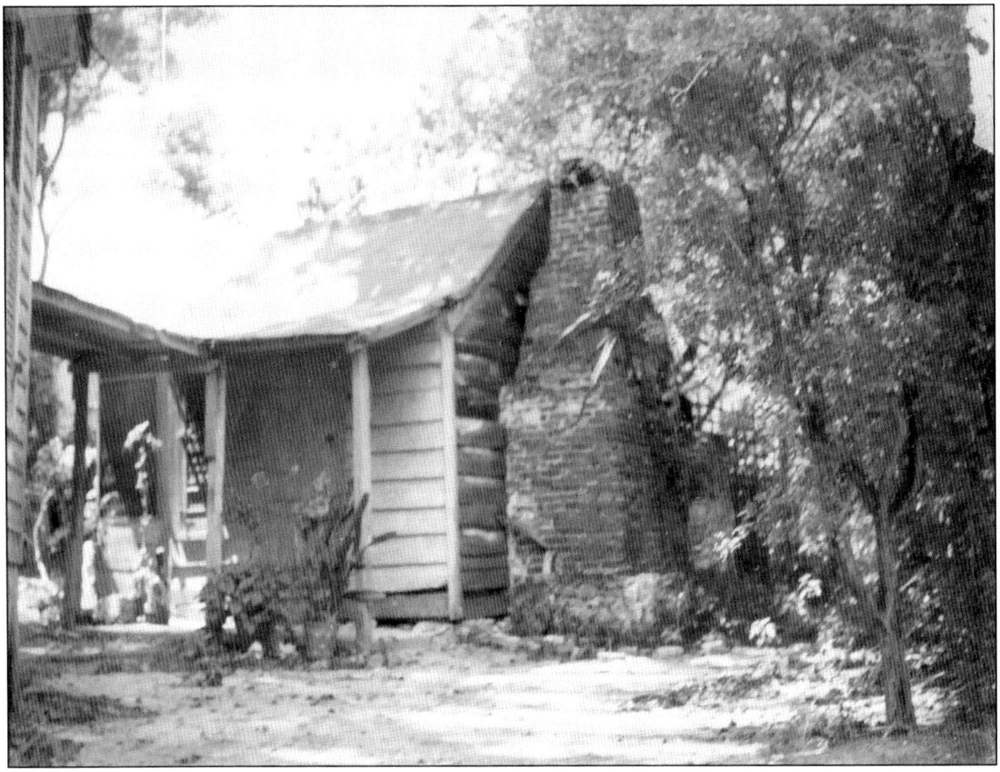

Behind the Oldest House was a cookhouse. These cookhouses were common in Key West and throughout the South because open cooking fires posed a serious hazard. It was wiser to confine cooking to a separate building to reduce the chances of the main house catching fire. Also, cooking created an infernal heat, which became truly unbearable in a hot Key West summer. (Courtesy of Monroe County Library, Key West.)

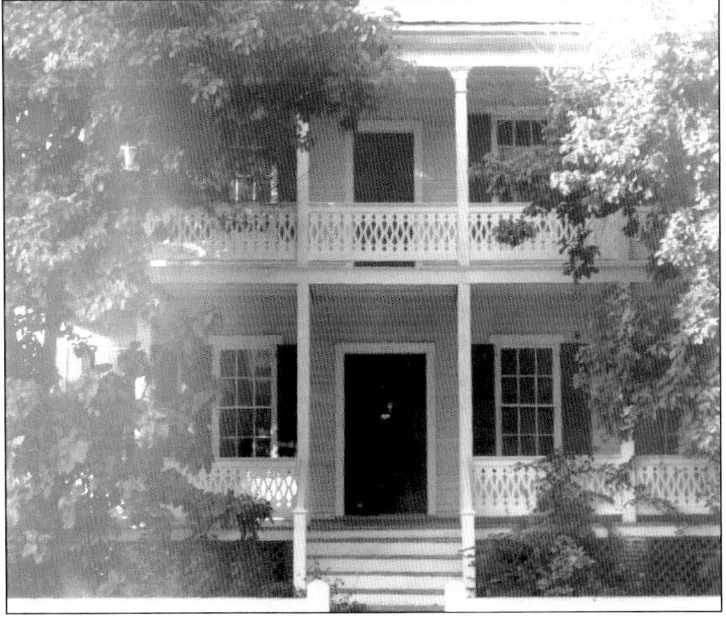

Near the Oldest House stands the "Oldest Schoolhouse," also called the Patterson-Baldwin House, at 336 Duval Street. It was moved to its present location in 1847 by owner and then mayor Alexander Patterson. A Madame Passaloque gave children lessons here from 1847 until 1860, when John Baldwin bought and expanded the property. Baldwins continued to own the home for 102 years. (Courtesy of Monroe County Library, Key West.)

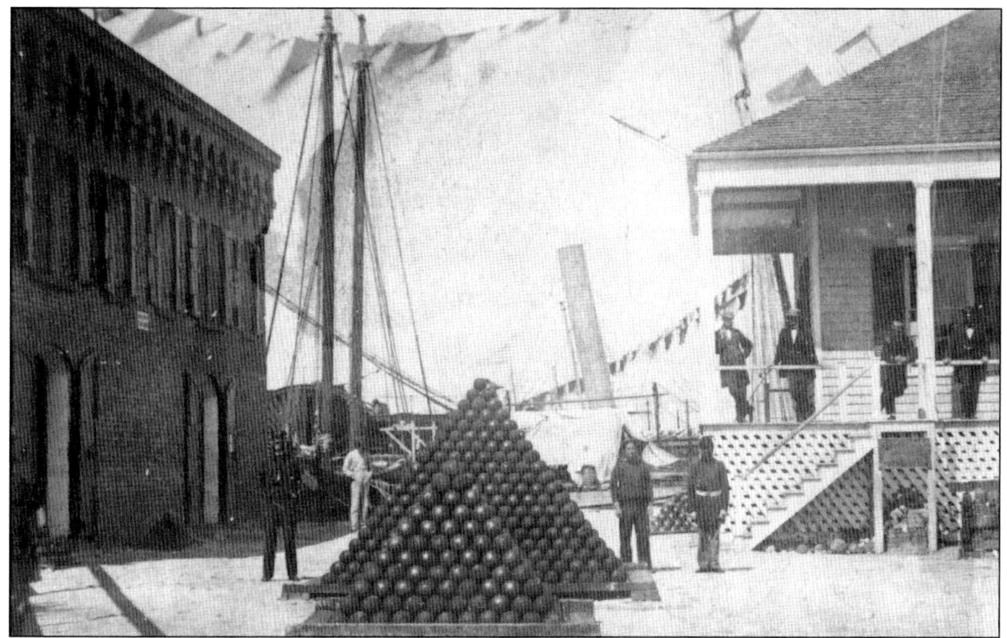

Men pose next to cannonballs stored at the naval headquarters on Duval Street during the Civil War. When the South seceded, Union forces secured Fort Zachary Taylor. Later, troops from New York and Pennsylvania were stationed on the island. Key West was the only southern town held by the Union for the war's duration. (Courtesy of Monroe County Library, Key West.)

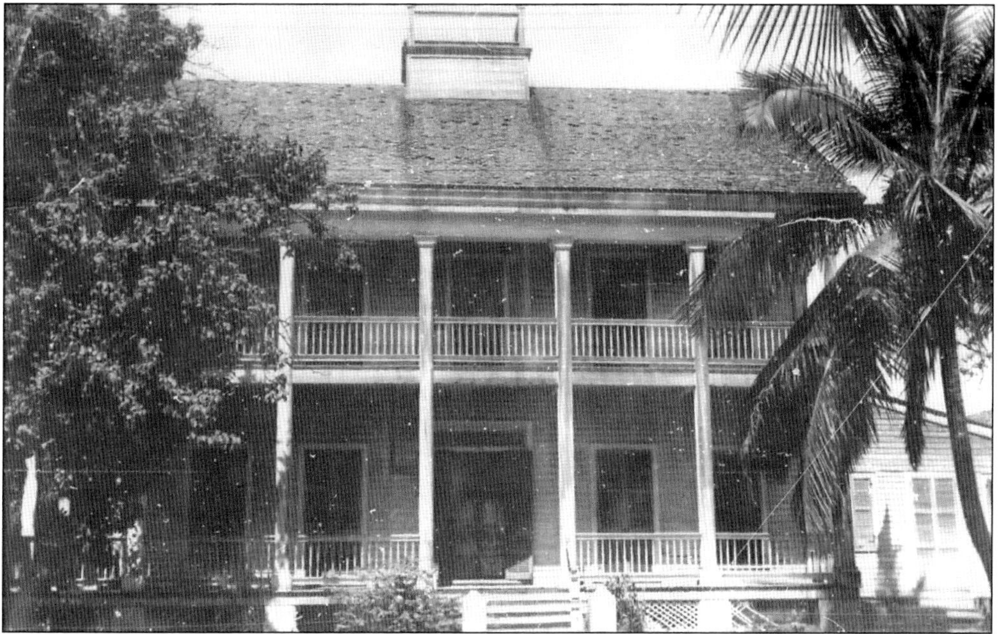

According to local lore, this house, which stood at 303 Duval Street, was home to a passionate Confederate sympathizer. Caroline Lowe defiantly flew the Stars and Bars from her house during a parade. Later, Union soldiers searched for but never found the flag, which Caroline had hidden in a secret compartment. Many in Key West supported the rebel cause; some men even sailed to Tampa to enlist. (Courtesy of Monroe County Library, Key West.)

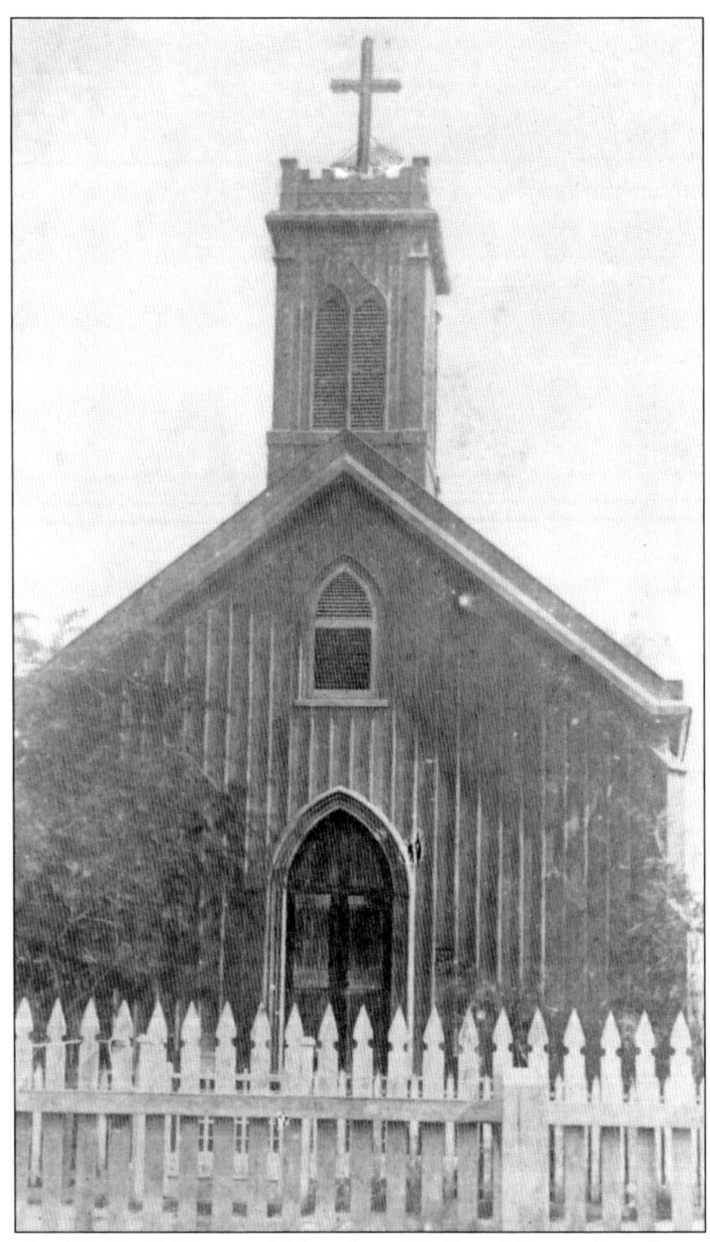

This photograph of St. Paul's Episcopal Church at 401 Duval Street dates from the Civil War. St. Paul's was the first church established in Key West, in 1831. Its first service was held in 1832, the same year that early settler Mary Rotch Fleeming (or Fleming) donated land for a church site. Her husband, John, had been buried on the property, and she asked that his grave not be moved. (It was not, although its exact location is not known today.) The first St. Paul's building, constructed of native coral rock, was completed in 1839. A mere seven years later, a hurricane demolished that structure. By 1848 a new, wooden church had been erected; it measured 28 feet wide by 66 feet long. Key West chronicler Jefferson Browne recalls that four pews at the back of the church were set aside for slaves and free people of color. In 1866 or 1867, writer Mark Twain attended services here and reported on the stylishness of its congregation. (Courtesy of Monroe County Library, Key West.)

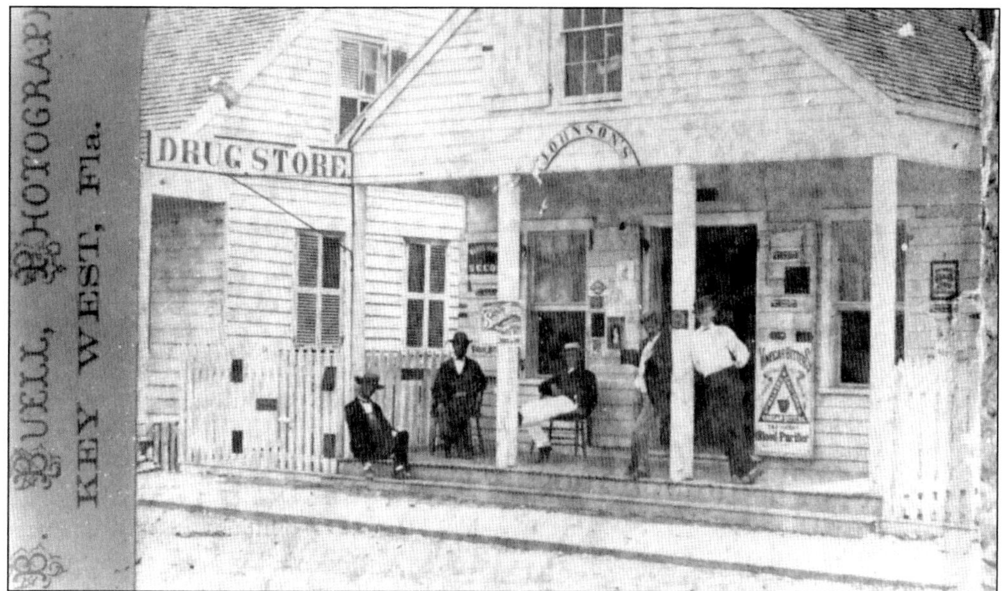

Five gentlemen lounge in front of Johnson's Drugstore on Duval Street around 1870. Signs advertise items such as seeds, soda water, and Dr. Walker's California Vinegar Bitters. The store was lodged inside a one-and-a-half story house with a wood shingle roof. The widespread use of wood as a roofing material in Key West would result in dire consequences 16 years later. (Courtesy of Monroe County Library, Key West.)

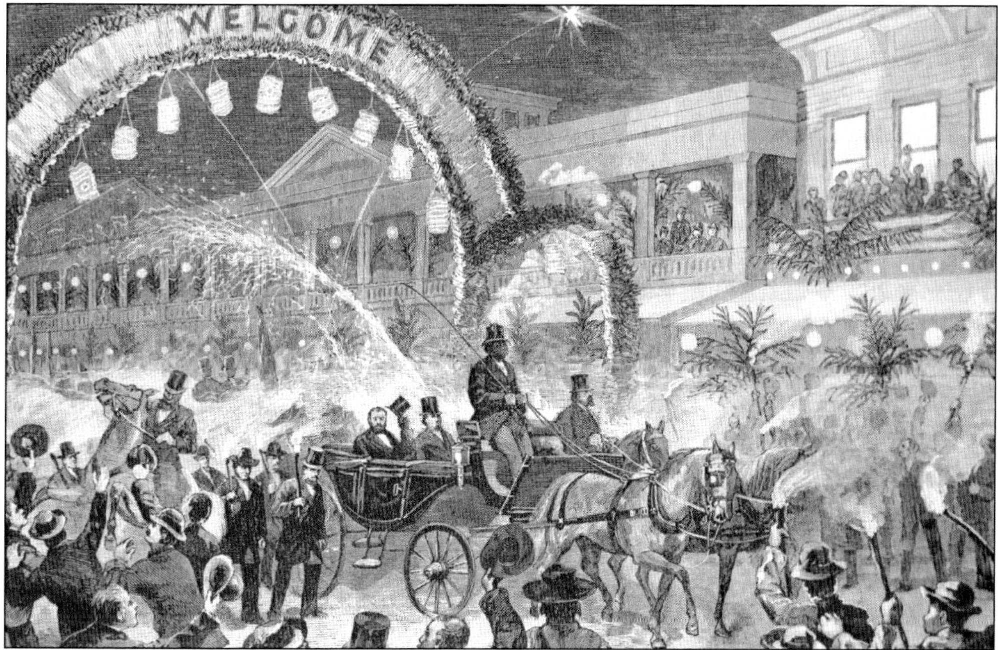

On his 1880 around-the-world trip with Gen. Phil Sheridan, former president Ulysses S. Grant visited Key West. Here, Grant rides under a welcome arch erected beside the Russell House hotel on Duval Street. The city also threw a reception and banquet in Grant's honor, and businesses closed to celebrate the occasion. Presumably, even some former Confederates turned out to cheer the famous man. (Courtesy of the State Archives of Florida.)

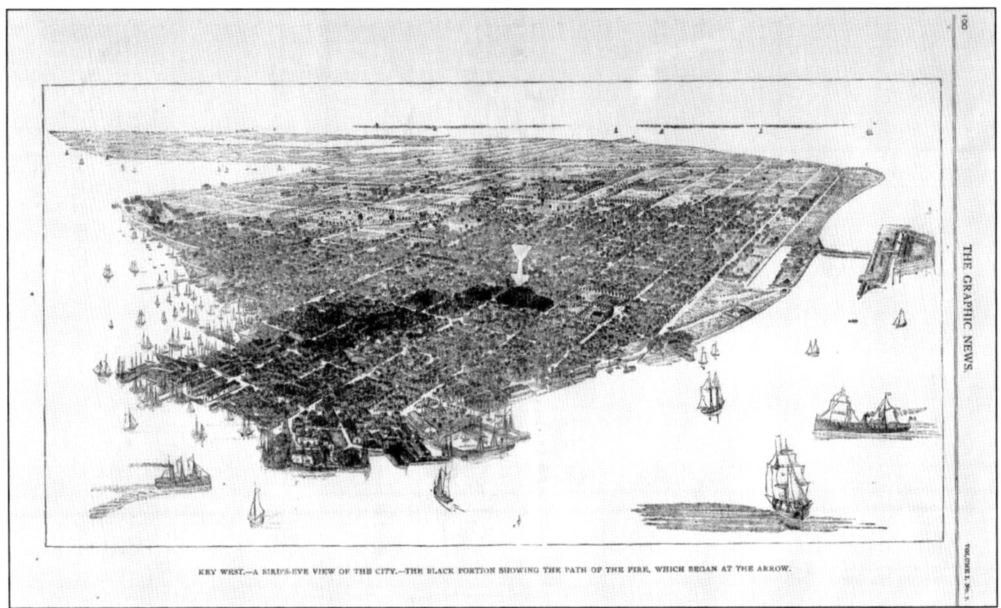

Key West's Great Fire of 1886 caused extreme devastation, particularly on Duval Street. The fire began on Fleming Street at the San Carlos Hall, a meeting place for Cuban expatriates, and quickly spread, with flames leaping from wooden roof to wooden roof. Rumors emerged that Spanish agents had deliberately started the fire to punish Key West's Cubans for supporting revolution. (Courtesy of Monroe County Library, Key West.)

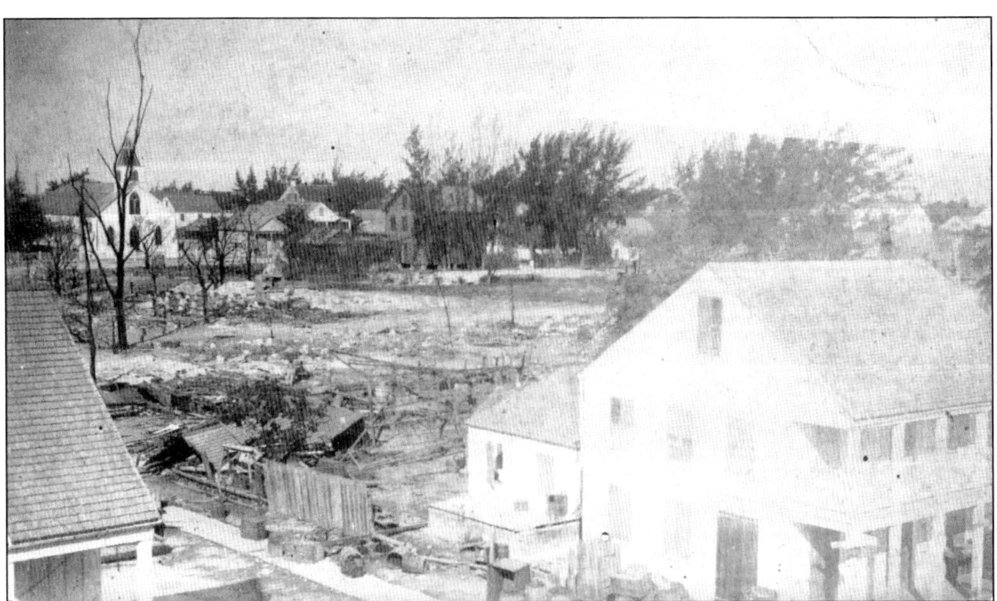

Key West's one fire engine had been sent out of town for repairs; when the Great Fire of 1886 broke out, it rampaged through the streets almost unhindered. Whole swaths of the city disappeared overnight. Looking from Fleming Street toward Duval, the photographer captured the desolation and St. Mary Star of the Sea Catholic Church (at that time on Duval Street), which miraculously survived. (Courtesy of Monroe County Library, Key West.)

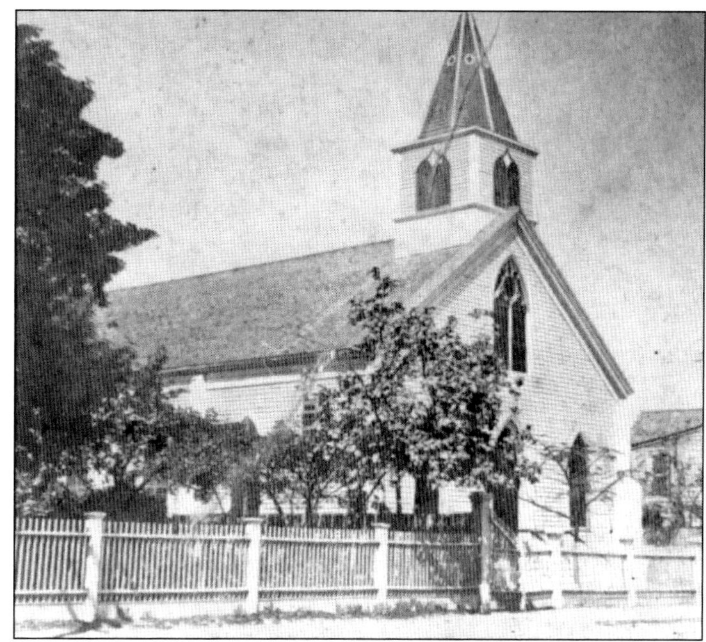

Built in 1852, St. Mary Star of the Sea Catholic Church stood at 406 Duval Street. Before emancipation, slaves attended services here along with whites and free people of color. When yellow fever broke out in Key West between 1850 and 1860, several priests died. After a fire destroyed it in 1901, the church was rebuilt at a new location on Windsor Lane. (Courtesy of Monroe County Library, Key West.)

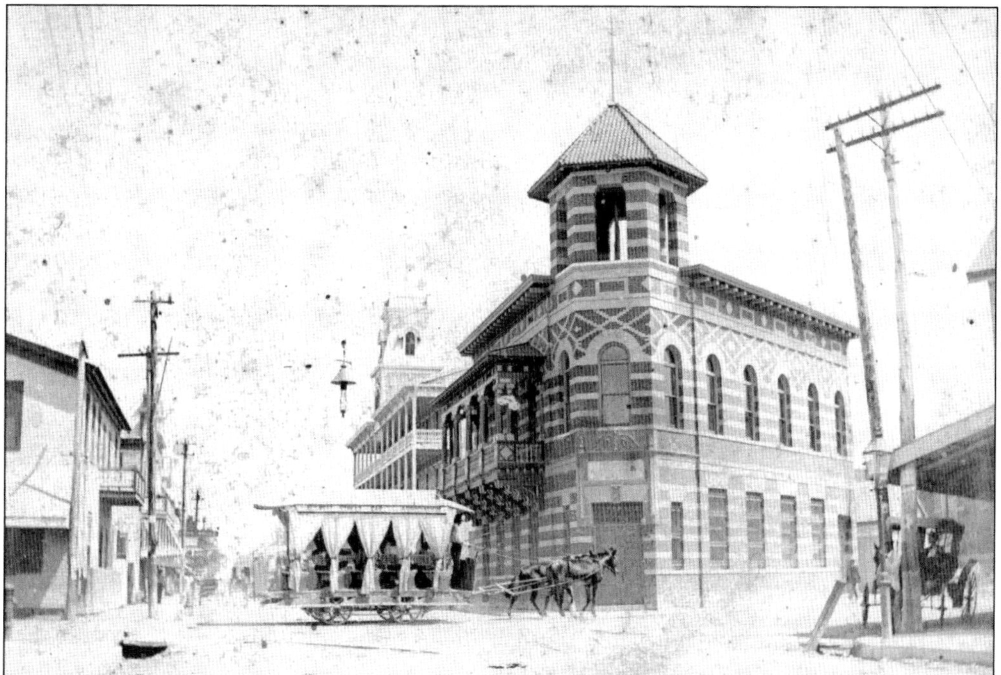

In this photograph, a mule-drawn streetcar passes by the distinctive brick First National Bank on the corner of Duval and Front Streets. Cuban cigar manufacturer Eduardo H. Gato founded the streetcar line to transport his workers to his factory. Many Cubans, including well-to-do cigar factory owners, immigrated to Key West during Cuba's ongoing struggles against Spanish rule. (Courtesy of Monroe County Library, Key West.)

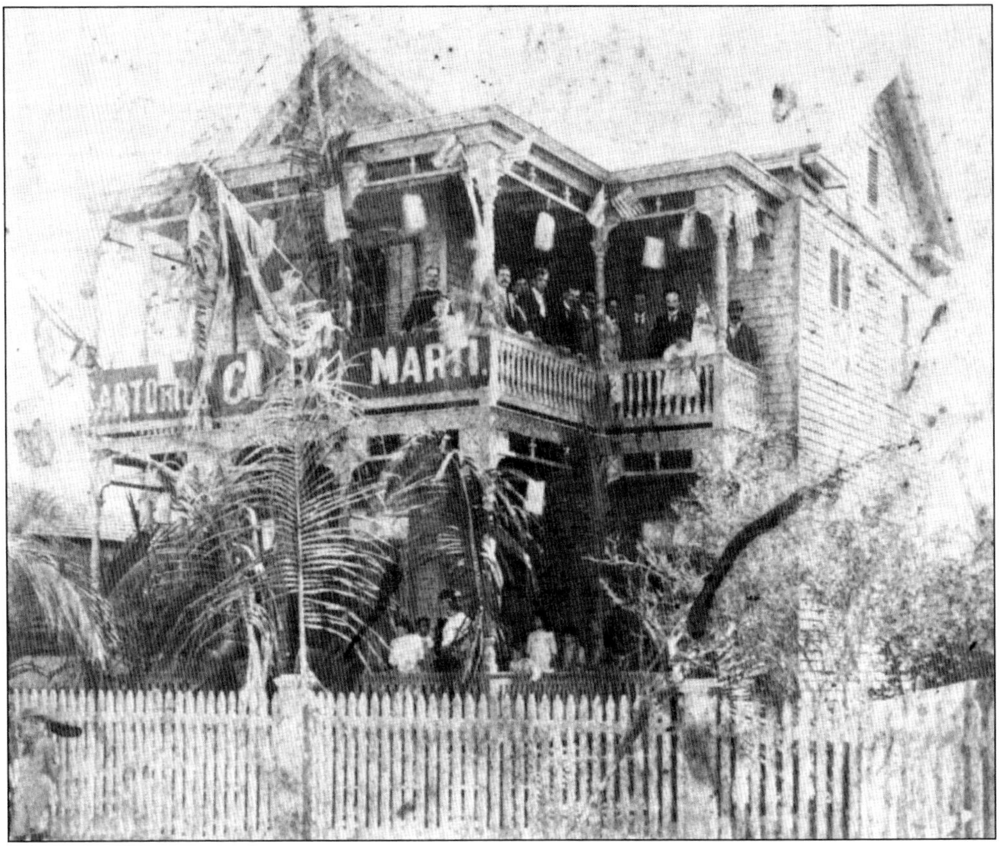

In 1892, Cuban revolutionary and poet Jose Marti delivers an inspiring speech about Cuban independence from Teodoro Perez's balcony at 1125 Duval Street. Marti stayed at the Perez home, which later became known as "La Terraza de Marti" in his honor. Revolutionaries found significant support among Key West's Cubans. Three years after his speech, Marti died at the Battle of Dos Rios. (Courtesy of Monroe County Library, Key West.)

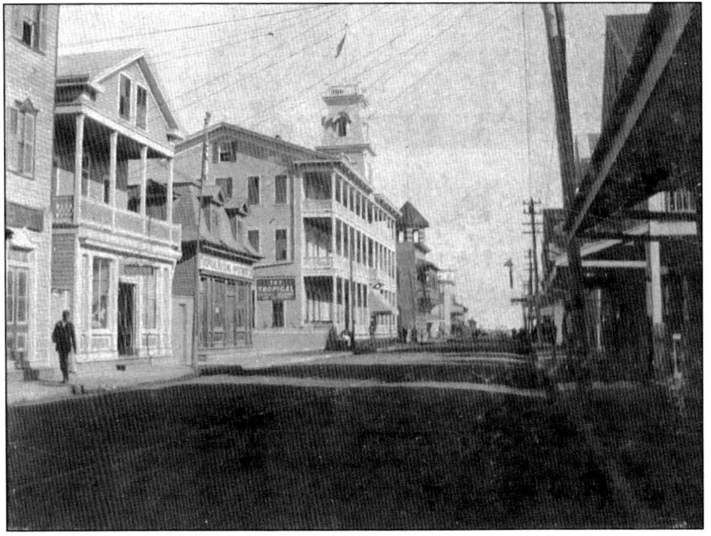

On the left, a man strides by one of the city's coffee shops. Behind him rise the Tropical Building and Investment Company, the imposing Jefferson Hotel, and the First National Bank. On Duval Street in 1898, a person could find almost anything: a bed for the night, money to borrow, clothing shops, carriage supplies, a strong shot of caffeine, and of course, saloons. (Courtesy of Monroe County Library, Key West.)

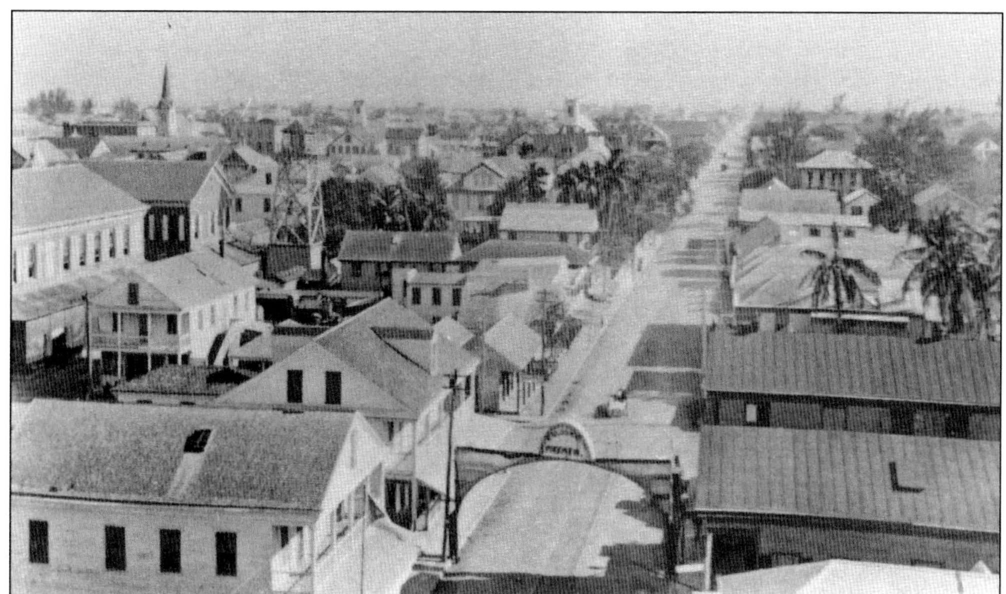
In 1898, Horatio Crain took this photograph that captures the 200 block of Duval Street looking south toward South Beach. Despite fires and hurricanes, as the 19th century drew to a close, Key West thrived. The banner in the foreground was erected for a firemen's convention. Even in the 19th century, Duval was a place where Key West gathered to celebrate. (Courtesy of Monroe County Library, Key West.)

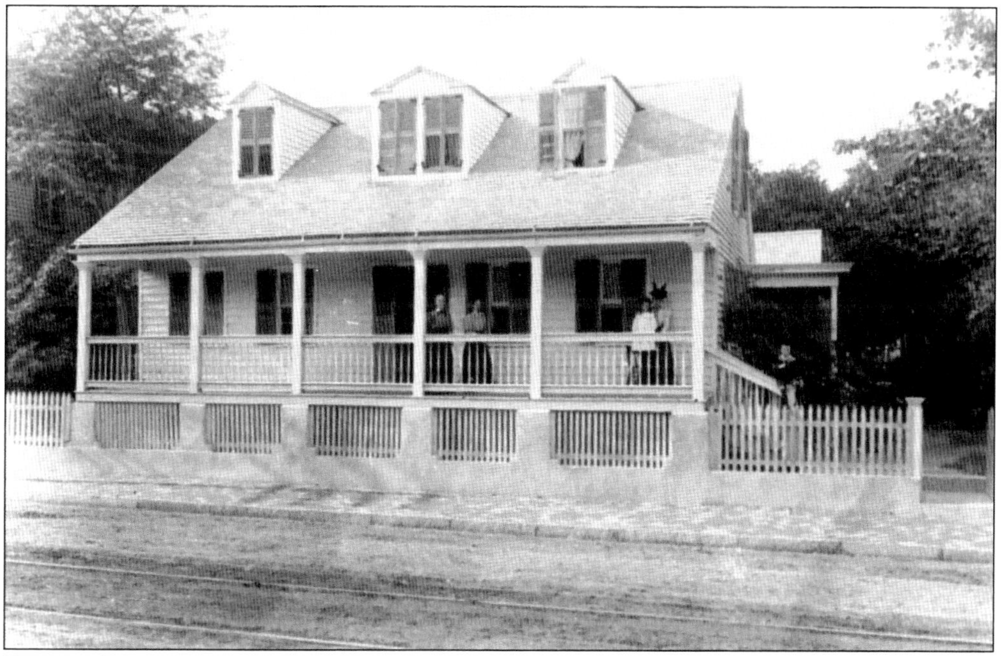
Despite the increasing number of banks, shops, and saloons on Duval Street, there were still plenty of Key West residents who called it home. Here, at the Oldest House, the Watlington family poses for a picture. The women wear leg o' mutton sleeves, which came into fashion in the 1890s. The boy on the right looks as though he has slid down the stair railing. (Courtesy of Monroe County Library, Key West.)

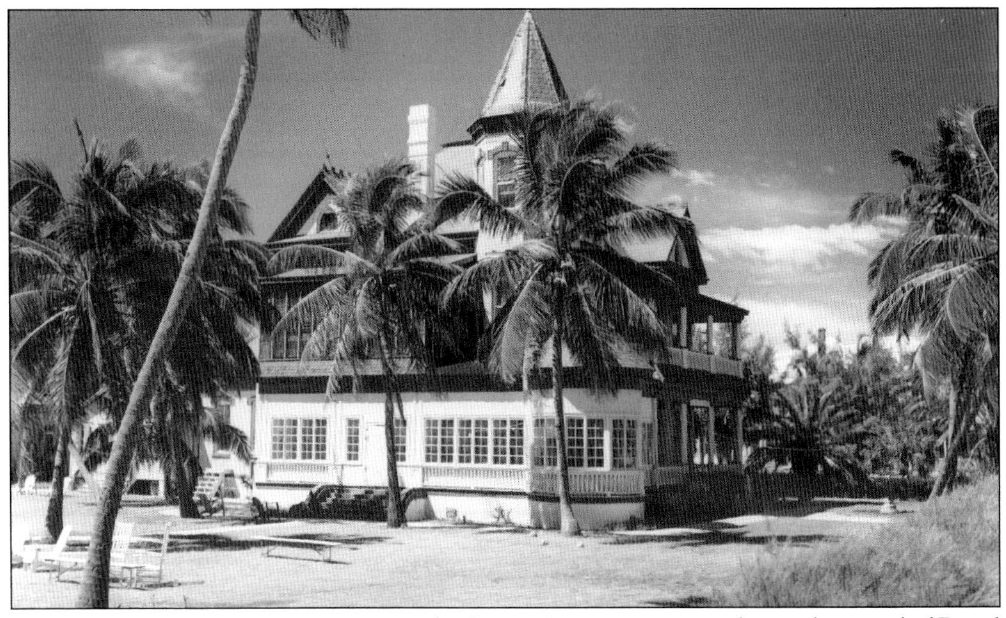

Judge Jeptha Vining Harris commissioned a Queen Anne mansion at the southern end of Duval Street in the late 1890s. The elaborate home with turrets and balconies was the southernmost house in the United States and cost a whopping $250,000 (or $6.7 million today). Queen Anne revival–style architecture came into vogue during the Victorian era in Great Britain before spreading to the United States. (Courtesy of Monroe County Library, Key West.)

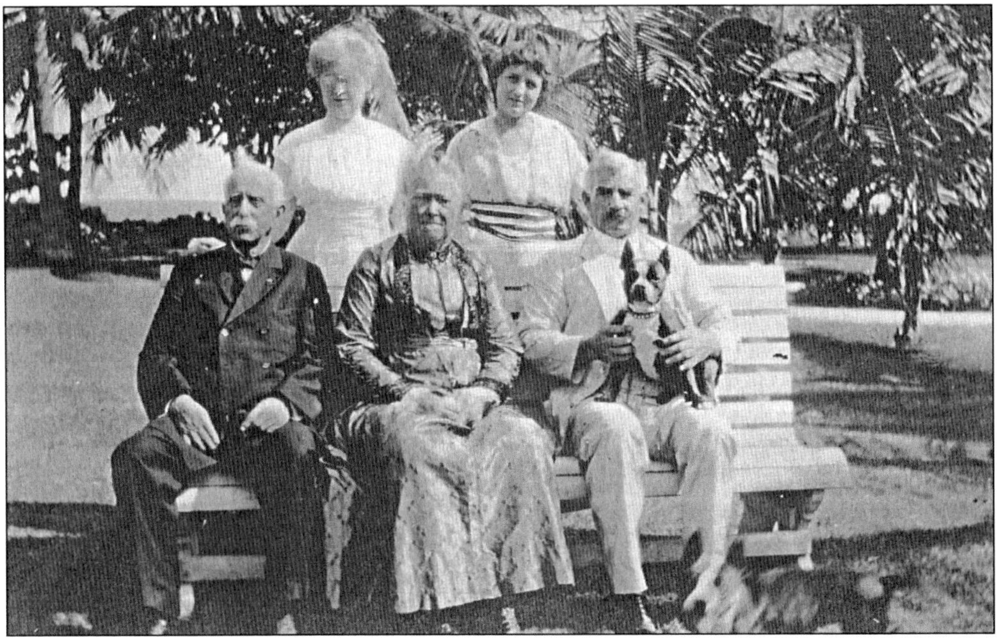

Jeptha Harris married Florida Curry, the daughter of Key West millionaire William Curry. Florida engaged no less a celebrity than Thomas Edison to supervise the installation of electricity in their home. Pictured at the Southernmost House are, from left to right, (first row) Dr. Jeptha Vining Harris, Mary Perkins Harris, and Judge Jeptha Vining Harris; (second row) Florida Curry Harris and daughter Marian E. Harris. (Courtesy of Monroe County Library, Key West.)

Two

A New Century

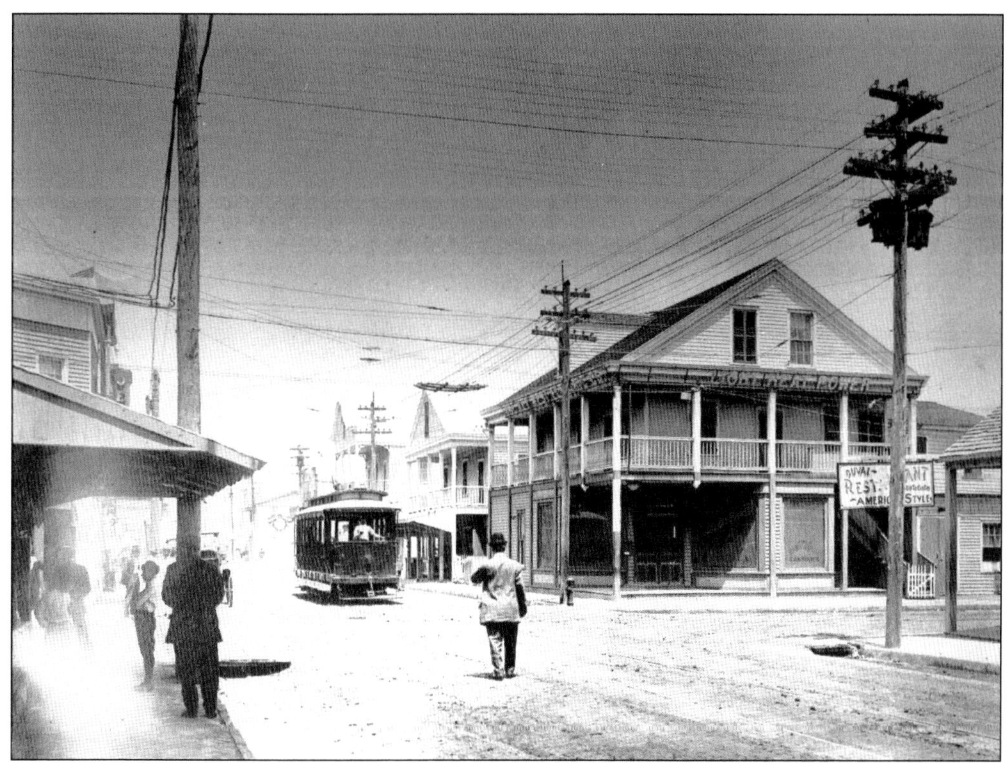

The year is 1900, and as a new century dawns in Key West, modernity clangs up and down Duval Street, like this new electric streetcar. As of 1899, the old mule-powered cars had been retired. Although still not paved, Duval Street was festooned with multiple electric power lines. Even the Duval Restaurant, pictured on the right, advertises that it is "up to date." (Courtesy of Monroe County Library, Key West.)

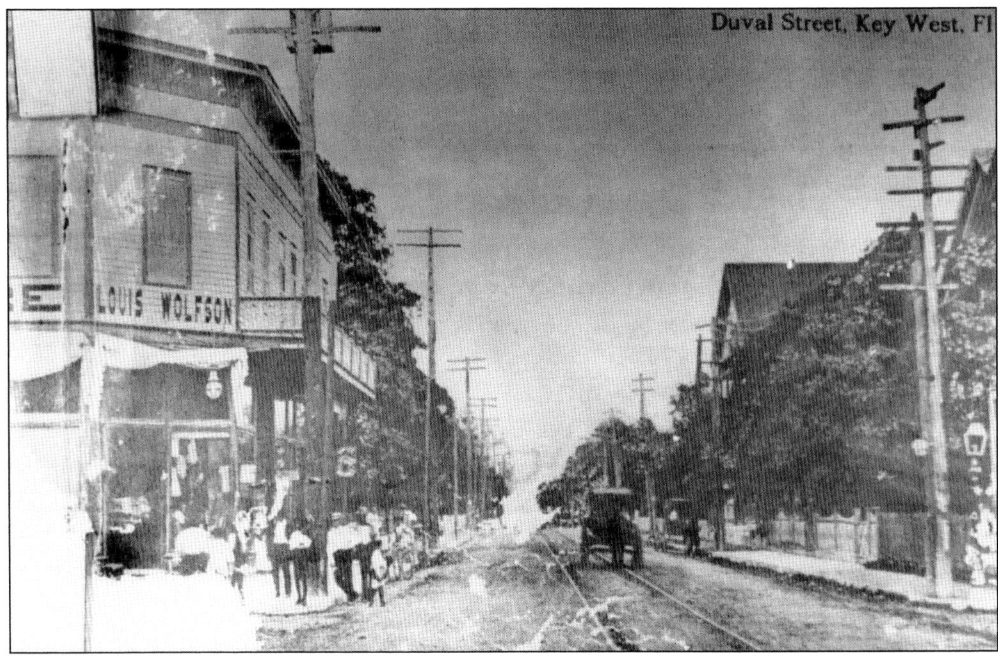

Men and children gather outside Louis Wolfson's store at the corner of Duval and Fleming Streets. One person leans against a bicycle while a horse-drawn carriage makes its way over the streetcar rails. In the early 1900s, in addition to Wolfson's, Duval Street boasted establishments like Island City Electrical Work, La Plata restaurant, J. Leibovit's Naval Store, Gallat's Shaving Parlor, and Jake's Trading Palace. (Courtesy of Monroe County Library, Key West.)

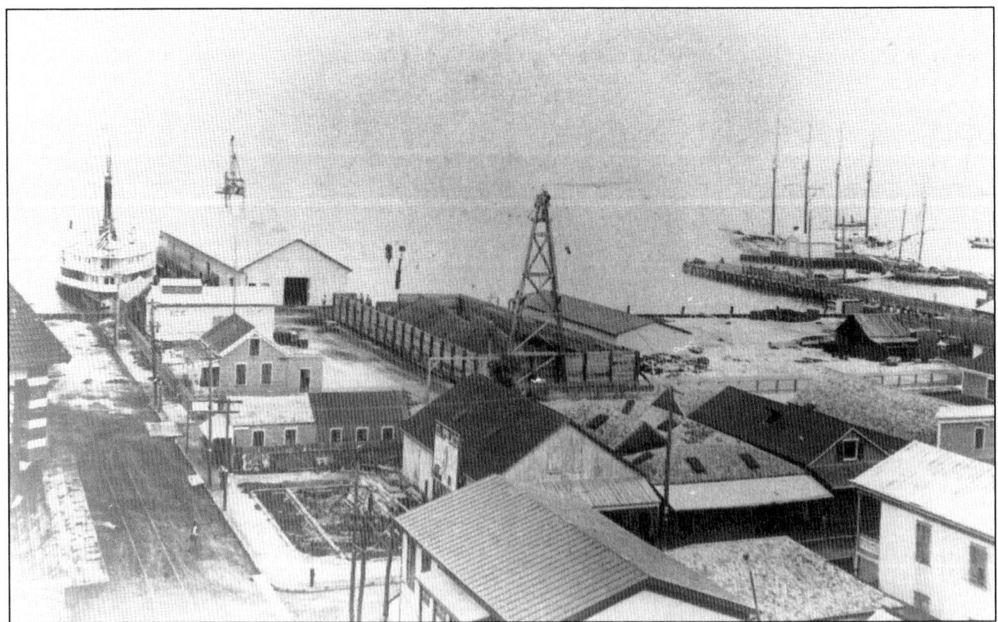

At the northern end of Duval Street, Peninsular & Occidental (P&O) Steamship Company steamers like the one at left docked to let off passengers and freight. In the early 1900s, Key West attracted few tourists, and those who came usually arrived by P&O ship. From Key West, travelers could voyage on to Cuba or other ports in Florida. (Courtesy of Monroe County Library, Key West.)

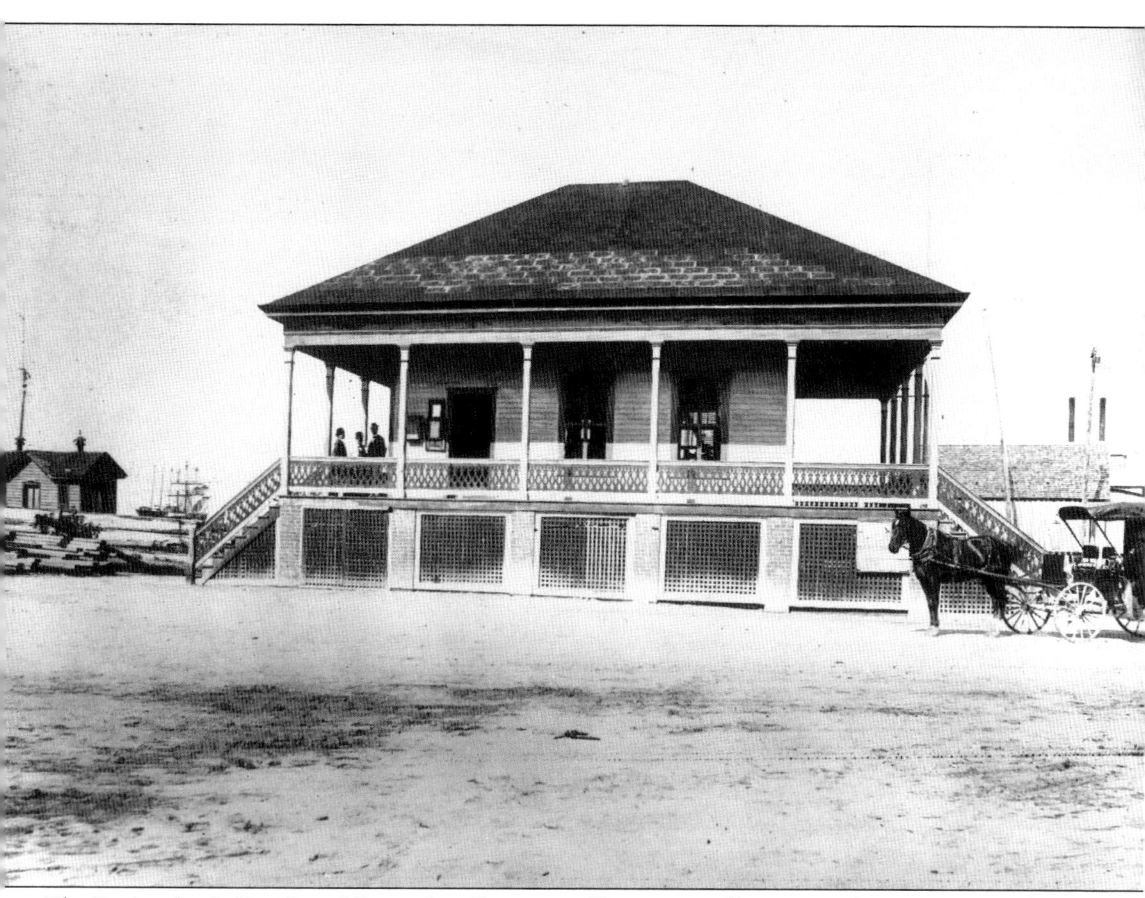

The Peninsular & Occidental Steamship Company office, pictured here around 1900, once stood on the waterfront at 0 Duval Street. (This building had once been the Phillinick residence.) In the early 1900s, the northern end of Duval served as a busy, working harbor and a transportation hub, as both passengers and freight were brought in by ship. The P&O advertised two routes in the *Key West Citizen* in 1908: one from Port Tampa to Key West to Havana, and another from Knight's Key to Key West to Havana. At that time, people could ride the train from New York or Jacksonville to Knight's Key (in the middle Florida Keys) and then take a steamer to Key West, where they would disembark at Duval Street. The steamship company's newspaper advertisement cautioned potential passengers that the schedule was "Subject to change and individual postponement without notice." (Courtesy of Monroe County Library, Key West.)

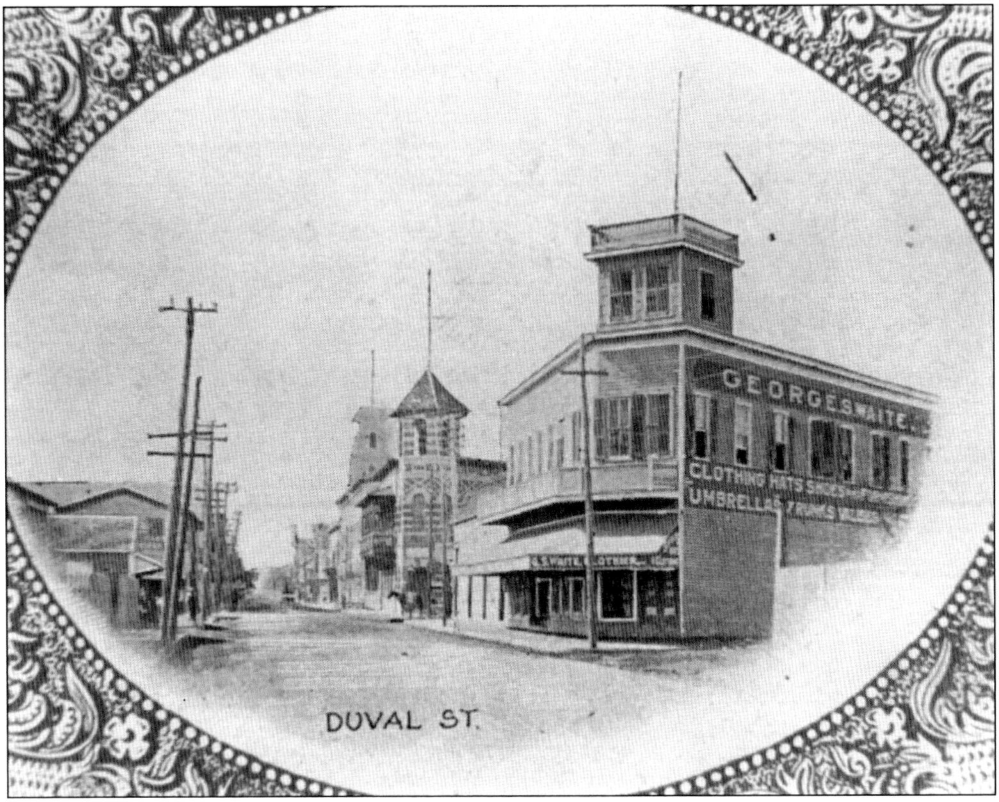

DUVAL ST.

An artist named Tom Jones drew this view of Duval Street for a series of "Scenic Souvenirs" published in 1904. On the right, the George S. Waite store at 92–94 Duval sold everything from hats to valises. One newspaper advertisement read, "Wear one pair of our shoes—and then you will know the best place to go for your next pair." (Courtesy of Monroe County Library, Key West.)

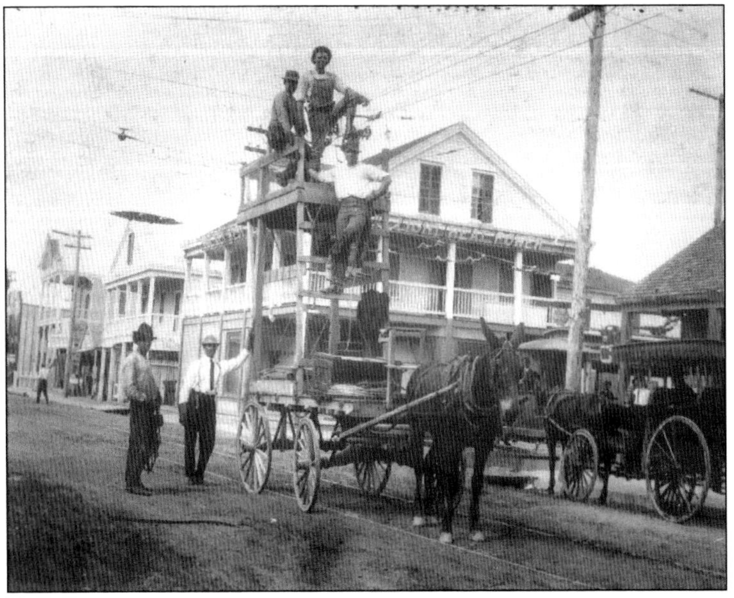

An electric company crew poses at 134 Duval Street in or around 1900. They have a wooden scaffolding built atop the cart, so they can reach the power lines. Key West got electricity in 1897, after which gas lights were converted to electric lights. Behind the workers stands the power company office, and beyond that, a sign advertises a shooting gallery. (Courtesy of Monroe County Library, Key West.)

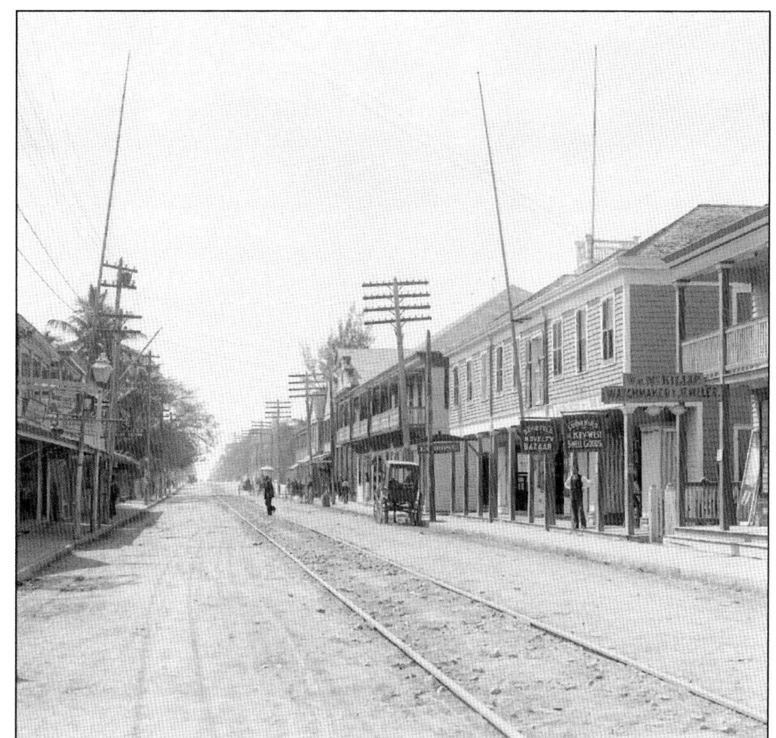

This photograph captures what it felt like to be in the middle of Duval in the early 20th century. On the left is P. Gonzalez's shoemaking shop, on the right David Fuld's Novelty Bazaar, selling souvenirs and shell goods. Next door on the 200 block is watchmaker and jeweler William McKillip's storefront. McKillip advertised in the *Key West Citizen*: "Complicated watch work a specialty." (Courtesy of Monroe County Library, Key West.)

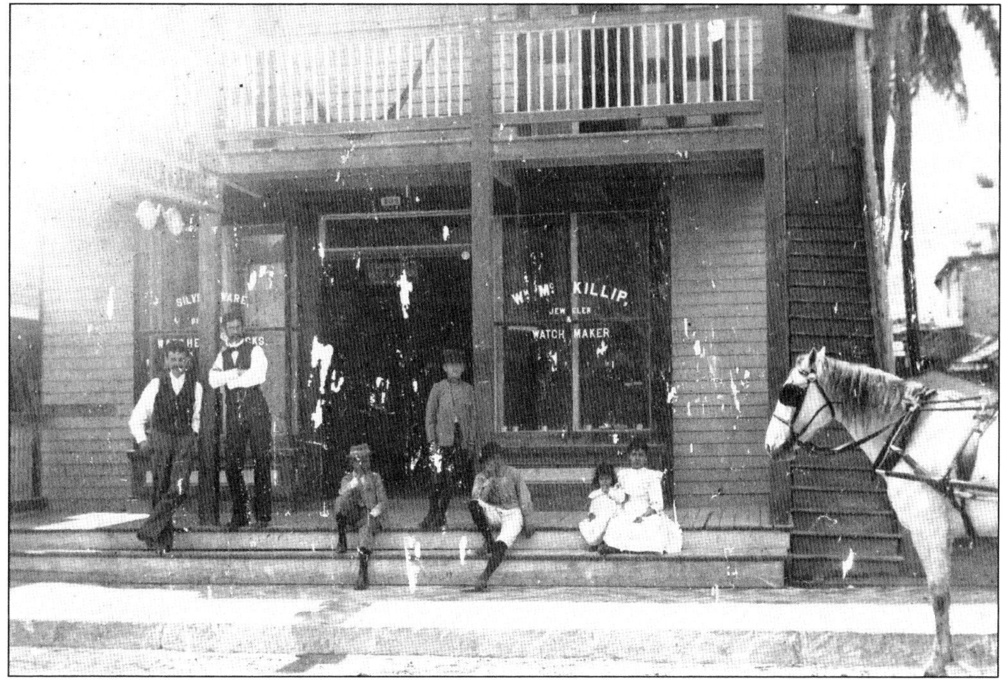

As the new century dawns, a horse pulling a carriage stands before William McKillip's store on the 200 block of Duval Street. Two gentlemen in shirtsleeves and five children pose for their photograph; perhaps the picture was taken with a Brownie camera, a model the Eastman Kodak company began selling in 1900. (Courtesy of Monroe County Library, Key West.)

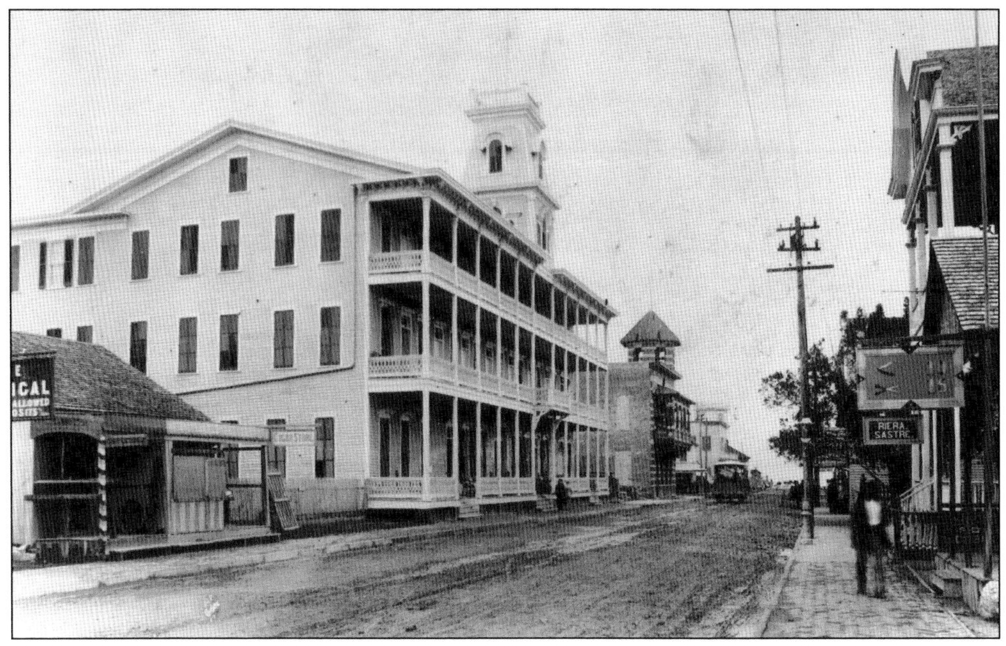

The imposing building on the left was the three-story Jefferson Hotel, one of the few hotels on the island at the time. It was called Hotel Key West until Henry Flagler's Florida East Coast Hotel Company bought the property in 1897 and changed the name. Hotel guests could walk across the street for a haircut at Riera Sastre's barbershop. (Courtesy of Monroe County Library, Key West.)

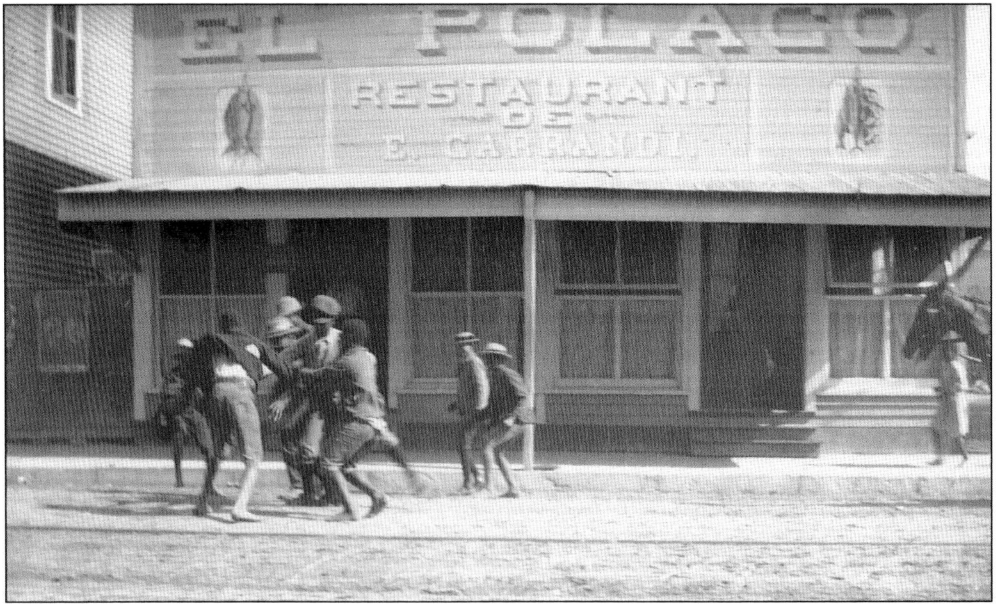

Outside El Polaco Restaurant at 111 Duval Street, some young men appear to be starting a fistfight. This was hardly the first street brawl—or even duel—on Duval. In 1870, one notorious duel took place inside the lobby of the Russell House, a hotel on Duval Street's 100 block. Visiting Spaniard Gonzalo Castañon was shot dead by Cuban exile Mateo Orozco. (Courtesy of Monroe County Library, Key West.)

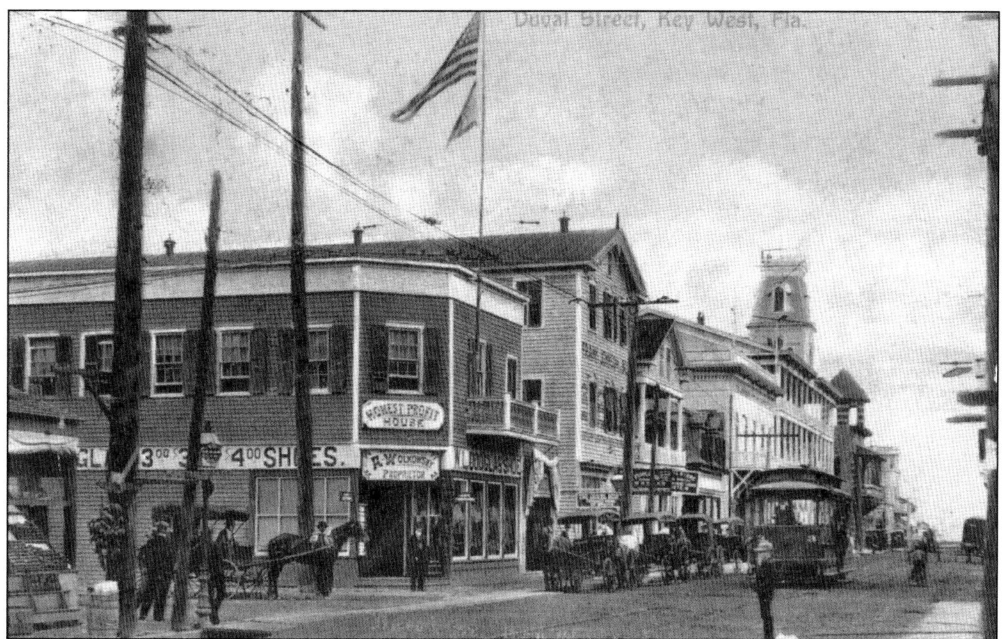

An electric streetcar rumbles down the 100 block of Duval Street. The image appeared on a postcard that visitors, whether in town for business or pleasure, could mail back home. On the far left, a humble stand sells fruit, including bunches of bananas, while across the way, the Honest Profit House, owned by A. Wolkowsky, hawks shoes for $3 and $4 a pair. (Courtesy of Monroe County Library, Key West.)

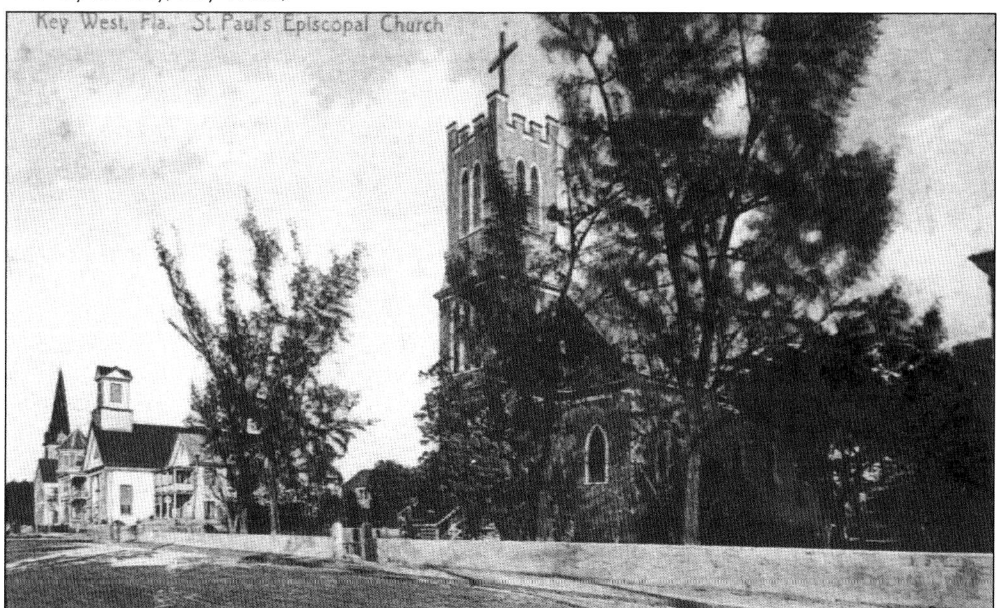

Another postcard shows a less commercial side of Key West. The impressive tower of St. Paul's Episcopal Church stands as a reminder that Duval Street has always had a dual nature: a street where elegant mansions and houses of worship contrast with shops selling every kind of merchandise, and saloons where hard drinking proves to be the rule. (Courtesy of Monroe County Library, Key West.)

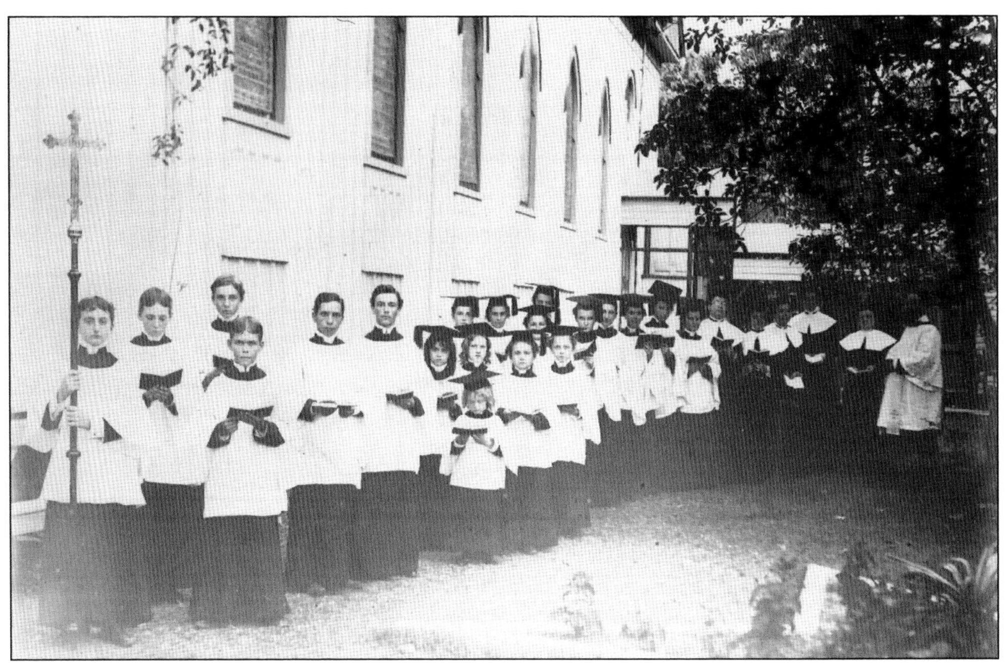

An altar boy and the St. Paul's choir pose in front of the church in the early 1900s. The third version of the church to be constructed on this spot measured 58 by 98 feet; the wooden church actually faced Eaton Street, although the building also fronted Duval. (Courtesy of Monroe County Library, Key West.)

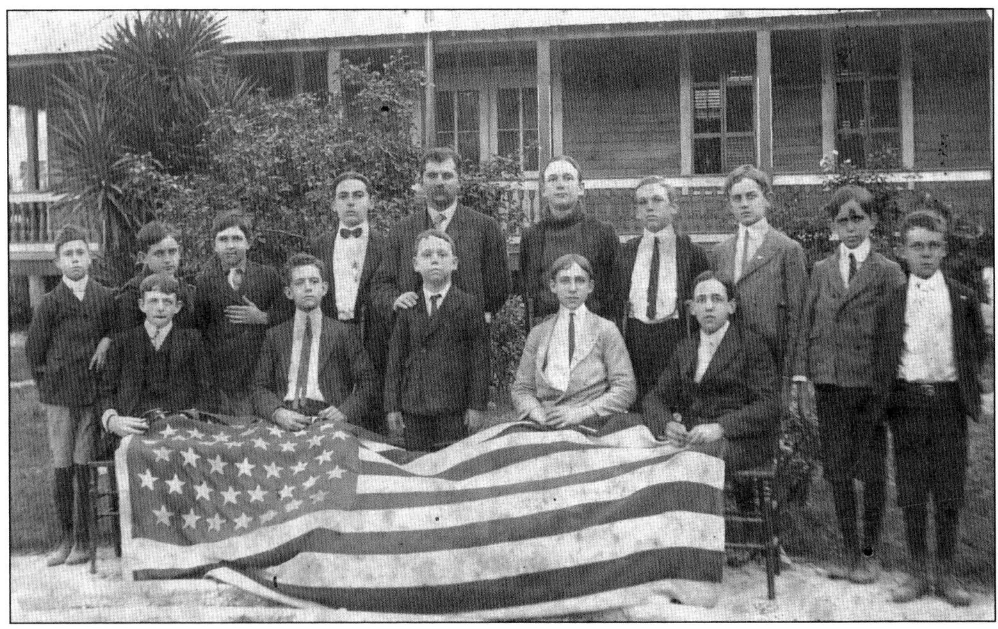

A teacher and students who attended classes at St. Paul's pose in front of the church hall. From left to right are (first row) Teddy Bailey, Ray Dobarganez, Sam B. Curry, Owen Sawyer, and Steward Hellings; (second row) unidentified, B. Curry Moreno, Porter Hellings, Ansel Arapian, unidentified, Norward Pinder, Carlisle Pinder, Kingman Curry, Newell Delaney, and Donald Williams. (Courtesy of Monroe County Library, Key West.)

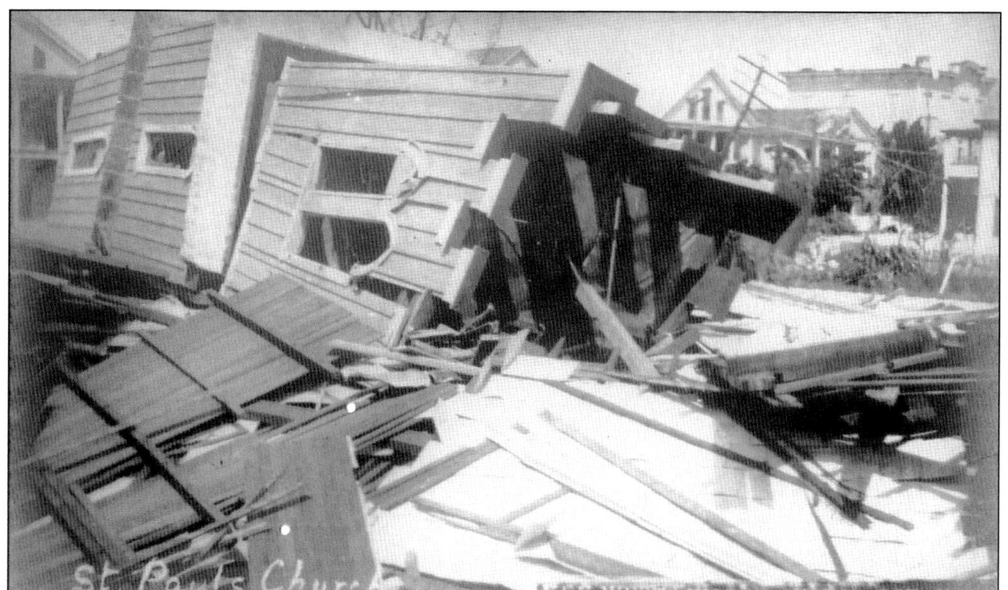

On October 11, 1909, a powerful hurricane swept over Key West and inflicted terrible damage. The *Key West Citizen's* headline on October 13 called it the "Greatest Disaster in History of the City" as the paper reported on the dead, the injured, and the destruction. One of the casualties was St. Paul's Episcopal Church at 401 Duval Street. Its wooden wreckage is pictured here. (Courtesy of Monroe County Library, Key West.)

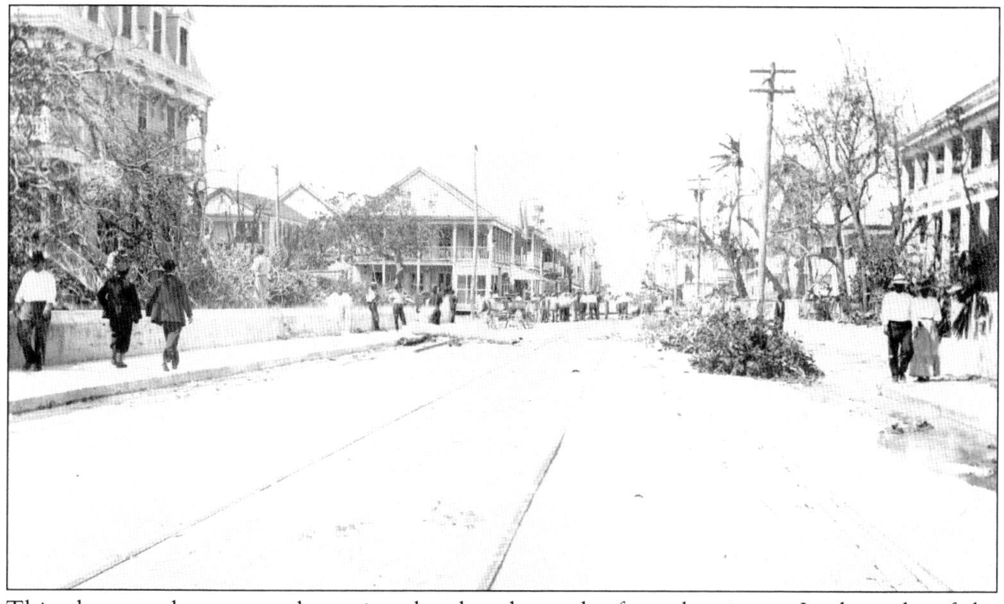

This photograph portrays the eerie calm that descends after a hurricane. In the wake of the 1909 storm, the city of approximately 17,000 people faced widespread damage. At the 300 block of Duval Street, citizens muster to clean up debris including tree branches that block the road. Key West residents also had to contend with downed power and telephone lines. (Courtesy of Monroe County Library, Key West.)

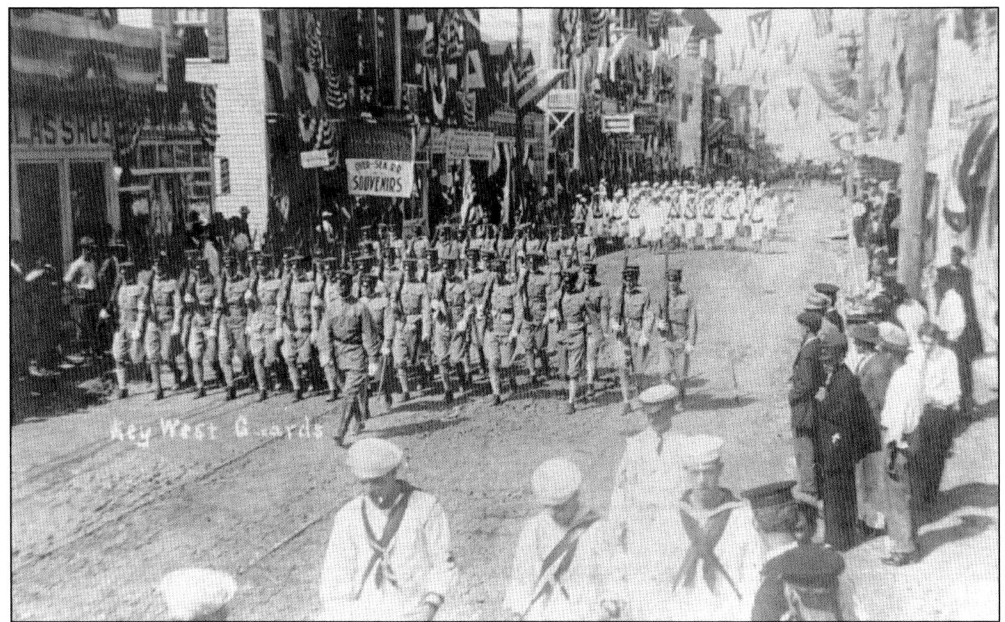

Duval Street was once again a center for celebrations when the Florida East Coast Railway's Key West Extension finally reached Key West. Railroad visionary and Standard Oil millionaire Henry Flagler rode the first train to Key West on January 22, 1912, an event celebrated with parades. Here, Key West Guards march past a shop already selling "Over-Sea R.R. Souvenirs." (Courtesy of Monroe County Library, Key West.)

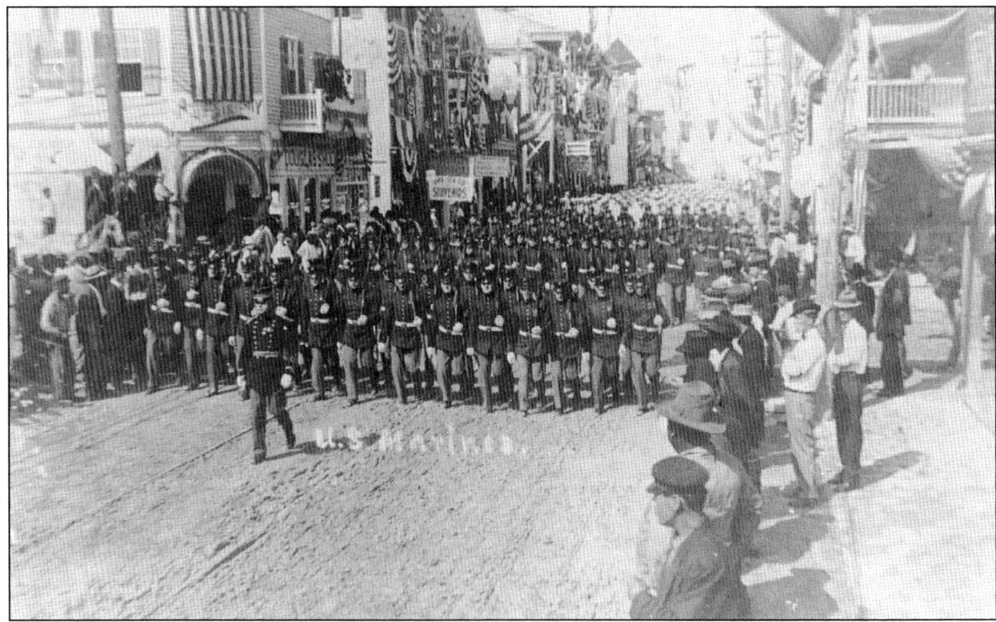

Flags flew over Duval as Key West's citizens lined up to watch US Marines and others parade in honor of the first FEC train to reach the city. The importance of this transportation link to the mainland cannot be overstated; it suddenly made the island much more accessible and opened up new possibilities for trade, shipping, and ultimately, tourism. (Courtesy of Monroe County Library, Key West.)

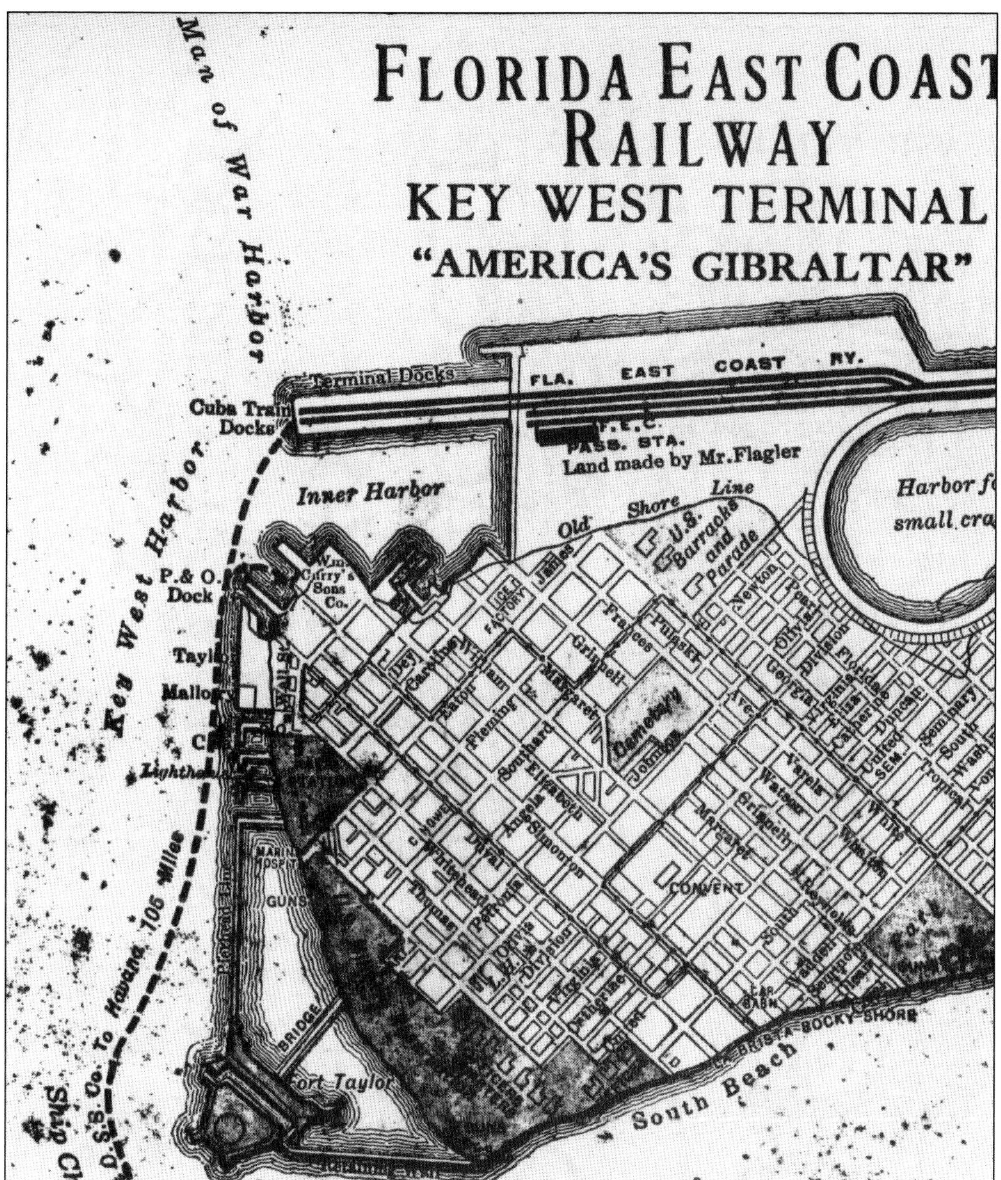

This detail from a Florida East Coast Railway map shows Duval Street with its Peninsular & Occidental Steamship Company dock at the northern end and South Beach at its southern end. Also visible is the terminus or final station for the train and the railroad's own docks. At the time, many tourists were eager to get to the tropical destination of Cuba, rather than spend a vacation in Key West. One dotted line shows the ship's route from the Cuban Train (FEC) dock and from the P&O dock at the end of Duval on the voyage to Havana. The map also shows a line with dots, which traces the streetcar route in Key West. The streetcar rode along Duval from Front Street to United Street, almost the entire length of the avenue. (Courtesy of Monroe County Library, Key West.)

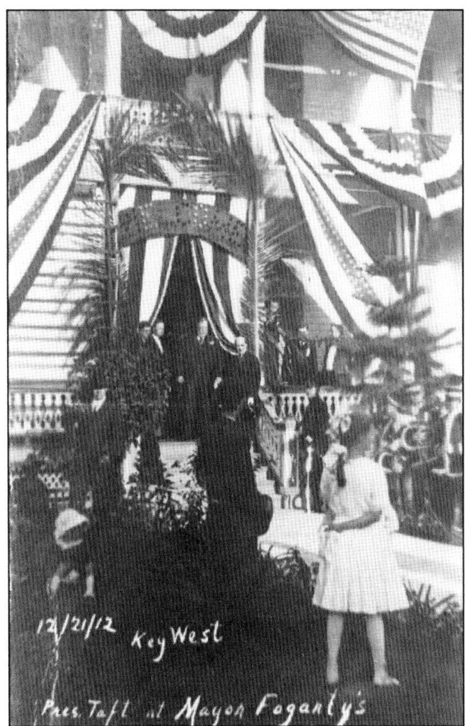

In December 1912, Pres. William Howard Taft arrived in Key West on the famed Overseas Railroad, or "railroad that went to sea," at the time considered one of the wonders of the world. Here, the president visits Mayor Joseph Fogarty's house, decked out with flags and banners, at 227 Duval Street. (Courtesy of Monroe County Library, Key West.)

President Taft (center) leaves Mayor Fogarty's house in December 1912. The house at 227 Duval Street was built by Charles Curry in 1875, then rebuilt in 1887 following the Great Fire. Curry's daughter Corinne became engaged to Joseph Fogarty, who purchased the house in 1900 as a wedding present for her. Fogarty would serve as Key West mayor for six years. (Courtesy of the State Archives of Florida, Wright Langley collection.)

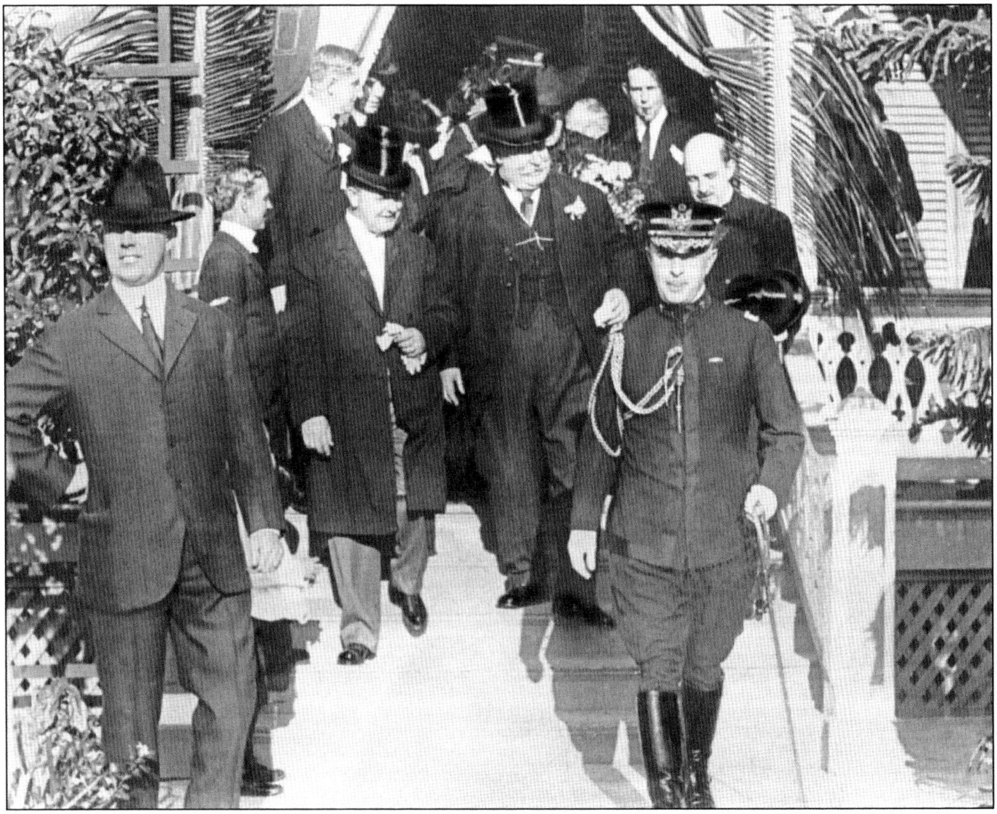

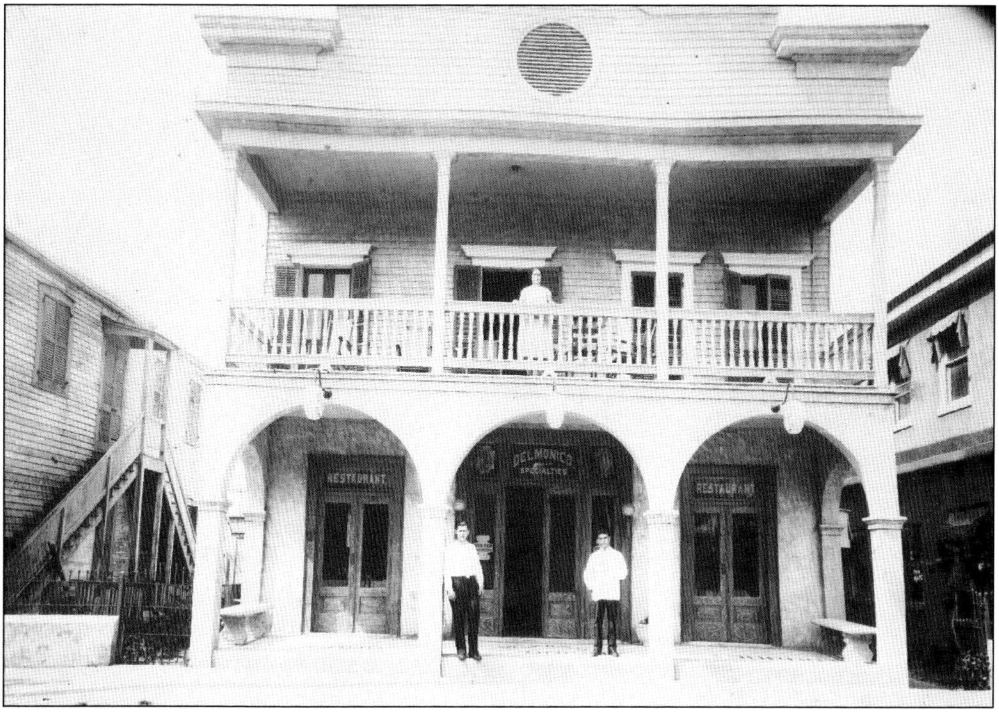

In 1912, Aquilino Lopez's restaurant Delmonico's at 218 Duval Street was one of the most popular places to eat in Key West. The owner's wife, Generosa Lopez, stands on the balcony, while head waiter Francisco Sanchez (left) and another waiter named Ovide ? pose at the entrance. House specialties included seafood, turtle steaks, and arroz con pollo. (Courtesy of Monroe County Library, Key West.)

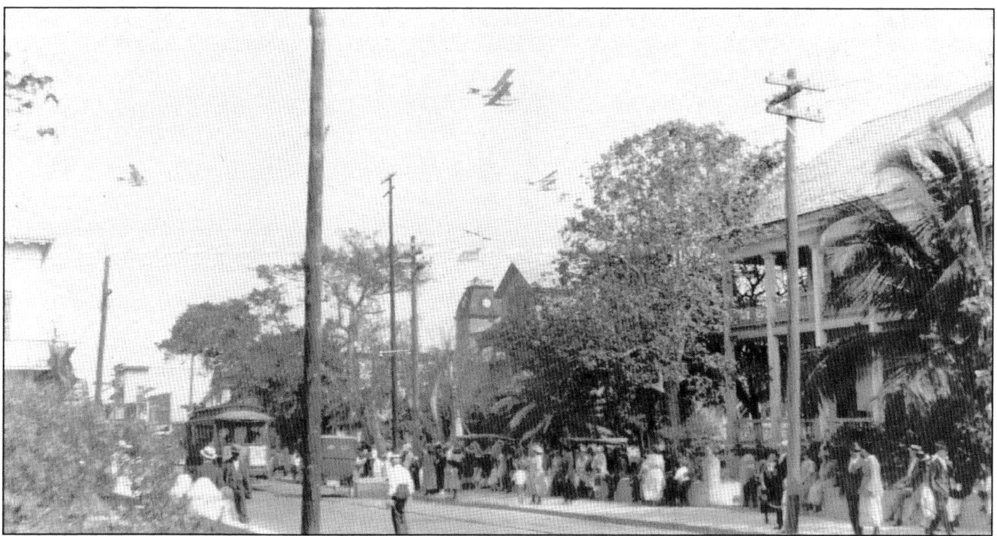

Navy seaplanes swoop over Duval Street. When the United States entered World War I in 1917, the US Navy constructed submarine and air bases in Key West. In September 1917, a Curtiss N-9 seaplane was the first naval plane to take flight from the island. By 1918, more than 1,000 military personnel were stationed here to train on seaplanes, airplanes, and blimps. (Courtesy of Monroe County Library, Key West.)

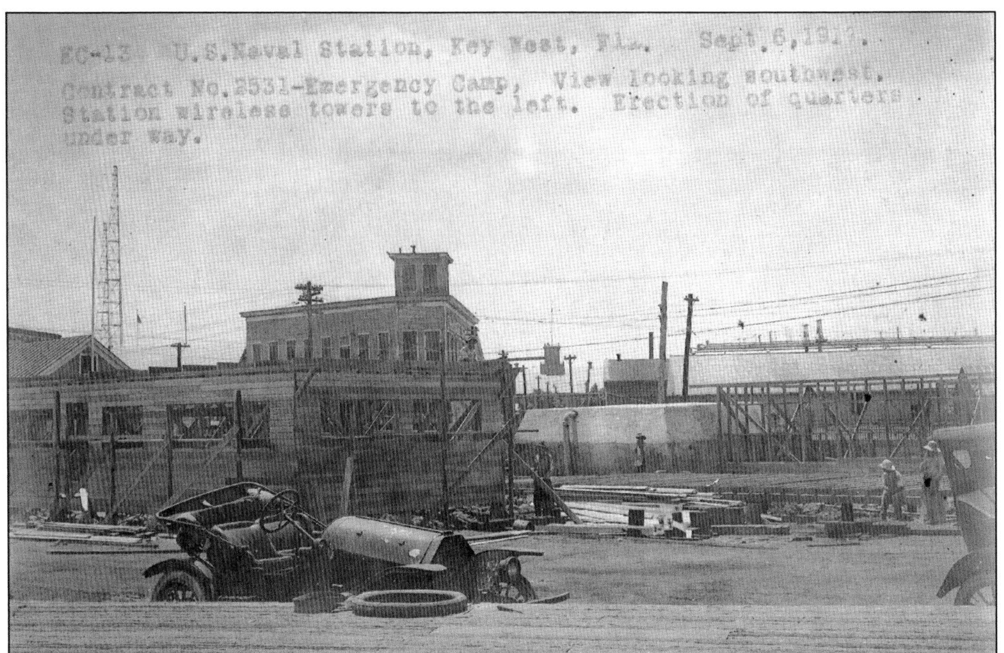

With America fighting in the war, the US Navy set to work building in Key West. This photograph shows the "emergency camp" being hastily constructed on Duval Street in September 1917, with wireless towers to the left and, in the foreground, military quarters in the process of being built. (Courtesy of Monroe County Library, Key West.)

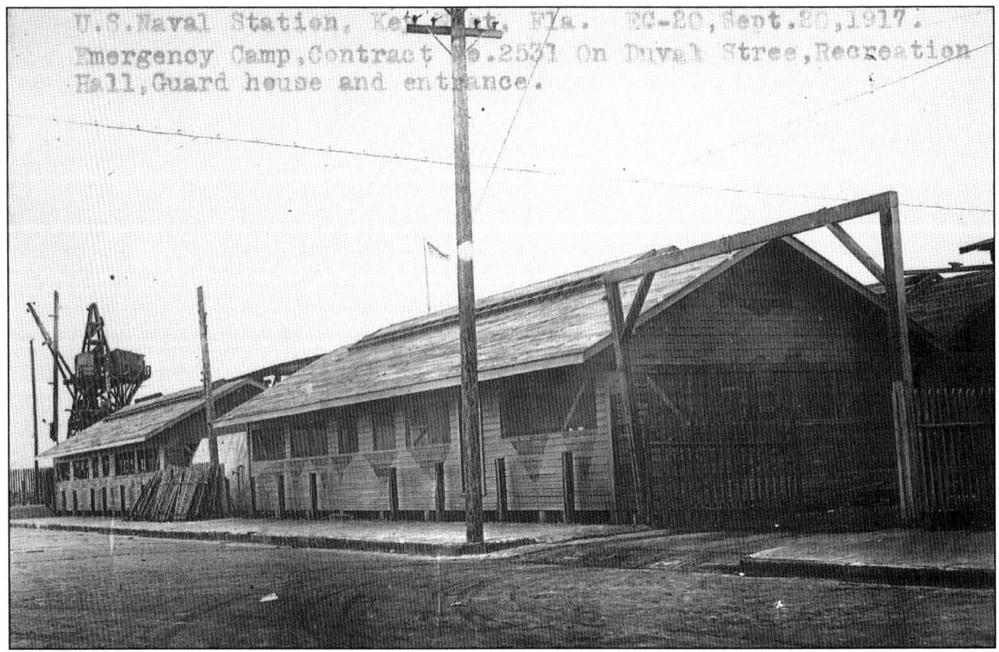

Another image shows more facilities of the naval emergency camp on the northern portion of Duval Street. A recreation hall for personnel, a guard house, and an entrance are visible in this photograph from 1917. Meanwhile, in Europe, the Battle of Polygon Wood raged near Ypres, Belgium. (Courtesy of Monroe County Library, Key West.)

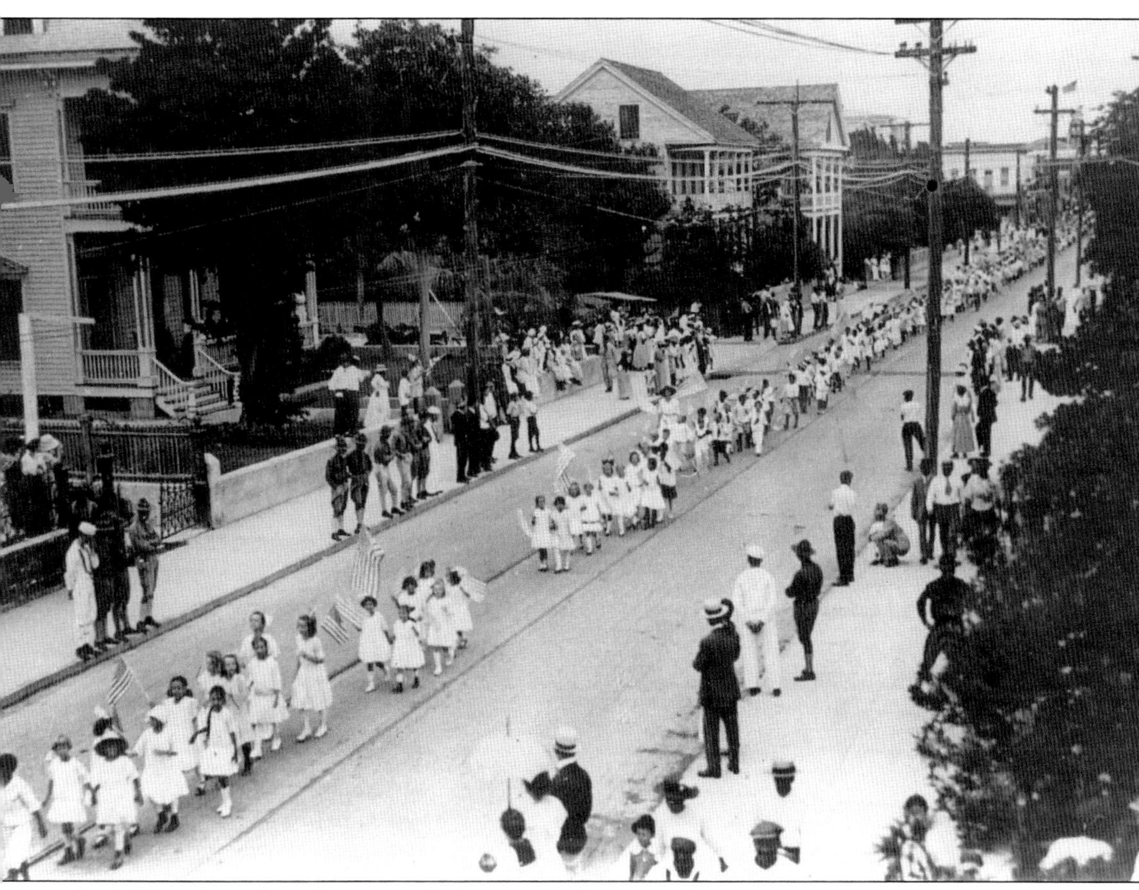

Little children dressed in white to symbolize peace take part in the Armistice Parade down Duval Street on November 11, 1918. Citizens, soldiers, and sailors line the 300 and 400 blocks of Duval Street to watch the event marking the end of the Great War. On that very day at 11:00 a.m., or "the eleventh hour of the eleventh day of the eleventh month," representatives of the Allies and Germany gathered at Compiegne in France to sign an armistice agreement, for the cessation of fighting. Key West, its citizens, and its naval forces had good reason to celebrate the peace. The war had exacted a terrible toll: approximately eleven million military personnel and seven million civilians died worldwide. Nevertheless, the naval presence and influx of so many new people in need of food, supplies, and entertainment had given a tremendous boost to the Key West economy. (Courtesy of Monroe County Library, Key West.)

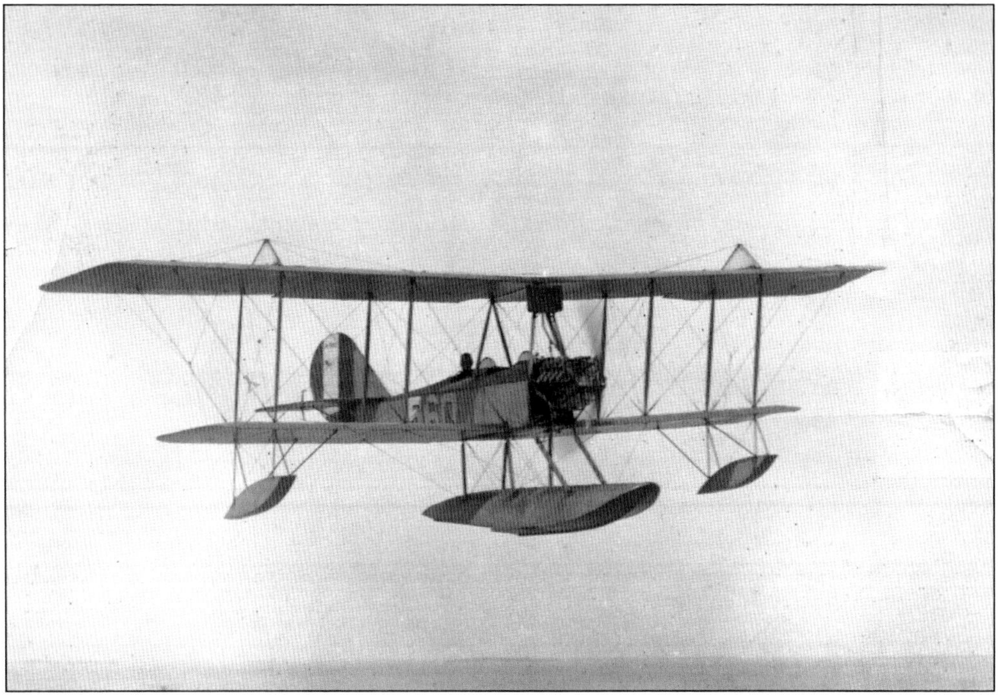

At the end of World War I, Navy seaplanes flew over Duval Street to celebrate the victory. This is one of the Curtiss biplanes that flew from the Key West base. Note the single pontoon in the center and the two floats, one under each wing. (Courtesy of Monroe County Library, Key West.)

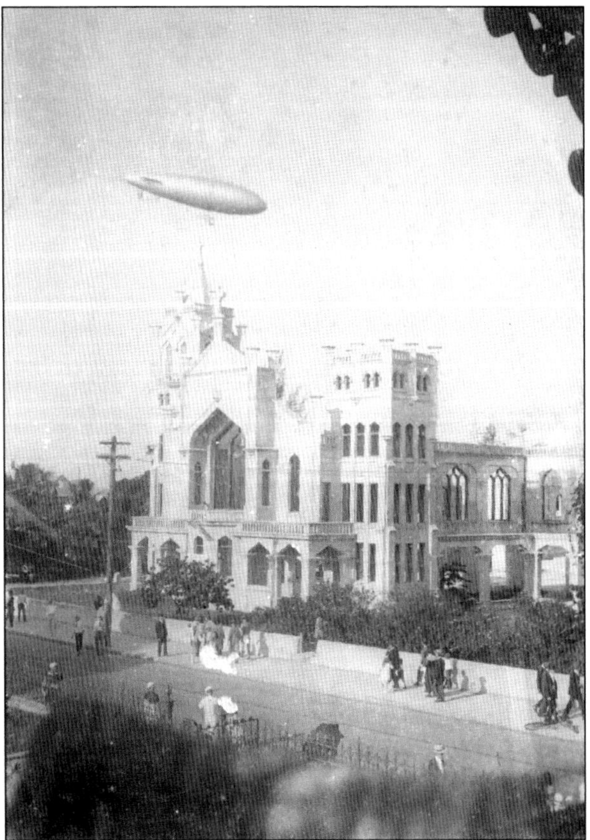

A military blimp hovers above St. Paul's Episcopal Church on Armistice Day in 1918. The crowds walking along Duval are scattering now that the parade and festivities have ended. At this point, the new St. Paul's was still under construction, as can be seen from the side of the building. The much-anticipated peace meant that Key West's wartime boom was about to end. (Courtesy of Monroe County Library, Key West.)

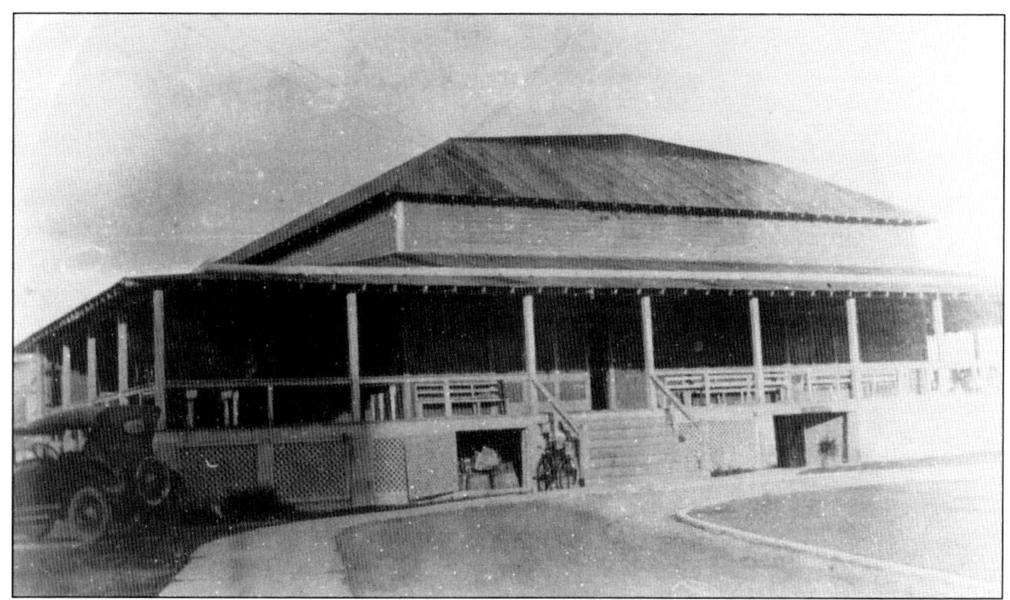

If the Navy had made its presence felt on the northern end of Duval Street, the southern end of the street was dedicated to residences and recreation. The Key West Athletic Club was located across from the Southernmost House, at South Beach, and housed a gymnasium and changing facilities. (Courtesy of Monroe County Library, Key West.)

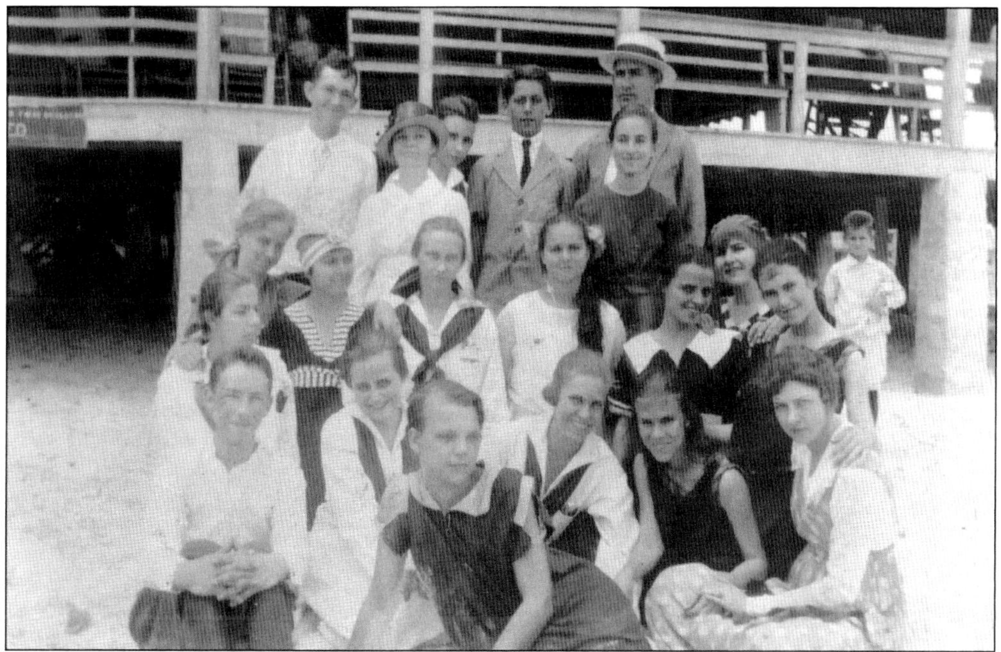

A class picnic gathers at the Athletic Club. From left to right are (first row) David Wientrub, Connie Warren, Golden Hanson, unidentified, Elizabeth Sharpley, and their teacher Annie Lois Hicks; (second row) unidentified, Gina Henson, Elois Curtis, Marque Curtis, Grace Romaguera, and Dorothy Pease; (third row) Edward Archer, Liza Gardner, Ansel Cleare, George Archer, Mabel Welch, and an unidentified teacher. (Courtesy of Monroe County Library, Key West.)

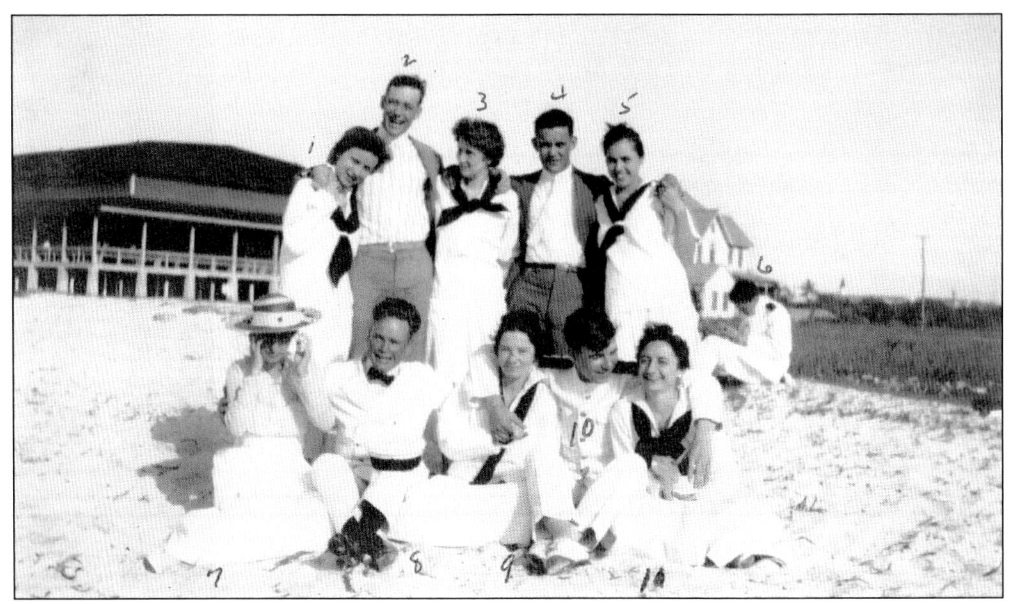

In the 1900s and 1910s, many Florida seaside towns erected athletic clubs of varying sizes, and Key West was no exception. Here, fashionable young people pose on the beach by the Athletic Club in 1917. Included are the names Billie Knowles, Curtis Stauton, Julia Sweeting, Ed Gato, Edna Macler, Lt. Crosby, Louie Ayala, Ruth Watkins, Lt. Huna, and May L. Haskins. (Courtesy of Monroe County Library, Key West.)

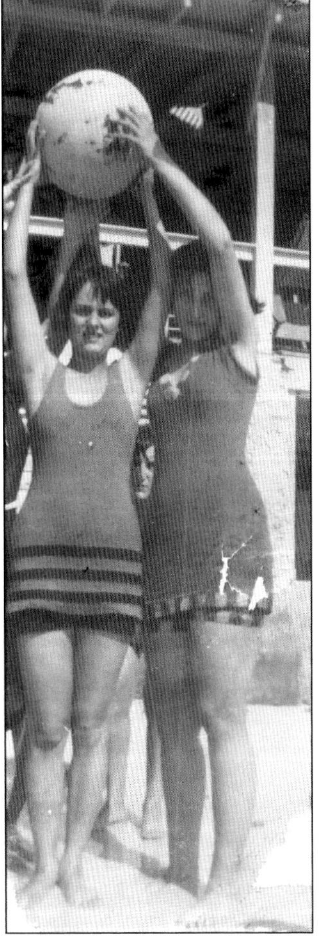

Alice Hambelt (left) and Georgette Edgerton pose at the Athletic Club at the end of Duval Street. The young women wear bathing suits that their grandmothers would probably have considered scandalous, although the suits seem quaintly modest today. Swimming's popularity as a sport for women was still fairly recent; women were only allowed to swim competitively in the Olympics in 1912. (Courtesy of Monroe County Library, Key West.)

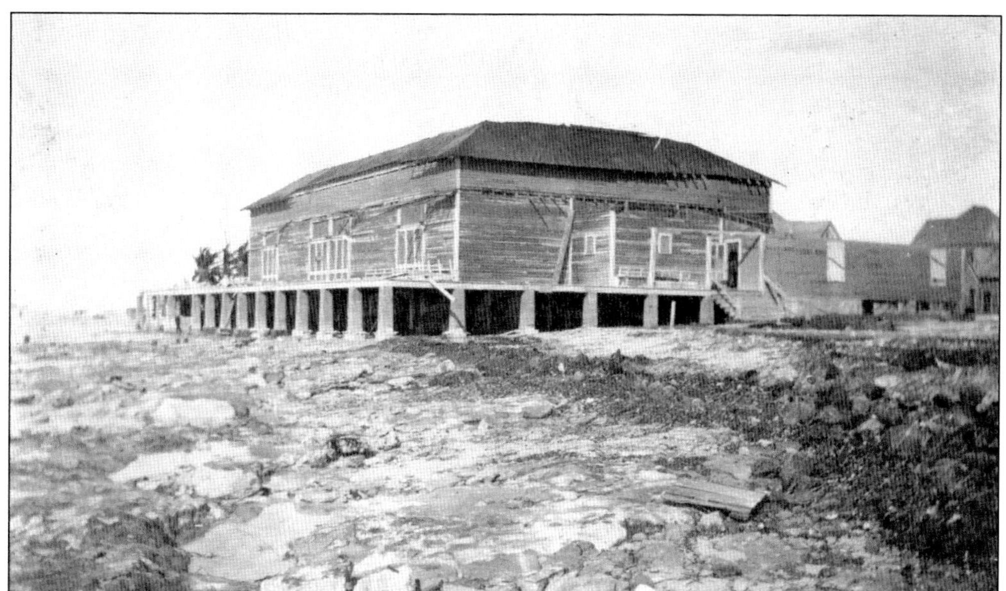

A 1919 hurricane walloped the Athletic Club at the southern tip of Duval Street and did some damage. But the building was apparently repaired, and Key Westers continued to frequent the club for exercise, swimming, and socializing. The building was torn down by the Works Progress Administration (WPA) during the Great Depression. (Courtesy of Monroe County Library, Key West.)

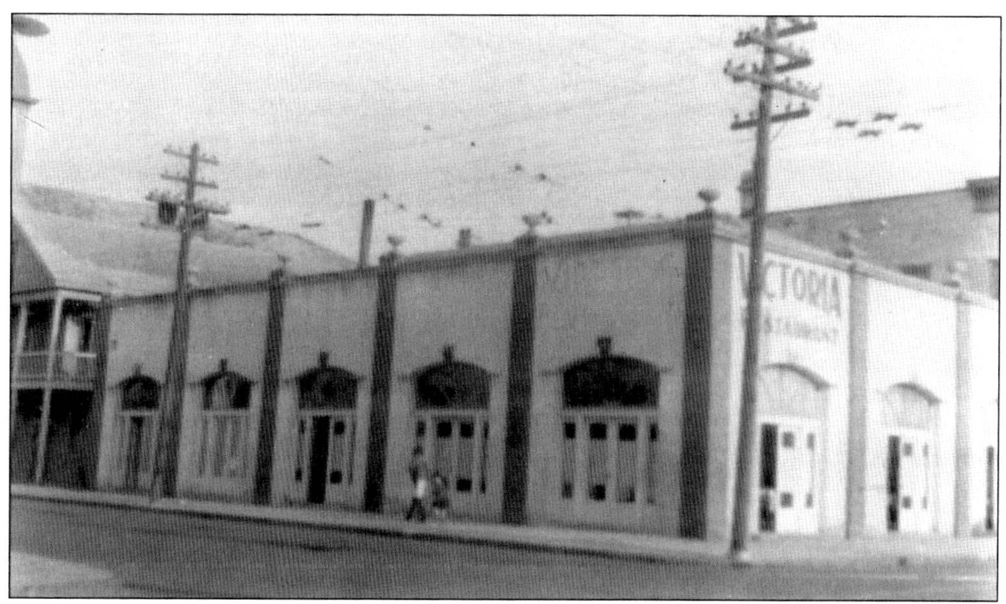

A Spaniard named Juan Farto chose the corner of Duval and Greene Streets to construct a new restaurant, the Victoria, in 1917. Architect Jose Castillo designed it using steel for strength, but inside, the atmosphere was all tropical elegance, with painted Cuban tiles and marble. The business thrived through the 1920s. Later, the place was transformed into Key West's most famous bar: Sloppy Joe's. (Courtesy of Monroe County Library, Key West.)

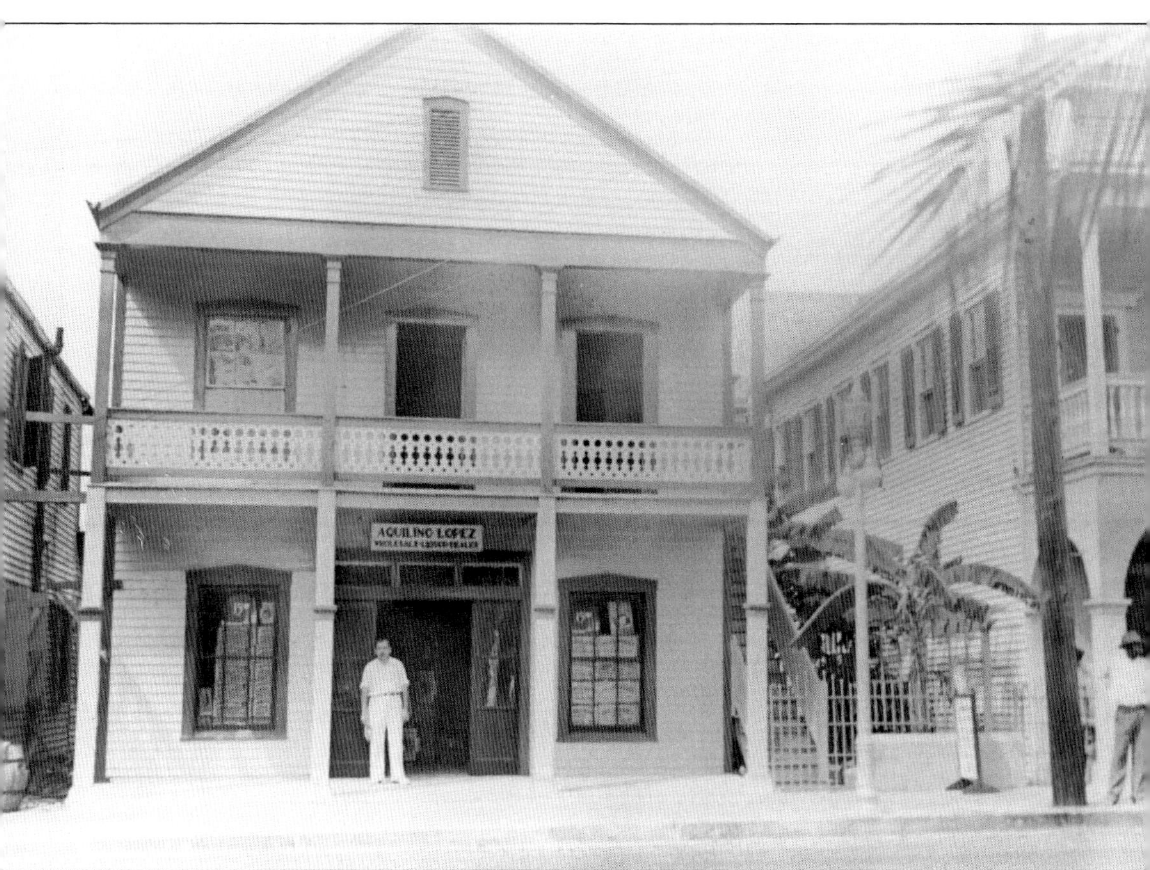

Aquilino Lopez poses in front of his store on the 200 block of Duval Street, where he sold liquor wholesale. His shop stood near Delmonico's, the successful restaurant Lopez owned at 218 Duval Street. Born in 1888 in Spain, Aquilino immigrated to the United States and settled in Key West with his wife, Generosa. Today, their home, the Lopez House, still survives on Duval Street, directly across from the Southernmost House, just steps away from South Beach. This photograph of Aquilino must have been taken sometime late in the 1910s, before Prohibition made the open sale of liquor illegal. The 18th Amendment to the US Constitution, passed in 1920, made it illegal to produce, import, transport, or sell alcohol. To say that many Duval Street business owners did not welcome this development would be an understatement. Soon, Key West would rely on rumrunners and speakeasies. (Courtesy of Monroe County Library, Key West.)

Three

Prohibition and the Great Depression

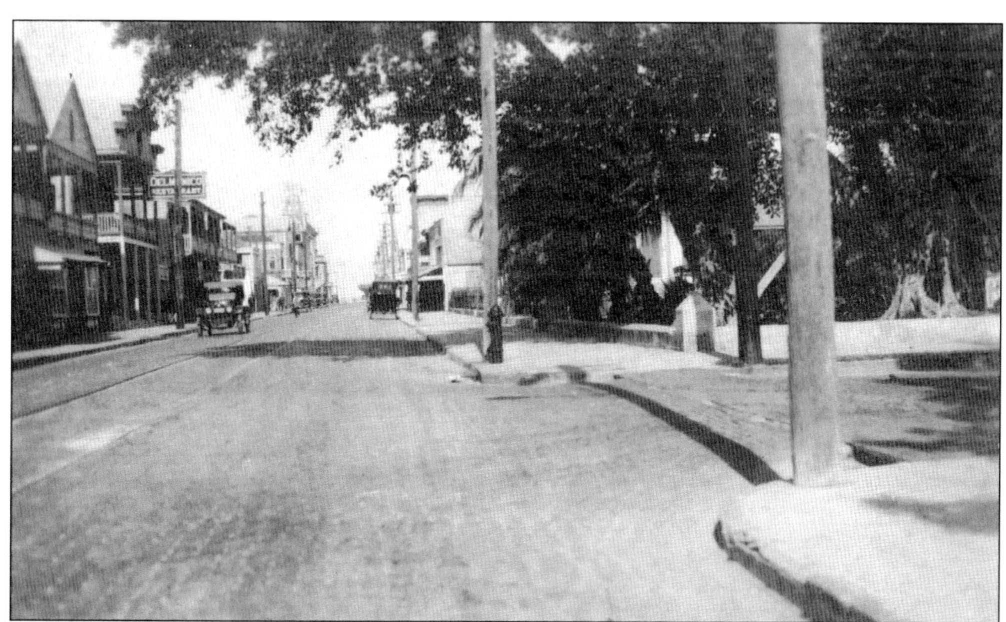

As the 1920s dawned, Duval Street reflected the profound changes Key West and America were undergoing. Automobiles edged out the horse and buggy, new Prohibition laws put a damper on the country's spirits, and movie theaters flourished. Later, the Great Depression enshrouded Key West in poverty and despair. But thanks to a new tourism scheme, Duval Street slowly began to bounce back. (Courtesy of Monroe County Library, Key West.)

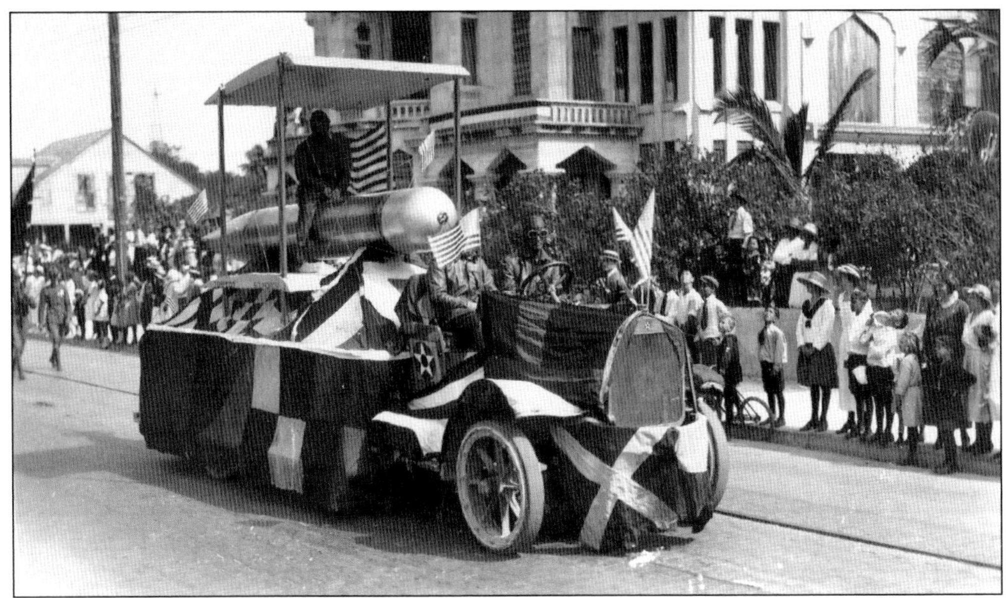

In the years following victory in World War I, America brimmed with a new confidence and patriotism; this parade passing in front of St. Paul's Episcopal Church in March 1922 captures that spirit. Men, women, and children gaze at the Torpedo Squadron's aviators, dashingly dressed in leather jackets and pilots' goggles, as they roll by. (Courtesy of Monroe County Library, Key West.)

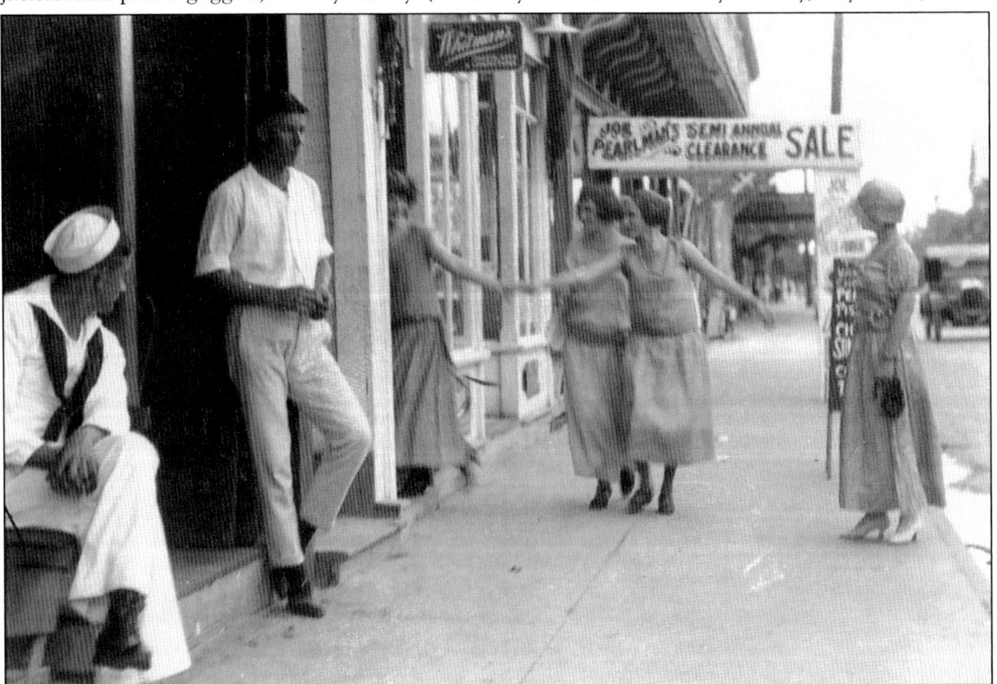

Duval Street witnessed plenty of changes in the 1920s; these young women wear daring, shorter dresses (and no corsets). Flappers and the Jazz Age were not far behind. The three dart into Whitman's chocolate shop, next door to Joe Pearlman's store on the street's 500 block. A sailor and another lady watch to see what the girls are getting up to. (Courtesy of Monroe County Library, Key West.)

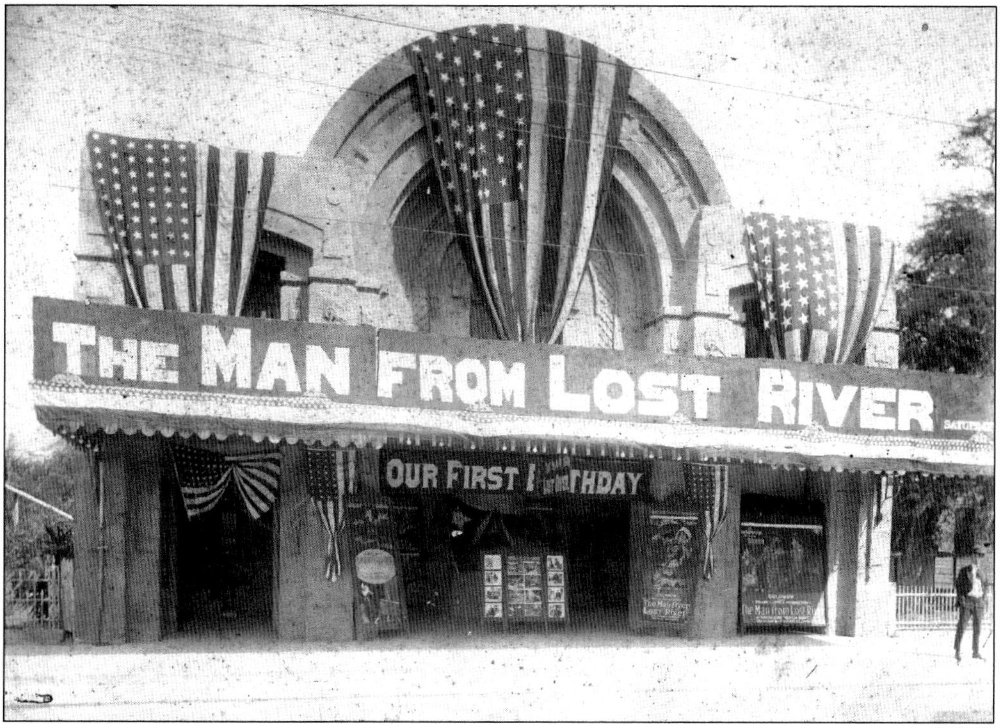

Key West flocked to Duval Street for entertainment, from live music shows to moving pictures. The impressive Strand Theater was built at 527 Duval Street in the early 1920s. Here, it is festooned with giant flags to mark its first anniversary; it is showing *The Man from Lost River*, a 1921 silent film about a young woman named Marcia torn between two loves. (Courtesy of Monroe County Library, Key West.)

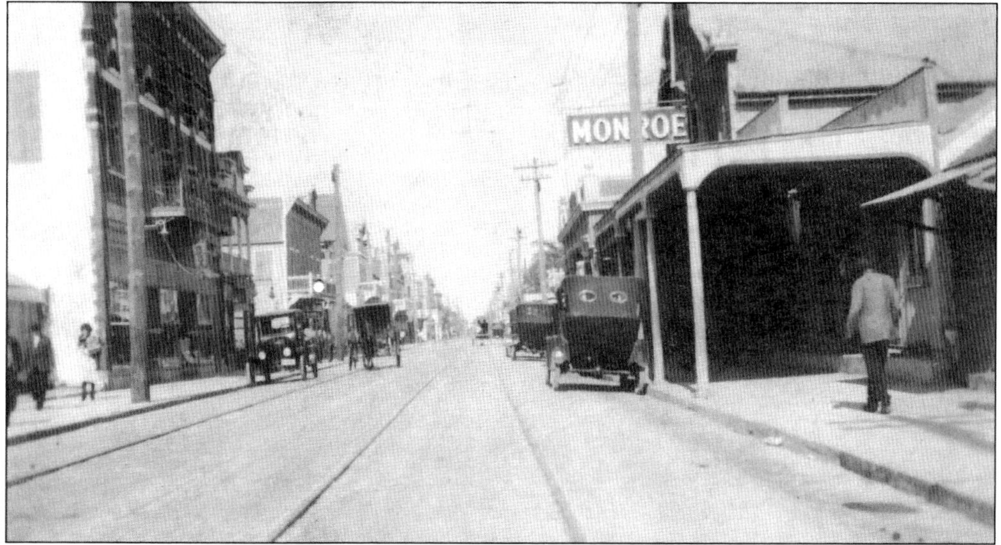

This view of Duval Street from the corner of Angela Street shows a horse and carriage riding over the streetcar rails, with automobiles parked on either side of the street. The Monroe Theater, which also showed movies, stood at 623 Duval Street. Unlike the Strand, this building no longer survives. (Courtesy of Monroe County Library, Key West.)

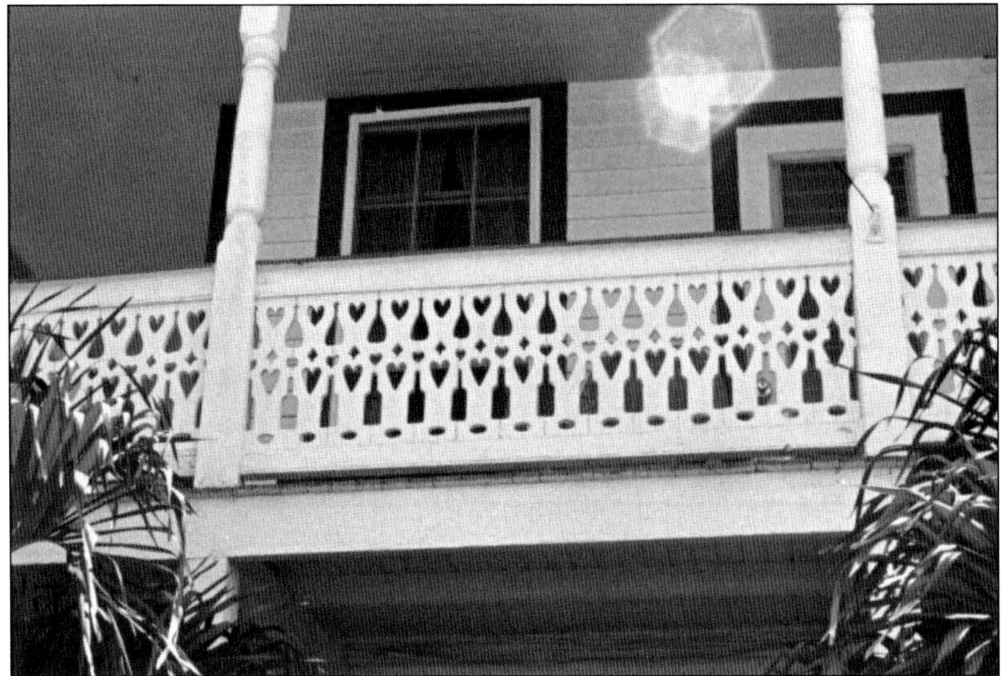

Note the liquor bottle pattern and playing card symbols (hearts and diamonds) carved into this balustrade at 1117 Duval Street. It indicated that a speakeasy operated at this address. The 1920 constitutional amendment that banned alcohol in the United States, known as Prohibition, was wildly unpopular in Key West and poorly enforced. Rumrunners made sure a steady supply of booze arrived from Cuba. (Courtesy of Monroe County Library, Key West.)

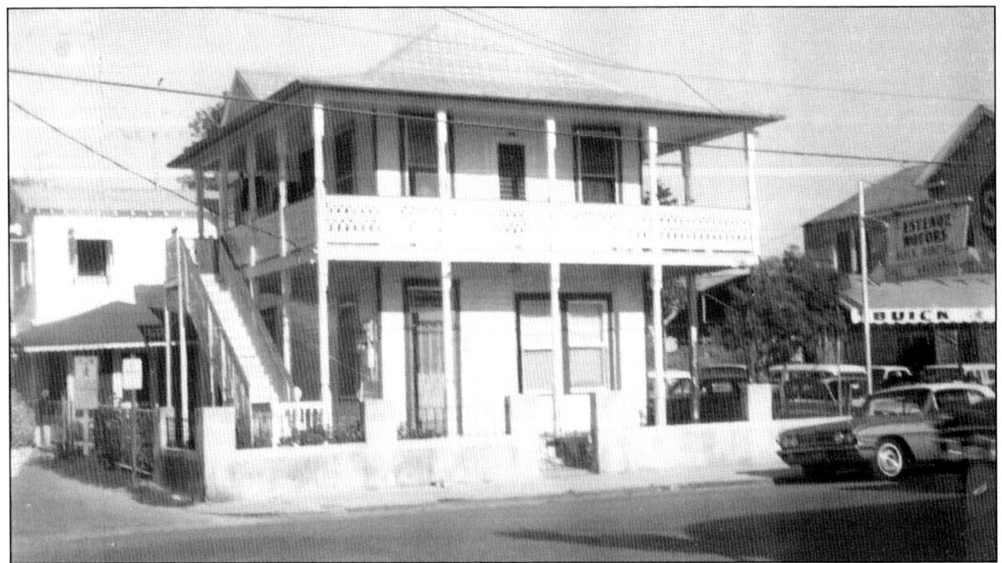

Although the house at 1117 Duval Street was built in 1889, rumrunner Raul Vasquez transformed the house during Prohibition by adding his own special balustrade with its liquor bottle motif. He acquired the balustrade in Cuba on one of his smuggling trips. Allegedly, Raul called his joint the Florence Club, since some of his regulars were married to women named Florence. (Courtesy of Monroe County Library, Key West.)

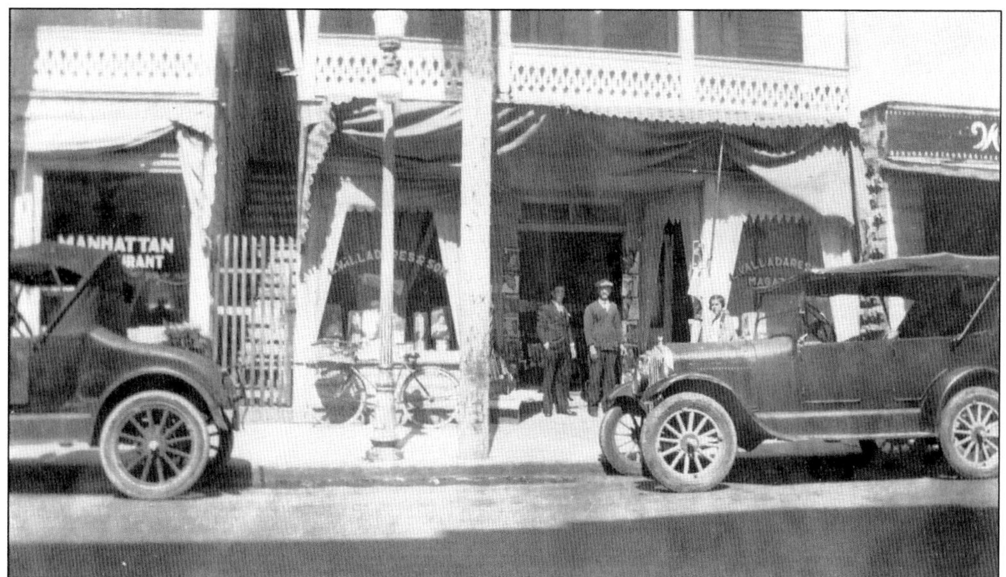

Duval Street still had plenty of legitimate businesses during Prohibition, like the L. Valladares & Son store that operated at 419 Duval Street, next door to the Manhattan Restaurant. Two men, possibly the father-and-son owners, pose at the entrance. Here, shoppers could buy magazines on women's fashion, movie stars, and other entertaining subjects. (Courtesy of Monroe County Library, Key West.)

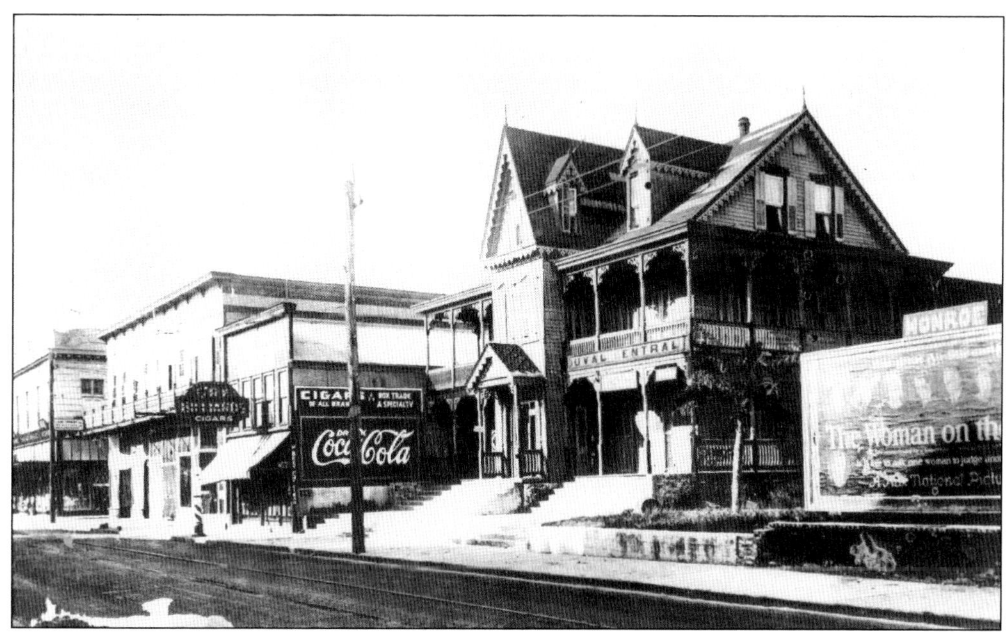

Visitors and Key West locals could buy cigars at this shop between Fleming and Eaton Streets; the Duval Central next door, with its elaborate gingerbread trim, was presumably a hotel. The sign at right advertises a 1924 silent film, *The Woman on the Jury*. These buildings would soon be pulled down to erect a modern hotel, La Concha. (Courtesy of Monroe County Library, Key West.)

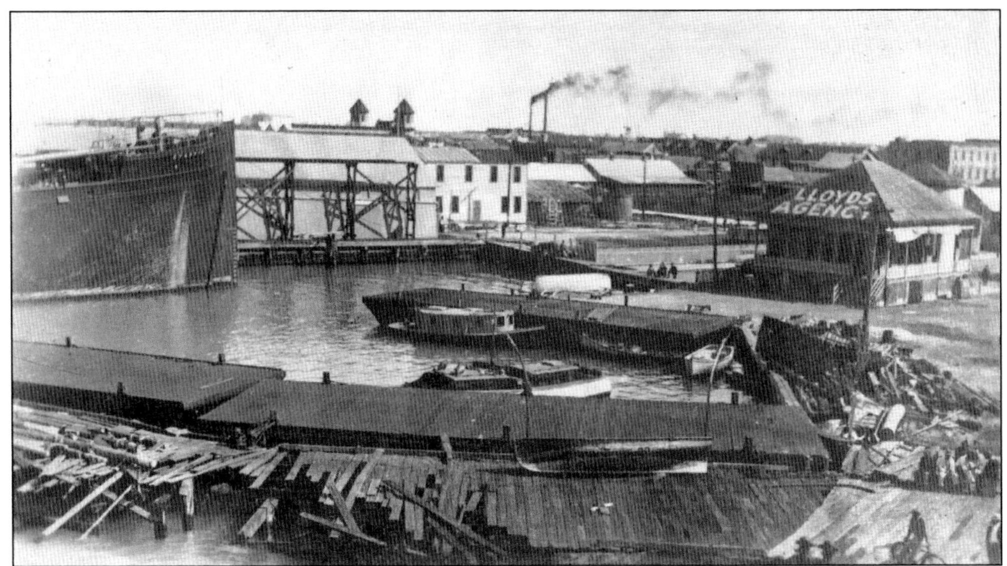

In this 1920s photograph, Duval Street's northern end, which was a working harbor, bustles with industry. In the foreground are two wharves, one apparently new and the other badly damaged. A mammoth freighter protrudes into the frame on the left, while a building, Lloyds Agency, stands on the right. This had once been the ticket office for the Peninsular & Occidental Steamship Company. (Courtesy of Monroe County Library, Key West.)

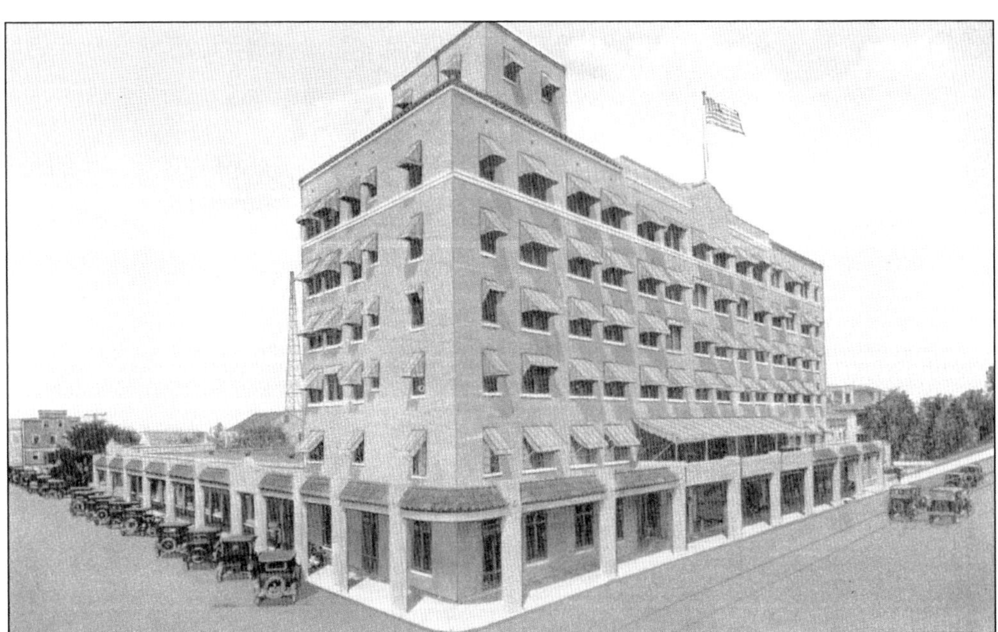

During Florida's 1920s land boom, luxurious hotels sprang up in seaside towns; in 1926, La Concha was Key West's "swell" new addition. With 100 rooms that would set guests back $3 a night, the hotel was expected to herald in a new wave of well-heeled tourists. Unfortunately, the grave economic crisis of the Great Depression lay only a few years off. (Courtesy of Monroe County Library, Key West.)

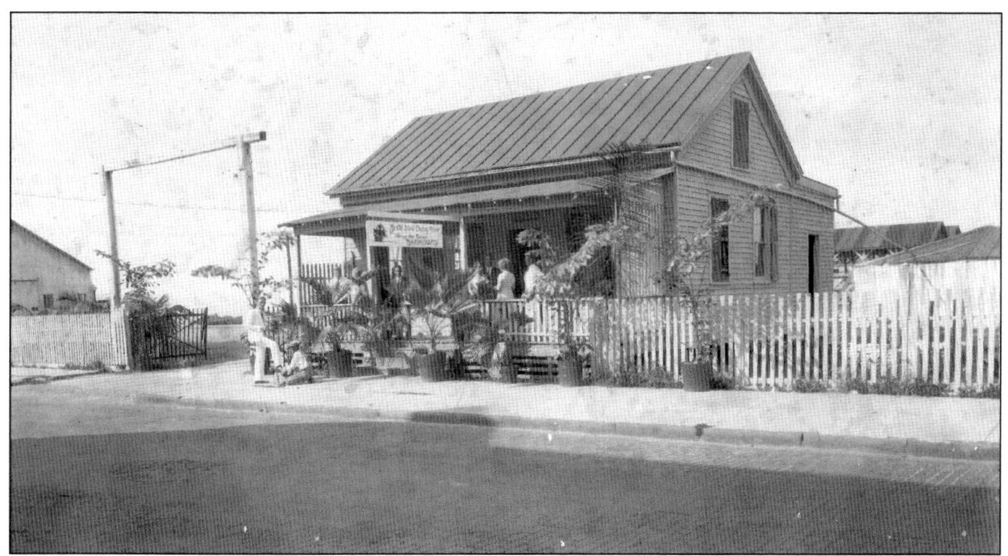

Here, fashionable men and women pose in front of Ye Old Island Trading Post, located at 89 Duval Street. This shop geared toward visitors sold "native and foreign handicrafts." Potted palms lent the property a tropical atmosphere. On the left, an African American boy is shining shoes. (Courtesy of Monroe County Library, Key West.)

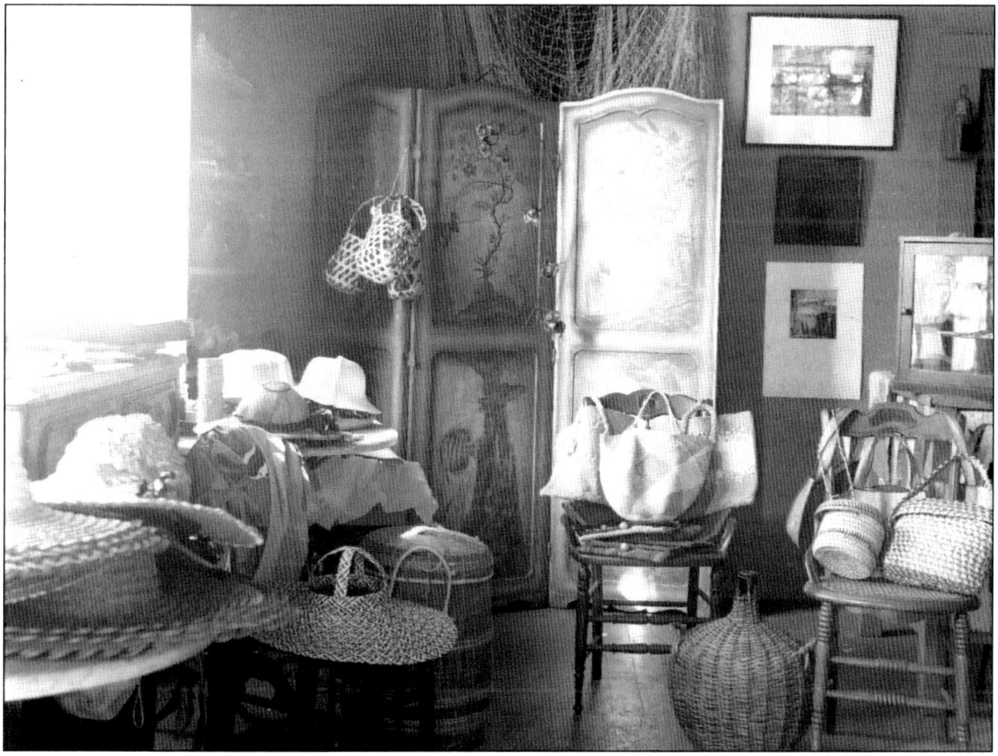

Inside Ye Old Island Trading Post, visitors to Key West could buy all kinds of straw bags and sunhats to protect faces from the intense tropical sun. Some of the "straw" was actually strips of palm frond, a resource that the Florida Keys had in abundance. (Courtesy of Monroe County Library, Key West.)

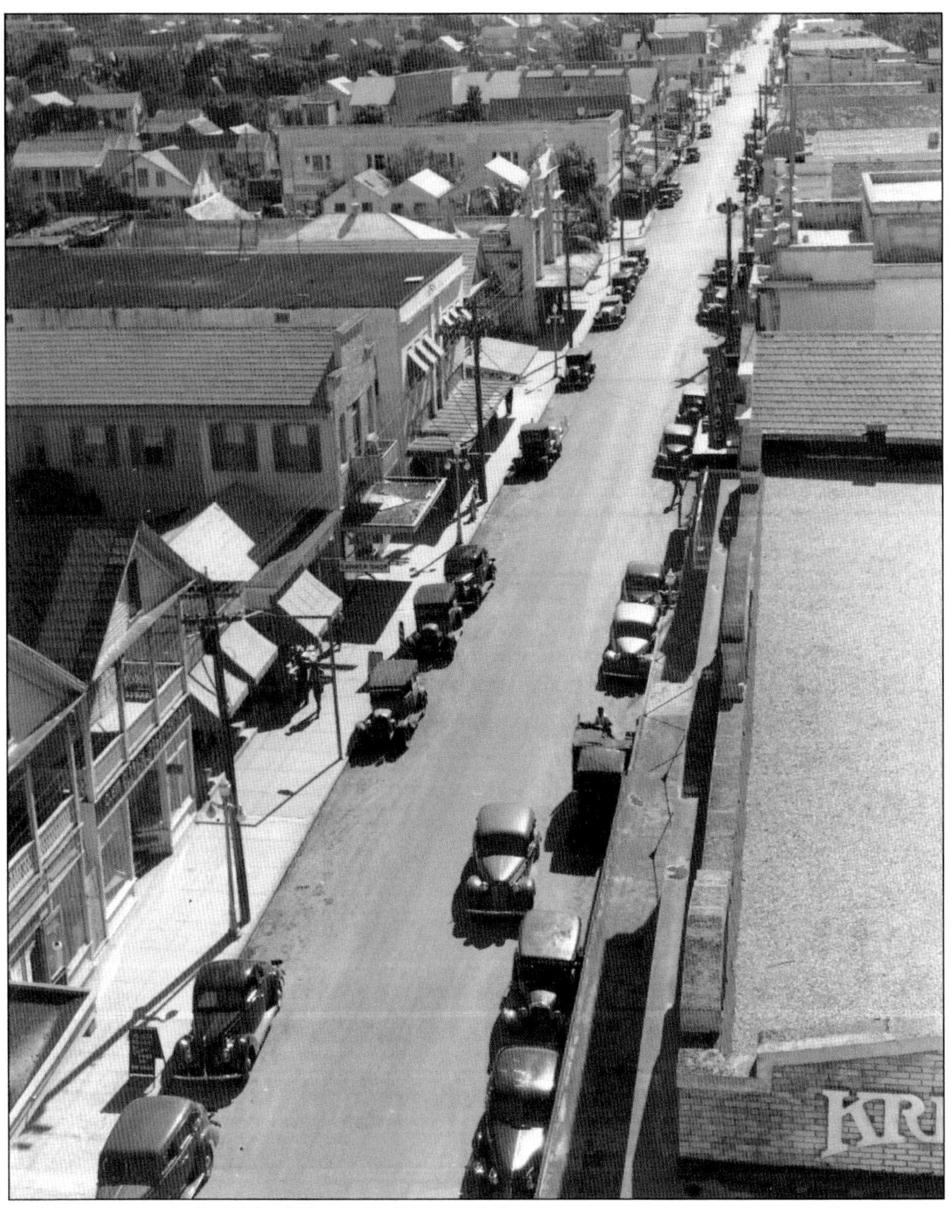

Duval Street—and all of Key West—had been sliding into an economic slump before the stock market crash of 1929: cigar factories relocated to Tampa, the sponging industry moved to Tarpon Springs, and then the Navy closed its airbase and submarine station. The Great Depression that followed forced the town to the edge of desperation. This photograph of Duval, taken from La Concha hotel in the 1930s, belies a grim reality of shuttered stores and increasing numbers of people with no work and little food. La Concha itself was on the skids and had to be sold off. Duval Street, the central commercial and entertainment artery of the island, grew shabbier with each passing month. By 1933, around 5,000 unemployed people vainly hunted for jobs. Some lived off a diet of "grits and grunts," cheap hominy grits and an easy-to-catch local fish. With Key West bankrupt and desperate, the federal and state governments needed to intervene. After this bleakest period, Duval Street's fortunes were about to change again. (Courtesy of Monroe County Library, Key West.)

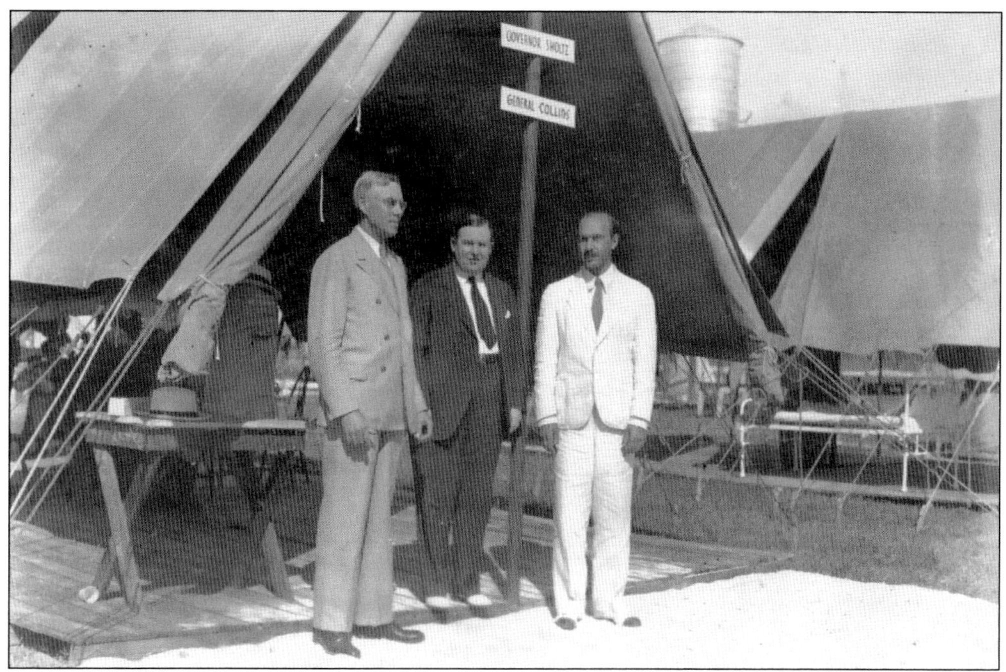

Florida governor Dave Shultz (center) appointed Julius Stone (right) director of the Florida division of Federal Emergency Relief Agency (FERA); to save Key West from penury, Stone hit upon the idea of promoting the city as a tourist town. He convinced residents to volunteer for a "Great Clean Up," painting houses and fences, including on Duval Street, and clearing beaches like South Beach of seaweed, all in an effort to attract travelers. (Courtesy of Monroe County Library, Key West.)

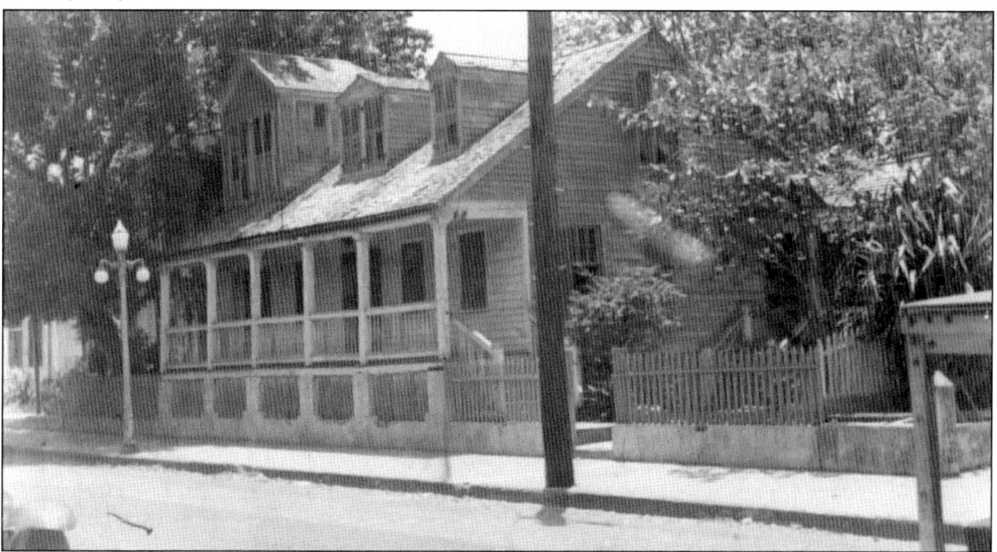

As FERA was replaced by the Works Progress Administration, more schemes were hatched to change Key West's fortunes and create jobs. Unemployed painters, writers, and photographers were sent to both document and beautify the island. This WPA photograph captures the condition of the Oldest House at 322 Duval Street; like many other homes in Depression-era Key West, it needed refurbishment and care. (Courtesy of Monroe County Library, Key West.)

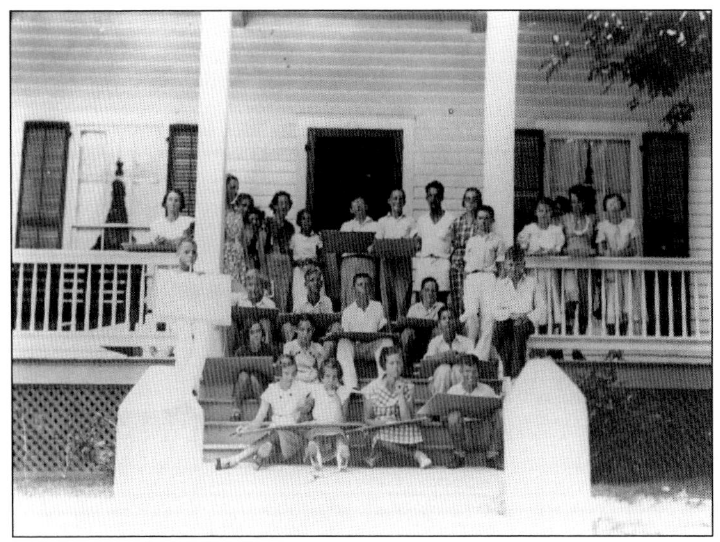

Caroline Lowe, alleged Confederate flag waver during the Civil War, may have been saddened to see the dilapidated state of her home as Key West entered the Depression. Fortunately, the house, located at 303 Duval Street, was restored in the 1930s and turned into Key West's first art gallery. Here, a group of art students gather on its steps in 1935. (Courtesy of Monroe County Library, Key West.)

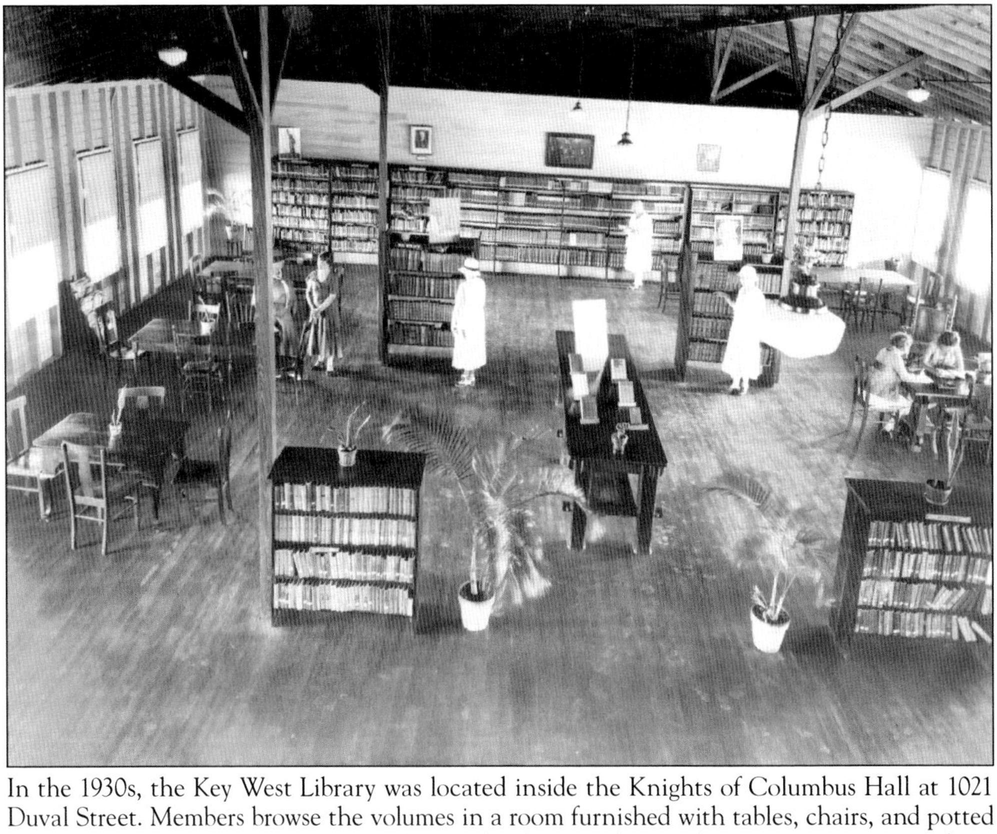

In the 1930s, the Key West Library was located inside the Knights of Columbus Hall at 1021 Duval Street. Members browse the volumes in a room furnished with tables, chairs, and potted palms. In those tough economic times, buying books was a luxury that many Key West residents could not afford, but the library gave people access to literature, knowledge, and entertainment. (Courtesy of Monroe County Library, Key West.)

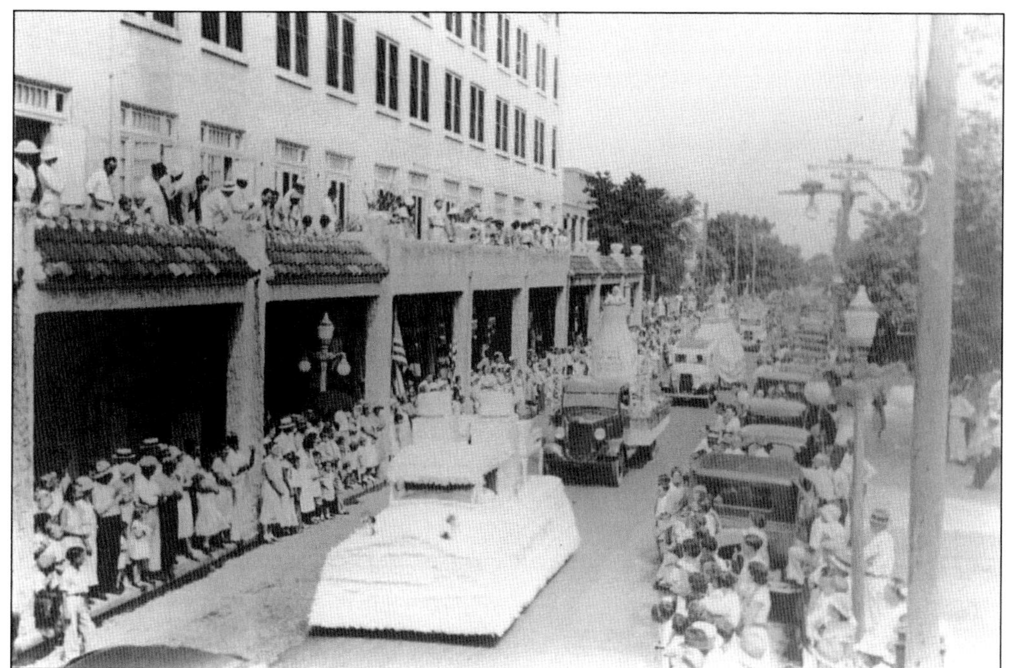

Even in the depths of the Depression, Key West would still turn out for a parade. It is a sunny Monday on September 3, 1934, as men, women, and children line Duval Street outside La Concha for the Labor Day parade. For some mysterious reason, on the second float, a woman poses atop a giant bottle of milk. (Courtesy of Monroe County Library, Key West.)

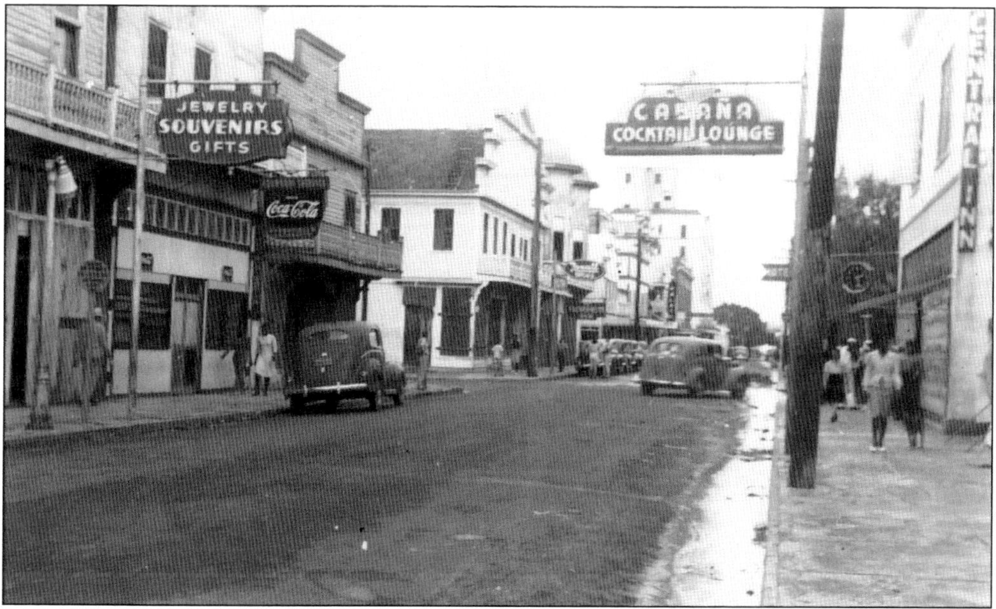

As this image of Duval at Southard Street shows, the restrictive days of Prohibition finally ended in 1933. At last, instead of lurking in speakeasies, locals and visitors could celebrate happy hour in public. Once again, Duval Street became known for its memorable bars; one of the places to open its doors to eager customers was the Cabaña Cocktail Lounge, pictured here. (Courtesy of Monroe County Library, Key West.)

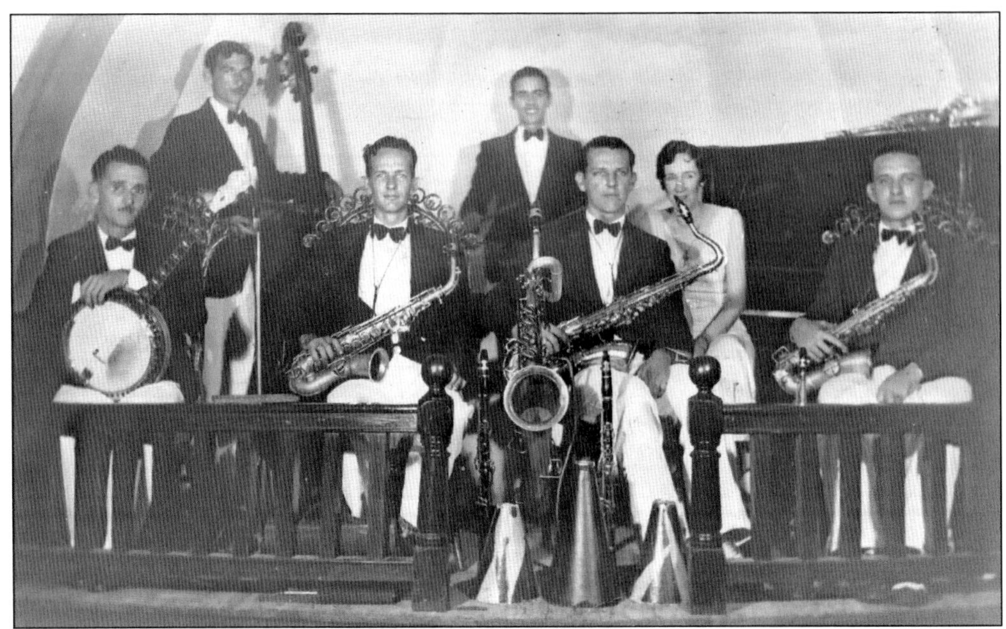

After Prohibition, good times rolled again. This sharply dressed band appeared at the Cuban Club (the Sociedad de Cuba) at 1108 Duval Street in the 1930s. The musicians, from left to right, are Pete Fernandez on banjo, Barry Barroso on double bass, Charles Curry on saxophone, Gould Curry on percussion, Jack Baker on sax, Miaiam Piodela (possibly the singer), and Joe Dorano, also on sax. (Courtesy of Monroe County Library, Key West.)

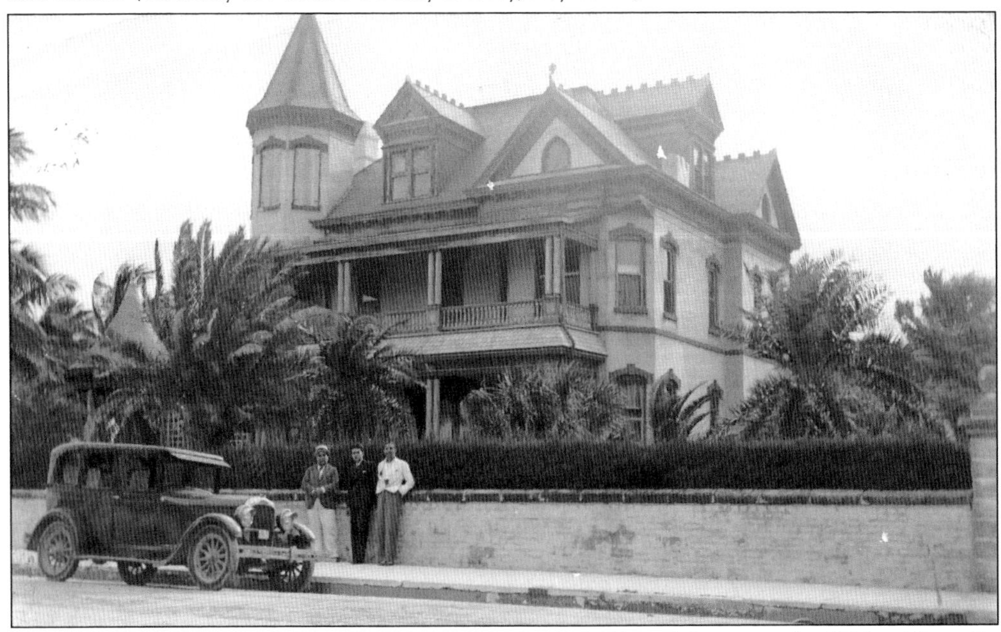

Three men pose outside the Southernmost House at 1400 Duval Street in the 1930s. Allegedly, even this splendid mansion had functioned as part speakeasy during Prohibition. Patrons could dine at a restaurant on the first floor or gamble their dollars away (presumably while consuming illicit hooch) on the second. With Prohibition repealed, it evolved into a legal nightclub. (Courtesy of Monroe County Library, Key West.)

Centrally Located
All Outside Rooms

Parking Free
For Guest Cars

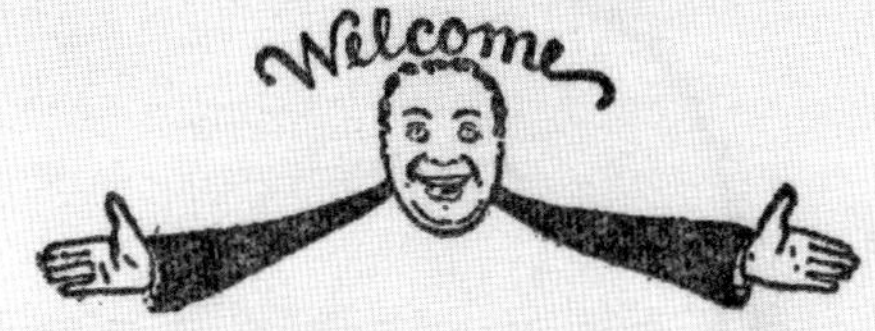

DUVAL HOTEL

FRANK JOHNSON, PROP.

Comfortable, Airy Rooms
Moderate Rates
$1.00 Per Night

130 Duval St.,
Key West, Florida

It seems almost inconceivable that at one time, travelers could enjoy a Duval Street hotel for $1 per night. Owned by Frank Johnson, the Duval Hotel offered "comfortable, airy rooms" and another coveted perk, free parking. As more tourists arrived on the island, the work of Julius Stone, the WPA, and countless local volunteers was finally bearing fruit. (Courtesy of Monroe County Library, Key West.)

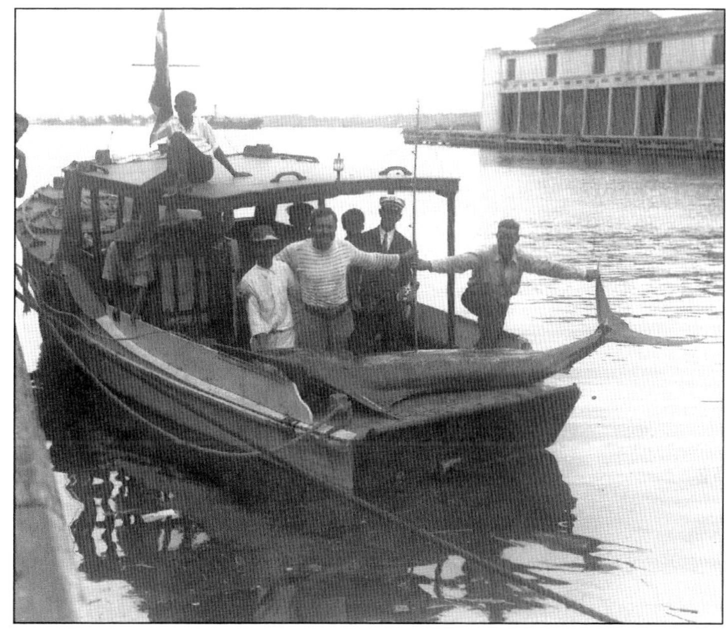

Celebrated writer Ernest Hemingway and his pal Joe Russell (far right) would make Duval Street famous. Russell had been one of Key West's most prolific rum smugglers, but with Prohibition over, he opened a legitimate place on Greene Street. After his landlord increased the rent in 1937, Russell and his customers moved Sloppy Joe's into the old Victoria Restaurant at 201 Duval Street. (Courtesy of the John F. Kennedy Presidential Library.)

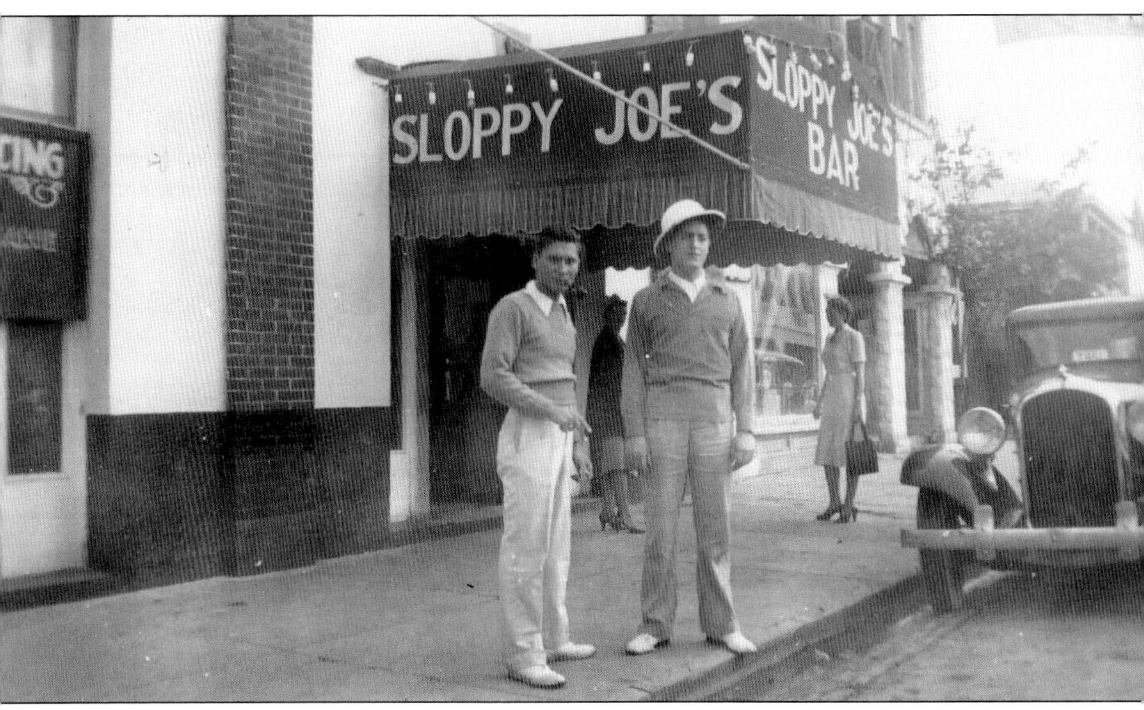

Two men stand on the sidewalk outside Sloppy Joe's bar in the late 1930s. Not only did Joe Russell's joint boast the longest bar in Key West, it also offered gambling in a back area called the Club Room. According to artist and historian Sharon Wells, at the time, "draft beer cost a nickel and a bowl of popcorn came with it." Ernest Hemingway became one of the bar's most reliable patrons, at least until he left Key West after splitting with his wife, Pauline, in 1939. But for a time, the new Sloppy Joe's on Duval Street was the unofficial Hemingway headquarters, where he drank with his pack of friends, also known as "the Mob." Hanging on one wall was a 119-pound sailfish caught by the great writer himself. On another wall was the WPA mural of Joe Russell, Hemingway, and "Big" Al Skinner, a favorite bartender. Not even a decade old, Sloppy Joe's bar was well on its way to becoming a legend. (Courtesy of Monroe County Library, Key West.)

Four

WORLD WAR II AND THE POSTWAR PERIOD

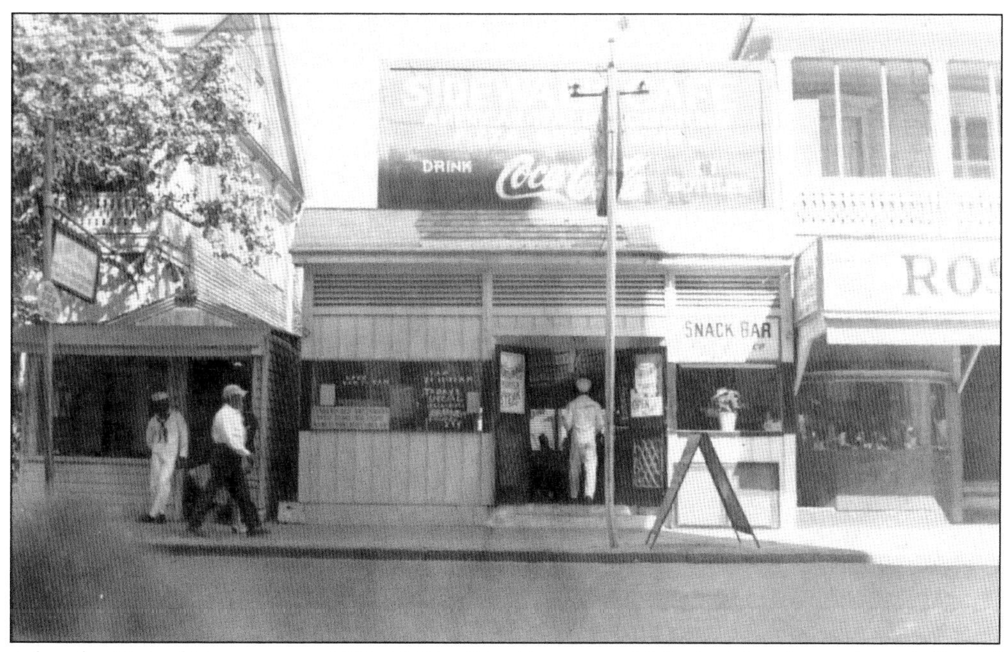

After the United States entered World War II in December 1941, the island saw a huge influx of military personnel and contractors, swelling in the war years to approximately 10,000. Suddenly, sailors flocked to Duval Street day and night. One Navy report noted that the street was "a wide-open honky-tonk area, studded with bars and so-called night clubs of fairly tawdry character." (Courtesy of Monroe County Library, Key West.)

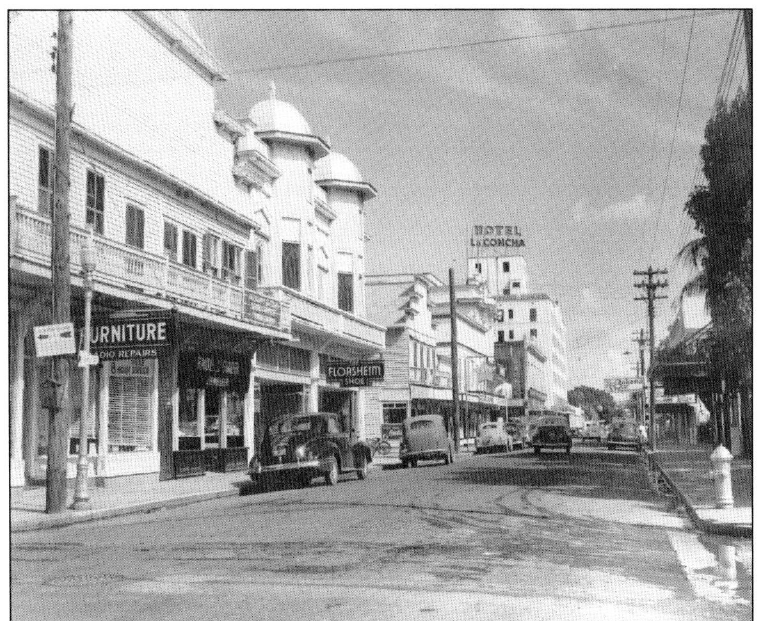

Even before America entered the war, the US Navy's presence in Key West was growing. Duval Street, with its many restaurants and bars, like the Bahama Bar (down the street on the right), became a magnet for soldiers and sailors who were far from home. (Courtesy of Monroe County Library, Key West.)

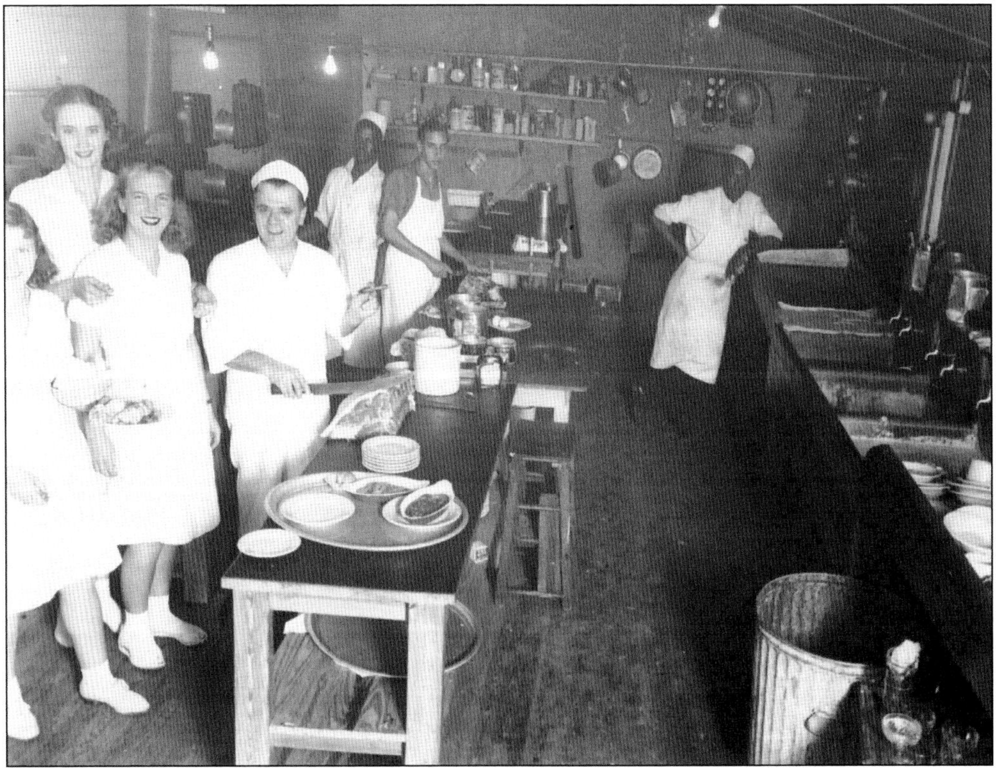

Cooks and waitresses smile inside a hotel kitchen at 1317 Duval Street, between United and South Streets. After the lean years of the Great Depression, businesses on Duval Street thrived, thanks to the presence of the US military on the island. Although tourism had already started to revive the city in the late 1930s, now there were many more job opportunities. (Courtesy of Monroe County Library, Key West.)

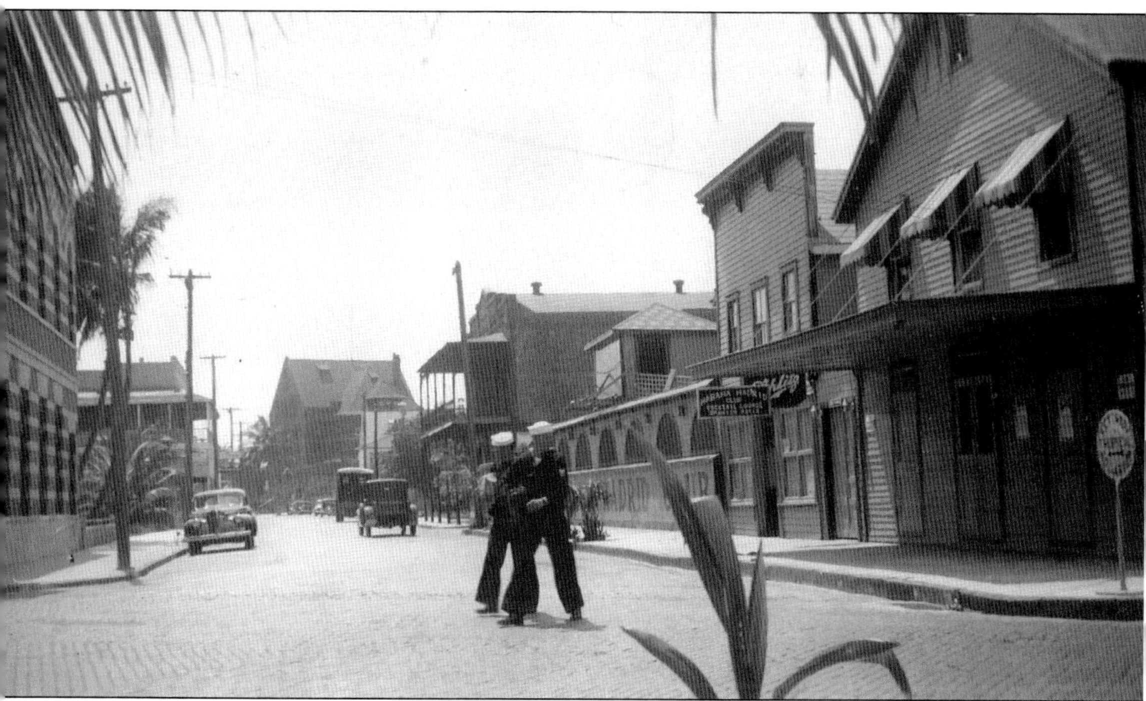

Here, two sailors go "on the town" at the corner of Duval and Front Streets. After Key West's naval station was revived in 1939, and the Fleet Sonar School relocated here in 1940, Navy men and women were a common sight along Duval. In fact, the whole city, not just its central artery, experienced a new burst of vitality, particularly once the United States entered the war. The Navy constructed buildings and brought a much-needed water pipeline through the Keys to Key West. Hotels were packed with personnel and contractors; bars like Sloppy Joe's poured endless drinks and held dances to keep servicemen entertained. Restaurants and coffee shops did a brisk business. Despite the party-time atmosphere on Duval Street, however, danger lurked offshore: Nazi submarines stealthily hunted for targets off the coast of Florida. (Courtesy of Monroe County Library, Key West.)

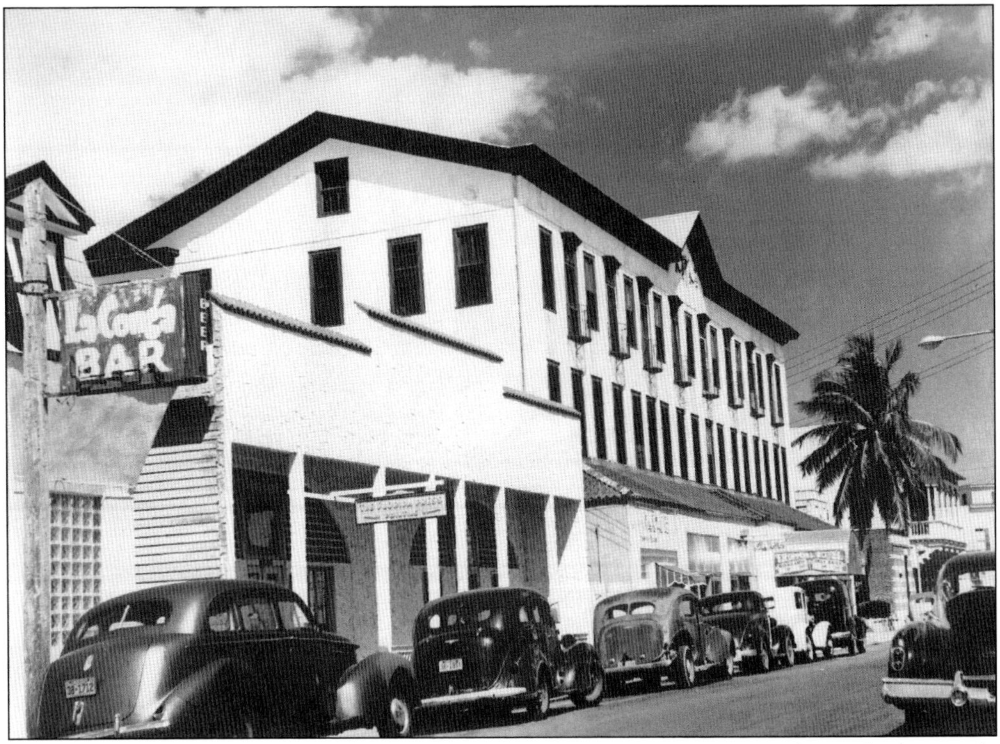

The Jefferson Hotel, built in the 1890s, had evolved by World War II; it no longer had a cupola but did boast a coffee shop. One Conch recalled that several civilian married couples stayed at the Jefferson while the men worked construction and other jobs at the naval yard. (Courtesy of Monroe County Library, Key West.)

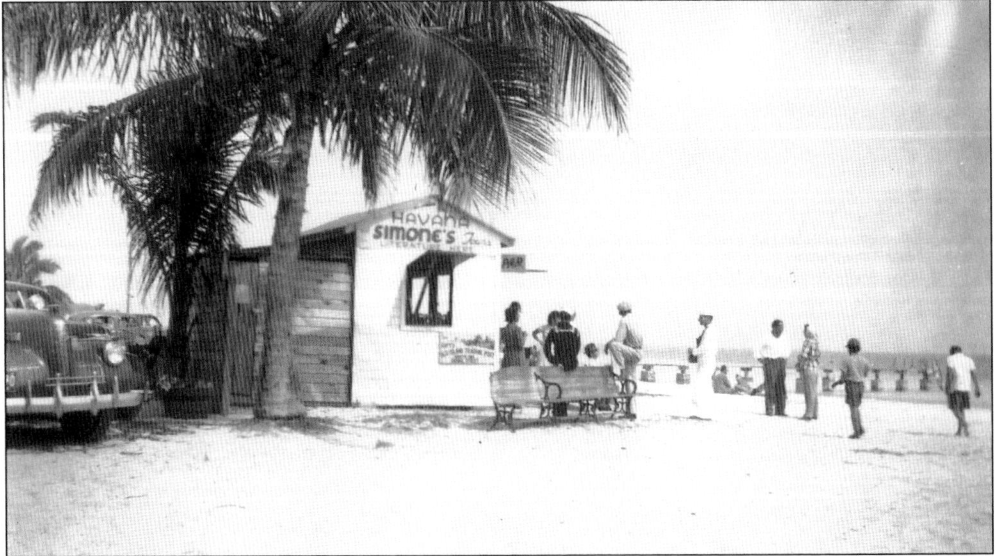

In the 1940s, sailors and civilians take a break and soak in the sun at South Beach, located at the southern end of Duval Street. For plenty of military, the beaches, bright sunshine, and sights of Duval Street were very exotic. The hut in the photograph advertises trips to another tropical city: Havana. (Courtesy of Monroe County Library, Key West.)

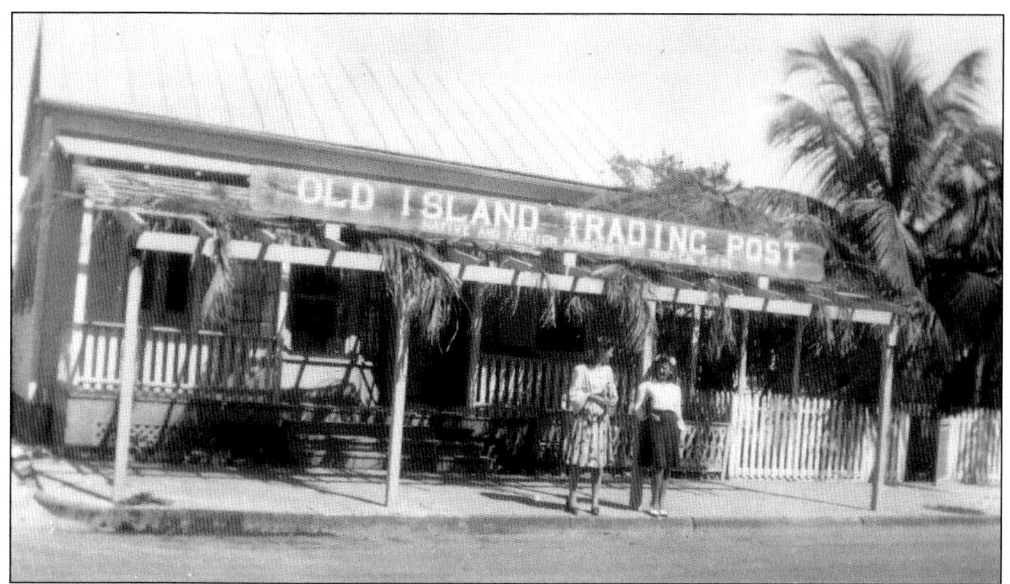

The Old Island Trading Post at 89 Duval Street (near Front Street) was a store that sold handicrafts and souvenirs to Key West's new surge of visitors. Two women pose in front of the store, and a pergola with palm fronds gives the establishment an especially tropical ambiance. (Courtesy of Monroe County Library, Key West.)

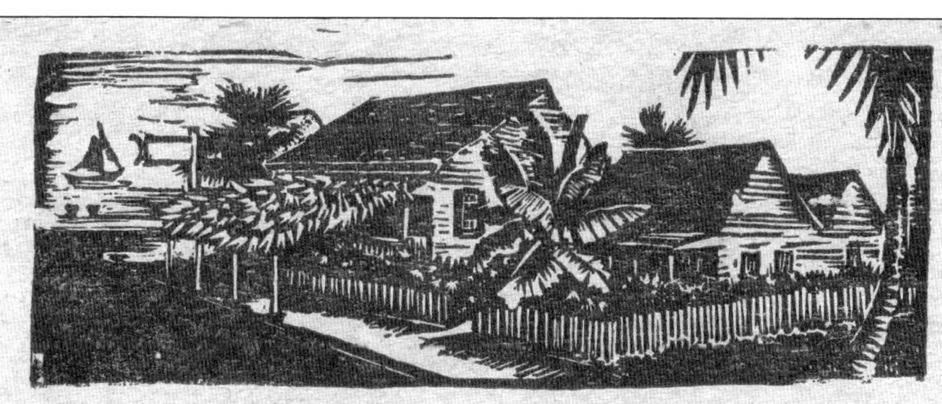

This Old Island Trading Post card features a woodcut illustration that captures the city's unique charms. Military personnel and civilians who worked on the island during the war could buy souvenirs and postcards on Duval Street to remember their time in Key West. (Courtesy of Monroe County Library, Key West.)

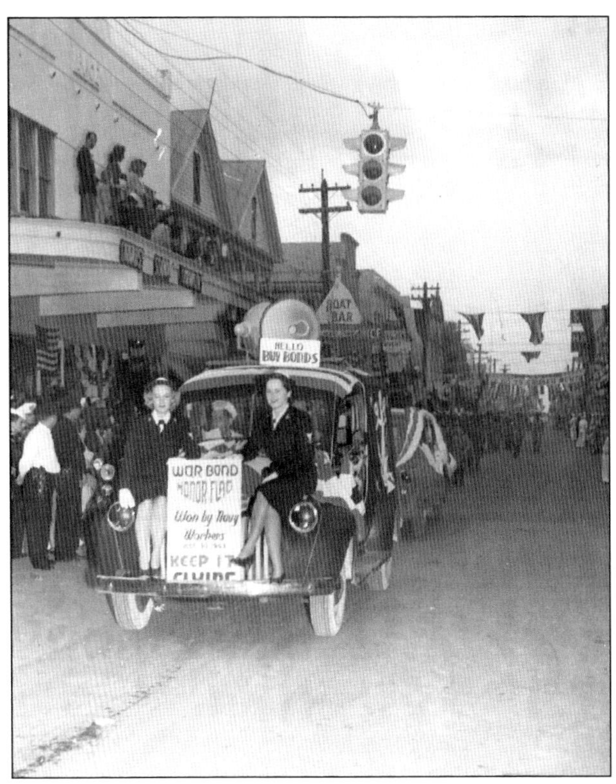

In October 1943, Key West residents watch the Navy Day parade roll down Duval Street. Here, two women ride on a car in celebration of the war bond campaign, which raised money to fund the American war effort. The honor flag they hold had been won by Navy workers on June 30 of that year. (Courtesy of Monroe County Library, Key West.)

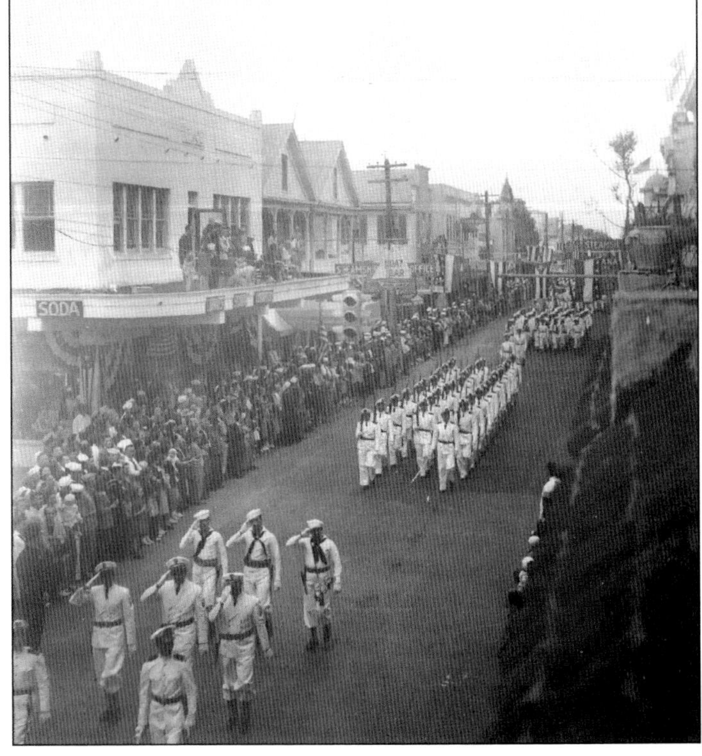

Men, women, and a child have climbed out onto the overhang of the building on the left to get a good view of the troops in the Navy Day parade in 1943. Although many prayed for victory, World War II would continue for almost two more years. (Courtesy of Monroe County Library, Key West.)

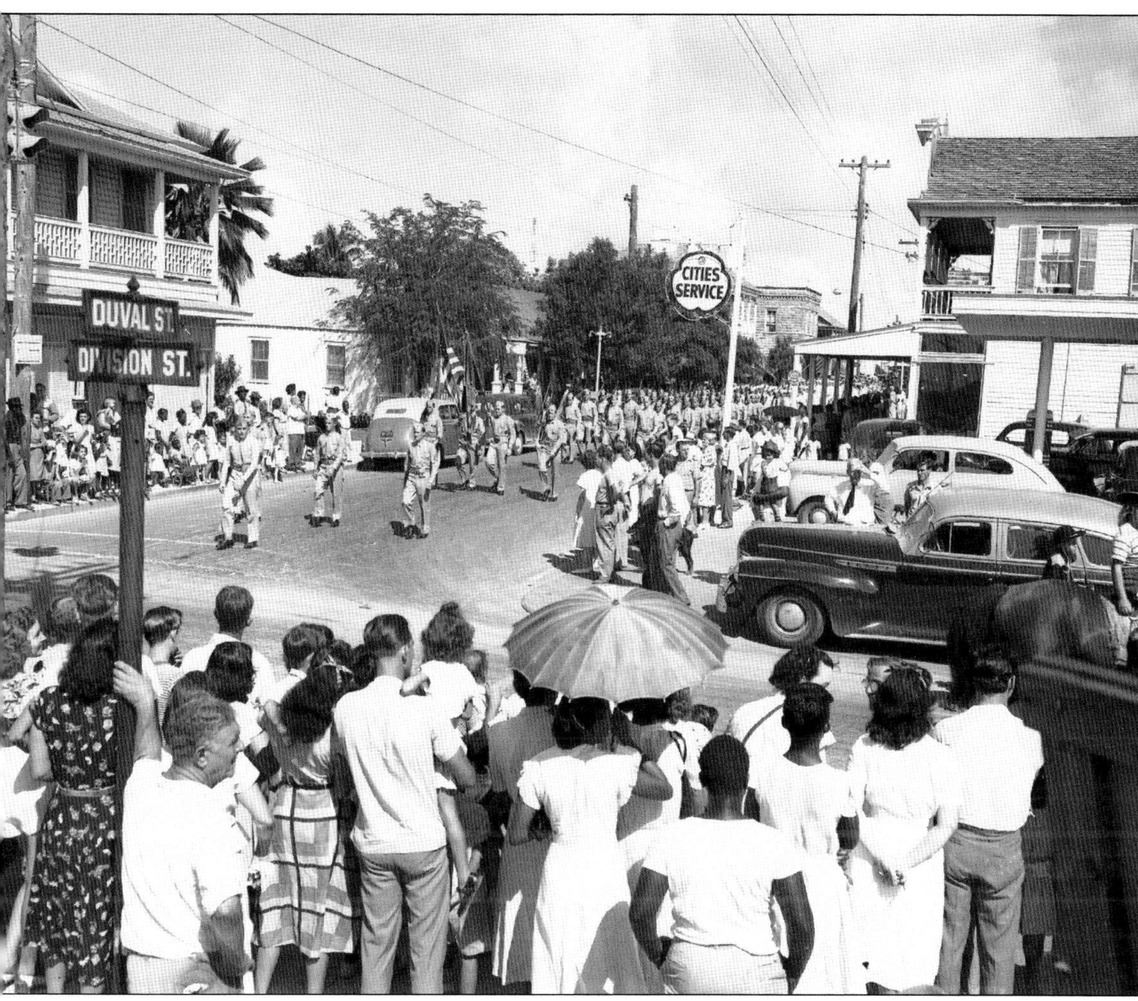

The war in Europe had ended on May 8, 1945, while the war in the Pacific ended with the unconditional surrender of the Japanese on August 15 of that same year. Key Westers have always loved a Duval Street parade and never more so during the wars years and the years that followed, when patriotism ran high. Here, Key West locals turn out to watch the Labor Day parade on Monday, September 6, 1948, as servicemen proudly march through the heart of the city. On the left, the street signs show this to be at the corner of Duval and Division Streets. Division Street's name was later changed to Truman in honor of Pres. Harry Truman, a beloved part-time resident who initially visited the island in 1946 and stayed at the Little White House. (Courtesy of Monroe County Library, Key West.)

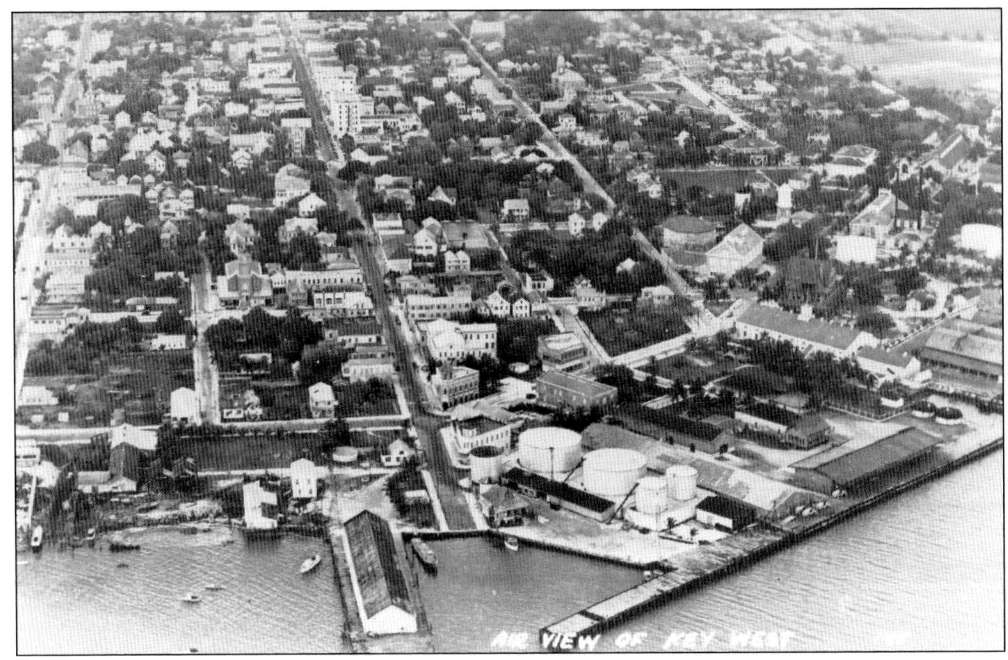

As the 1950s dawned, the northern end of Duval Street remained an industrial, working harbor. This aerial view captures the wharves jutting into the ocean. Also visible are the brick First National Bank building at Front Street (right) and Sloppy Joe's one block south (left). (Courtesy of Monroe County Library, Key West.)

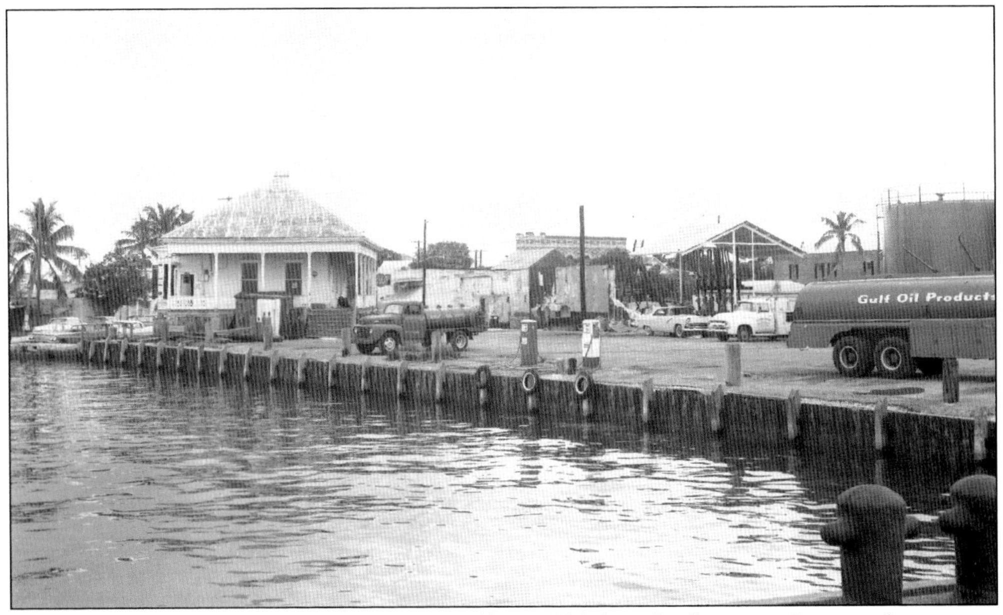

The building at 0 Duval Street was now owned by Gulf Oil. In the foreground are gasoline pumps with long hoses to reach boats docked alongside. Although certain historic buildings were torn down in the name of "modernization," others were adapted for new uses. (Courtesy of Monroe County Library, Key West.)

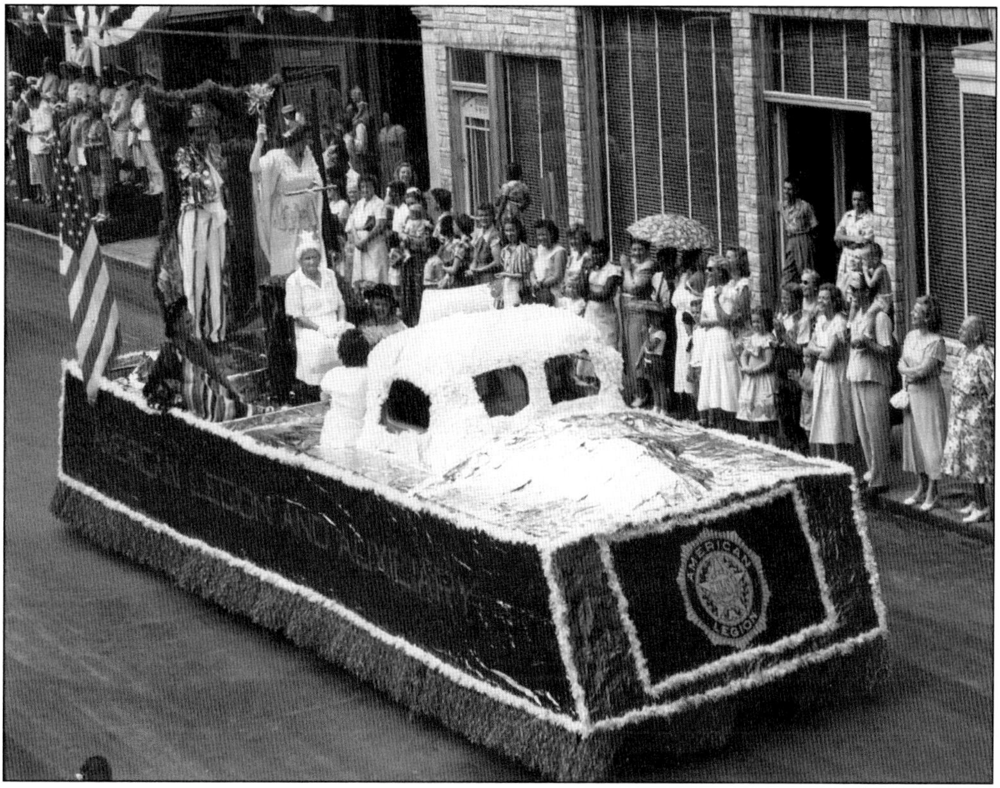

Patriotism continued to flourish in the wake of World War II. Here, citizens line the route to watch the Armed Forces Day parade on May 20, 1950, as the American Legion Auxiliary's float carrying Uncle Sam and the Statue of Liberty rolls down Duval Street. (Courtesy of Monroe County Library, Key West.)

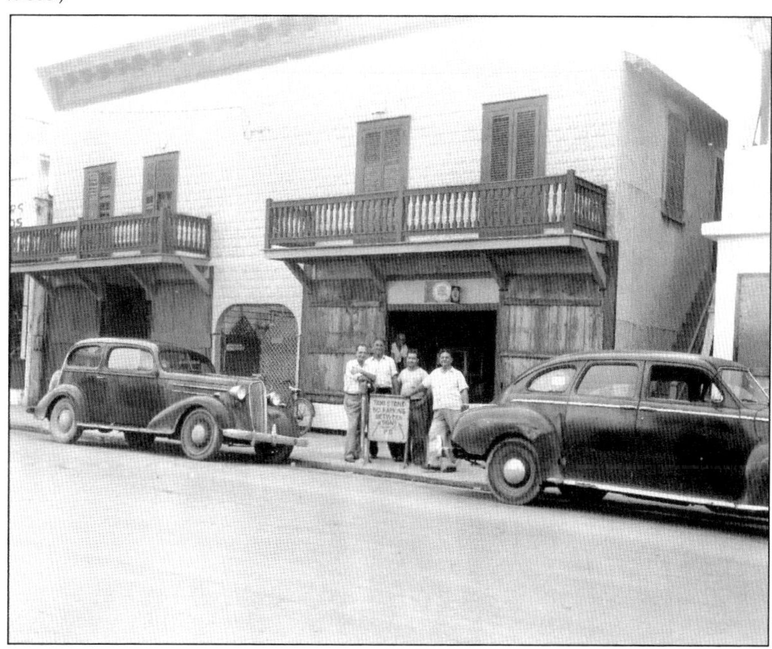

A group of men, probably including taxi drivers, pose for a photograph at a taxi stand at 612 Duval Street. Next door to the humble taxi stand is a jeweler's shop. In the 1950s, shoppers could buy anything on Duval, from a gallon of milk to extravagant diamond bracelets. (Courtesy of Monroe County Library, Key West.)

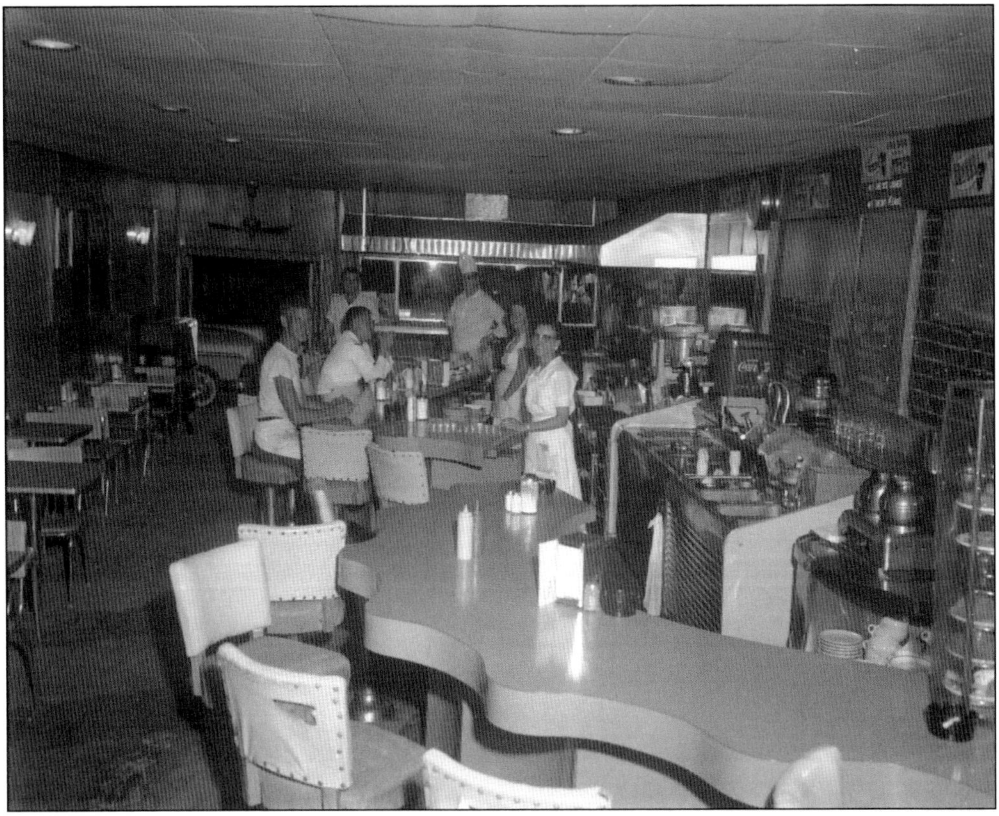

This view of the interior of the Charcoal Hut on the 500 block of Duval Street captures what it felt like to be inside a typical American diner. From the wavy design of the luncheon counter to the waitress's glasses and the whitewall tires on the car outside, this image encapsulates 1950s style. (Courtesy of Monroe County Library, Key West.)

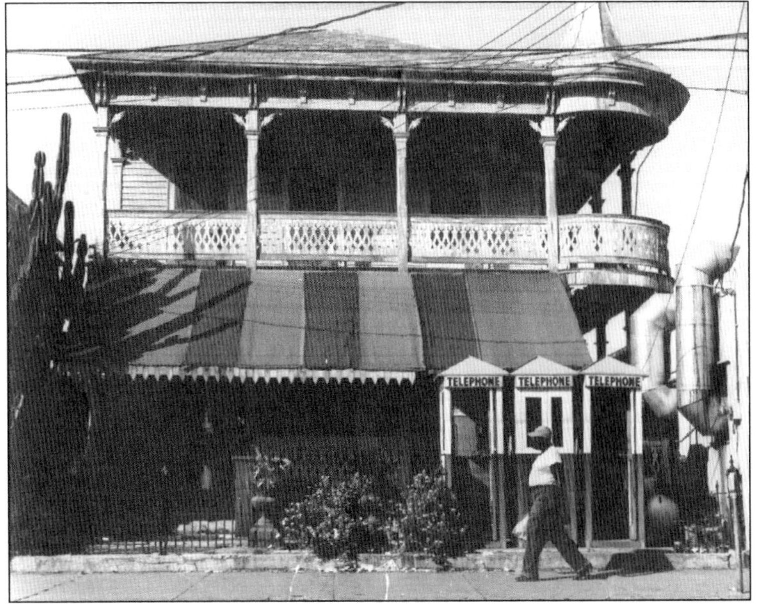

A man strolls by a beautiful, if neglected, home at 525 Duval Street with a Queen Anne–style turret and graceful Bahamian trim on the balustrade. Sadly, this building did not survive the vagaries of time. Telephone booths are also mostly a thing of the past. (Courtesy of Monroe County Library, Key West.)

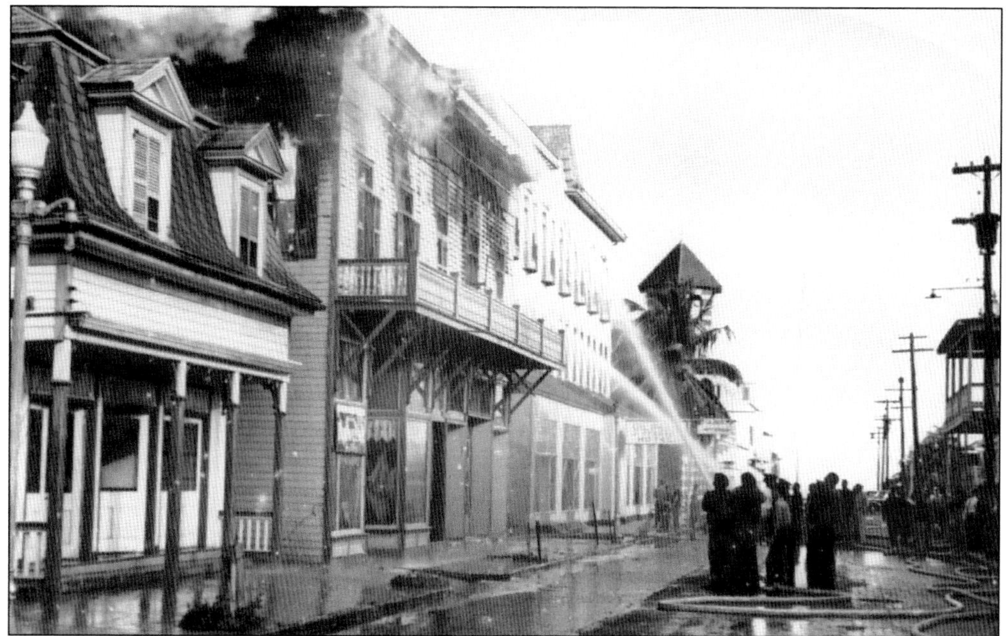

Firefighters work to put out the flames at 116 Duval Street, right next to the Old Customs House. Fires have been a serious threat to Key West's historic architecture for many decades; replacing wood shingle roofs with metal roofs decreased the spread of fire, but Duval Street and the island must still combat conflagrations, which threaten both lives and architectural heritage. (Courtesy of Monroe County Library, Key West.)

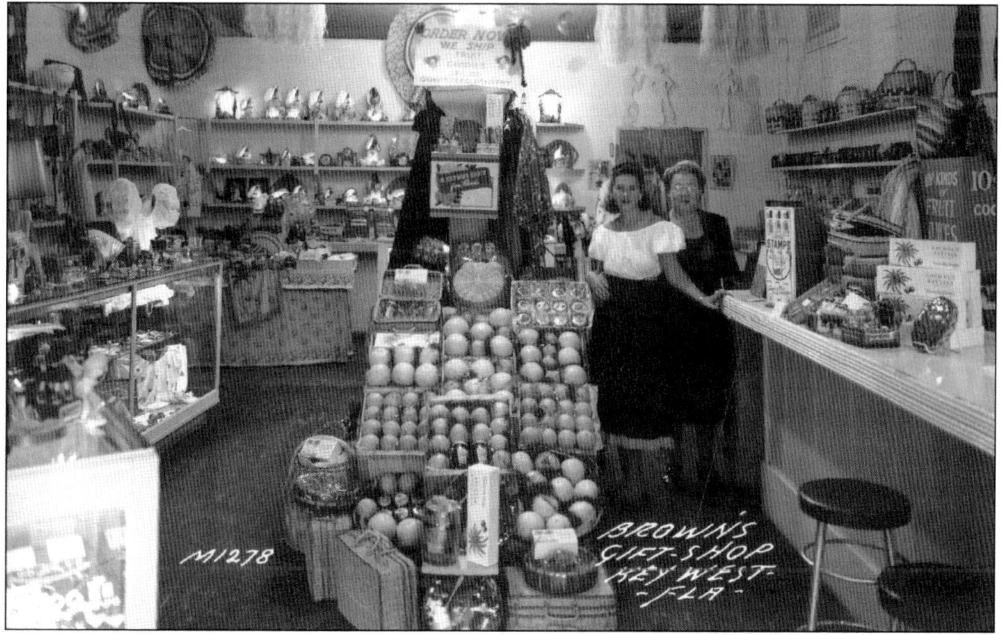

Two women pose inside Brown's Gift Shop, located at 609 Duval Street between Southard and Angela Streets. The shop sold conch shell souvenirs; there were also boxes of oranges and grapefruit ready to be shipped to northern destinations by tourists and military personnel stationed on the island. (Courtesy of Monroe County Library, Key West.)

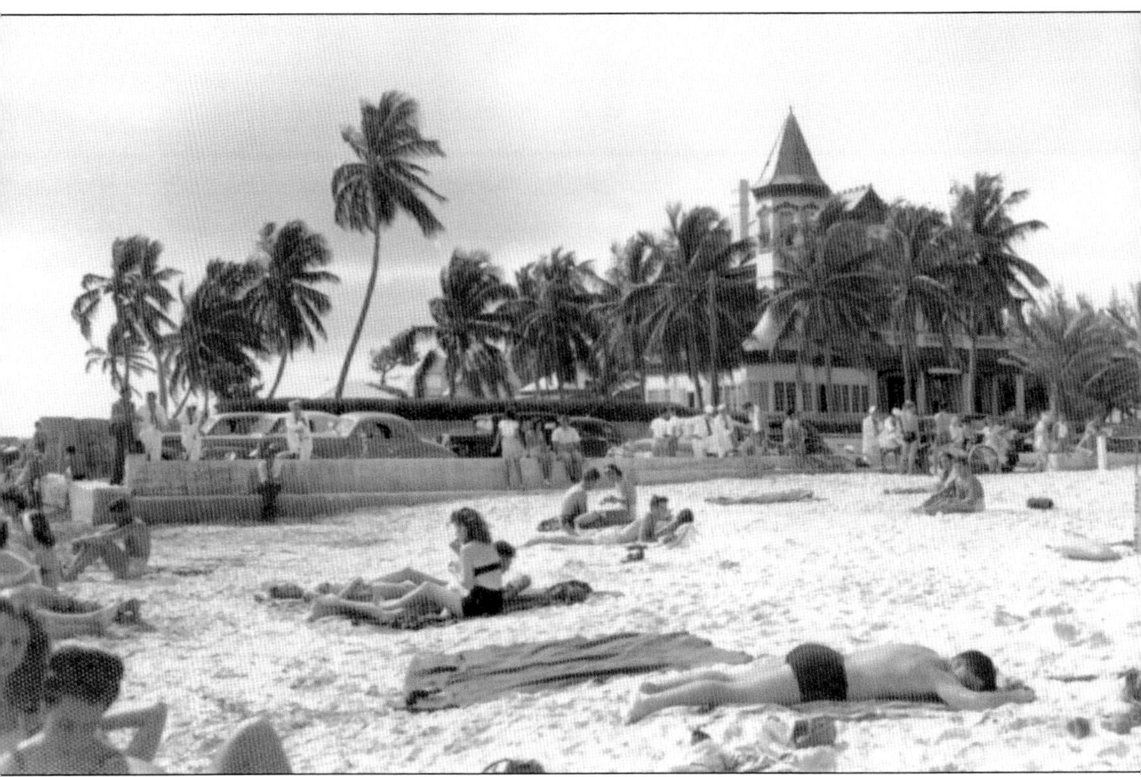

Sunbathers relax on South Beach, at the southern end of Duval, much as people do today. A few of the women wear two-piece swimsuits, a style that gradually became popular during World War II. Just off the beach, sailors and civilians lounge near cars. The Southernmost House rises up in the background, with a sign on the far right advertising that inside the mansion one could find the swanky "Casa Cayo Hueso" nightclub. The Casa Cayo Hueso featured a cocktail bar and a dining room. After serving as a private home to the Harris family and then a speakeasy during Prohibition, the nightclub lured in celebrities and the literati, including Charles Lindbergh, Gloria Swanson, Louis Armstrong, Tennessee Williams, Gore Vidal, and Truman Capote. In 1954, the club was converted back to a private home. (Courtesy of Monroe County Library, Key West.)

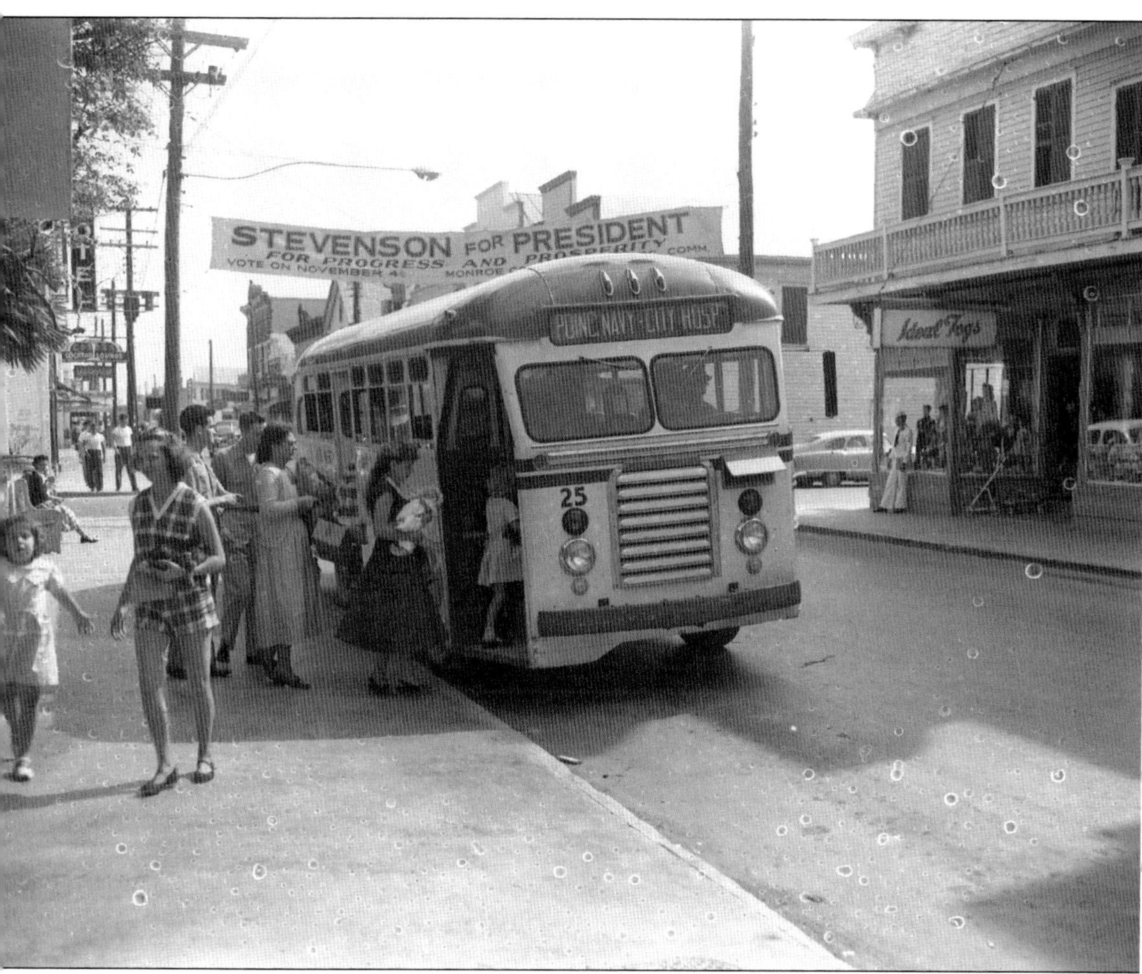

A local bus takes on passengers at Duval near Southard Street. One little girl boards the bus, followed by her mother, who has an infant in her arms. Another woman cradles parcels, probably purchased at stores on Duval Street. In the distance on the left, the Cabaña Cocktail Lounge advertises a "Jam Session;" on the right, a sailor stands in front of Ideal Togs, a shop displaying children's clothes in its windows. Despite the popular bars and hotels, Duval Street was nonetheless home to businesses that catered to the needs of Key West citizens, with everything from barbershops to groceries. In a sign of the times, the banner hanging overhead proclaims "Stevenson for President." Adlai Stevenson, the Democratic nominee, was defeated by Dwight Eisenhower in both 1952 and 1956. (Courtesy of Monroe County Library, Key West.)

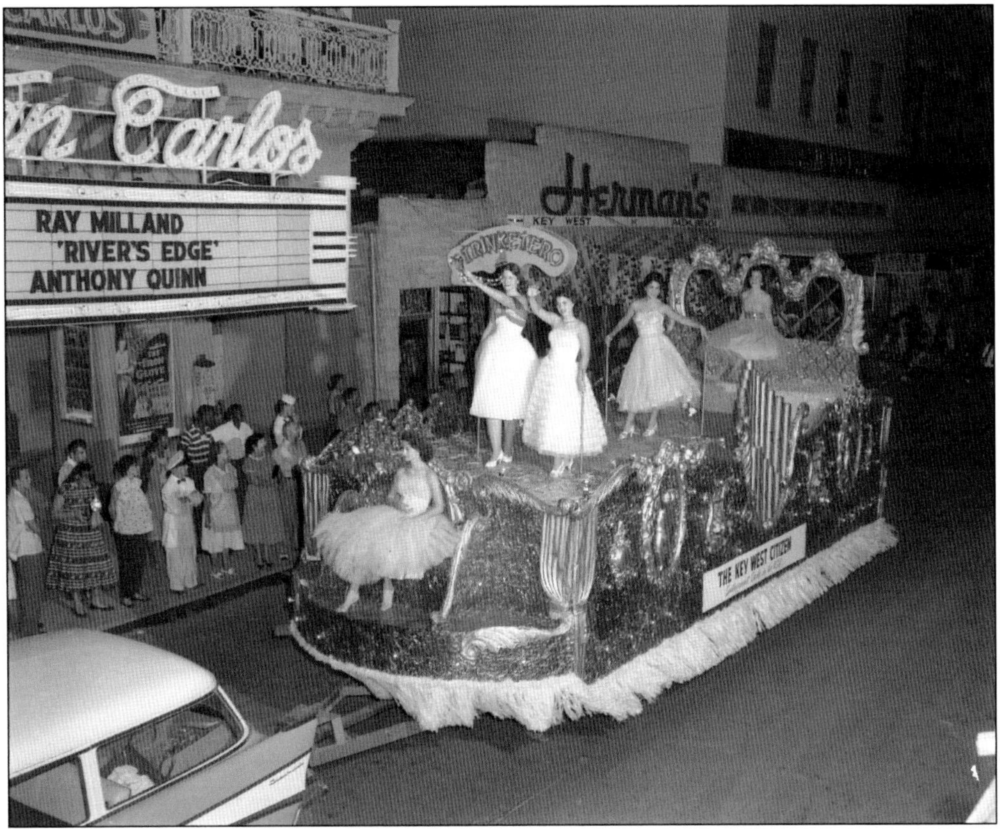

A float sponsored by the *Key West Citizen* newspaper heads down Duval during a parade. The young women are decked out in dresses with fashionable full skirts; the austerity of the war years is well and truly over. The San Carlos theater shows *River's Edge*, a 1957 film starring Anthony Quinn. (Courtesy of Monroe County Library, Key West.)

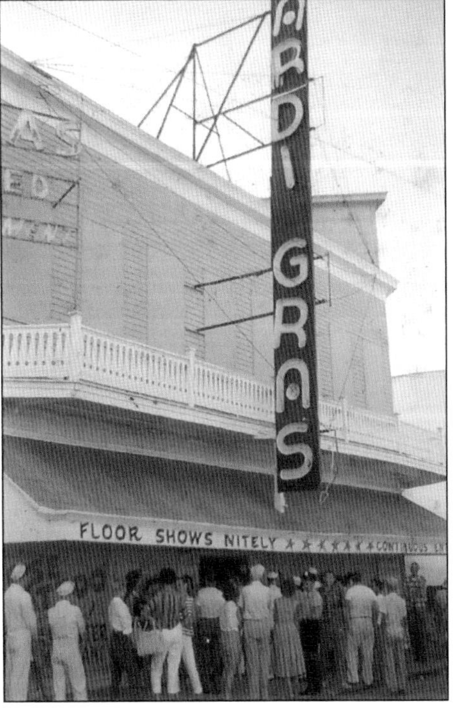

Duval Street's colorful atmosphere began to attract the attention of filmmakers. In this photograph, onlookers try to catch a glimpse of the filming of *The Rose Tattoo* at the Mardi Gras club on Duval. Key West resident and Pulitzer Prize–winning playwright Tennessee Williams wrote the play, which opened on Broadway in 1951; filming of the movie took place in 1954. (Courtesy of Monroe County Library, Key West.)

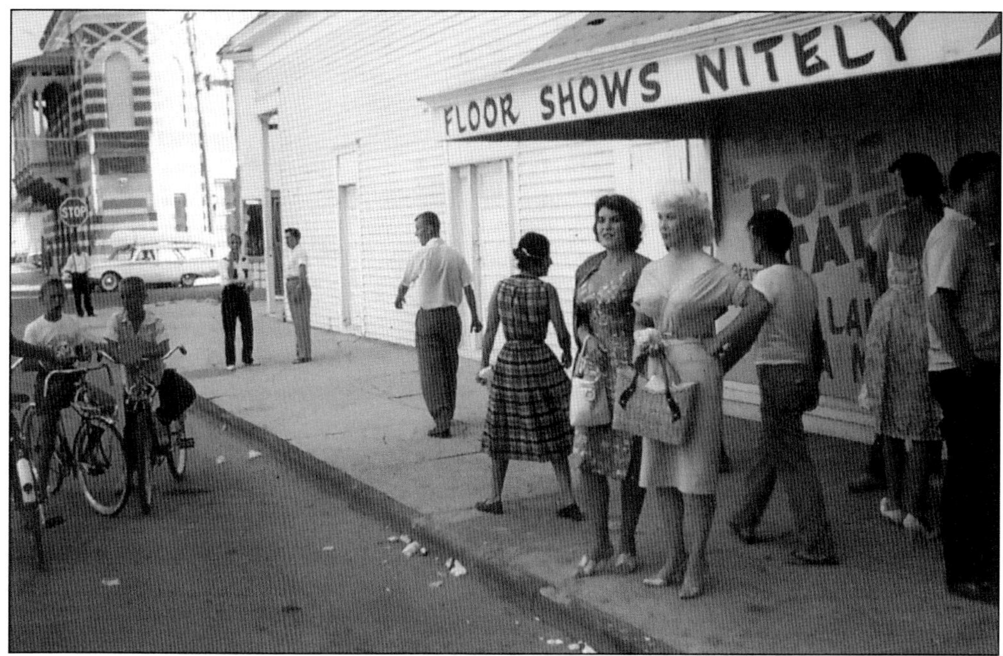

Another photo captures the Mardi Gras nightclub at 92 Duval Street during the filming of Tennessee Williams's *The Rose Tattoo*. In this tempestuous love story, a seamstress named Serafina Delle Rose discovers that her deceased husband had been unfaithful, while her daughter Rosa falls in love with a young sailor named Jack. (Courtesy of Monroe County Library, Key West.)

One of the most gifted American playwrights, Tennessee Williams (right) spent years in Key West and even finished his play *A Streetcar Named Desire* at La Concha hotel at 430 Duval Street. He is pictured here with the stars of *The Rose Tattoo*, Burt Lancaster and Italian actress Anna Magnani (far right), who won an Academy Award for her performance in the film. (Courtesy of Monroe County Library, Key West.)

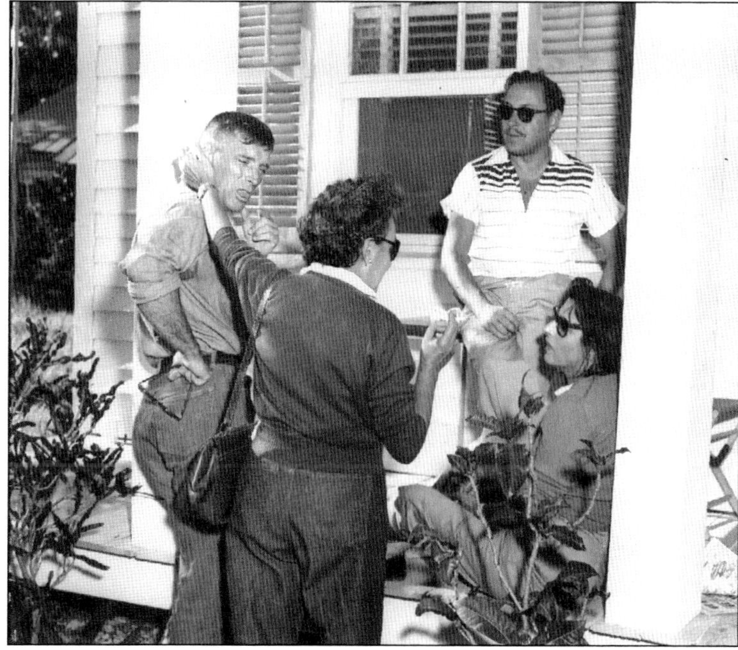

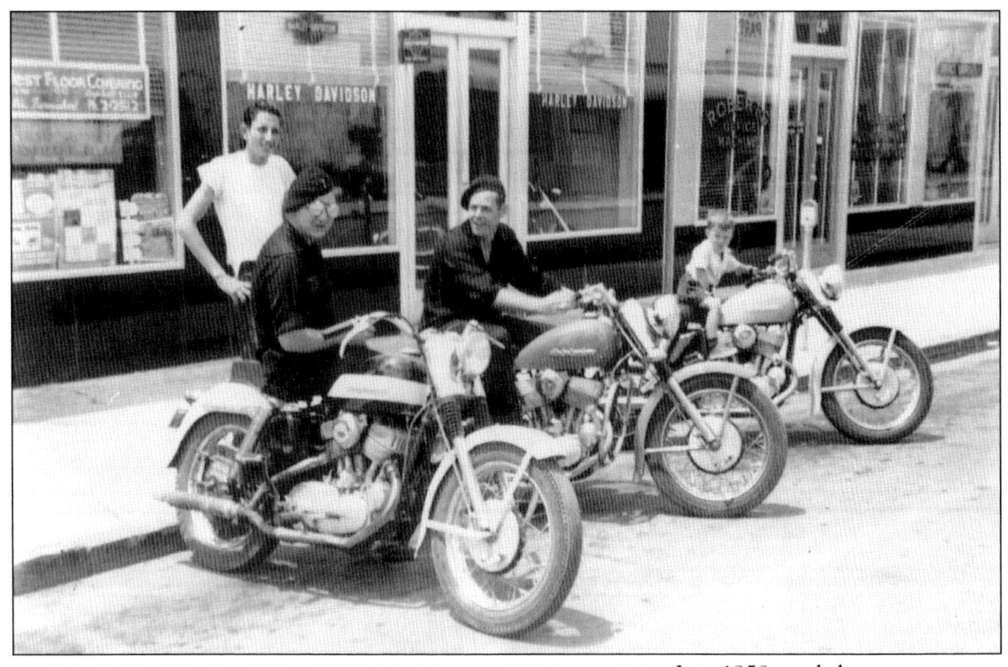

It is 1958, and the guys outside Phil Peterson's Harley Davidson shop are channeling James Dean with their clothes, caps, and even haircuts. Movies like *Rebel without a Cause* signaled a shift in America's youth culture, and foreshadowed social changes to come in the 1960s. (Courtesy of Monroe County Library, Key West.)

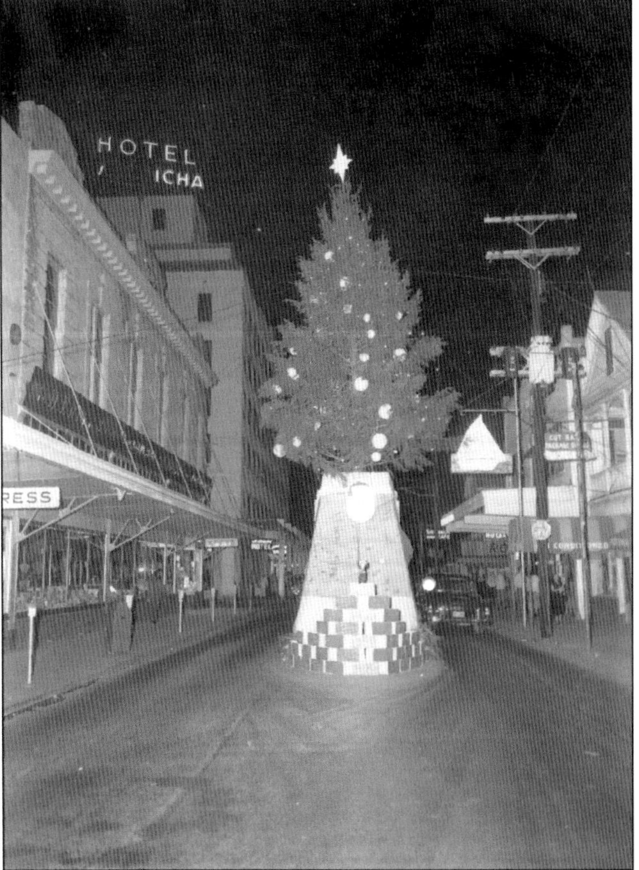

Key West celebrates Christmas with a decorated tree positioned smack in the middle of Duval Street. The tree has been raised high above the street at the 500 block, between the Kress department store and the Boat Bar (on the right), sometime in the 1950s. (Courtesy of Monroe County Library, Key West.)

Five

Times Change

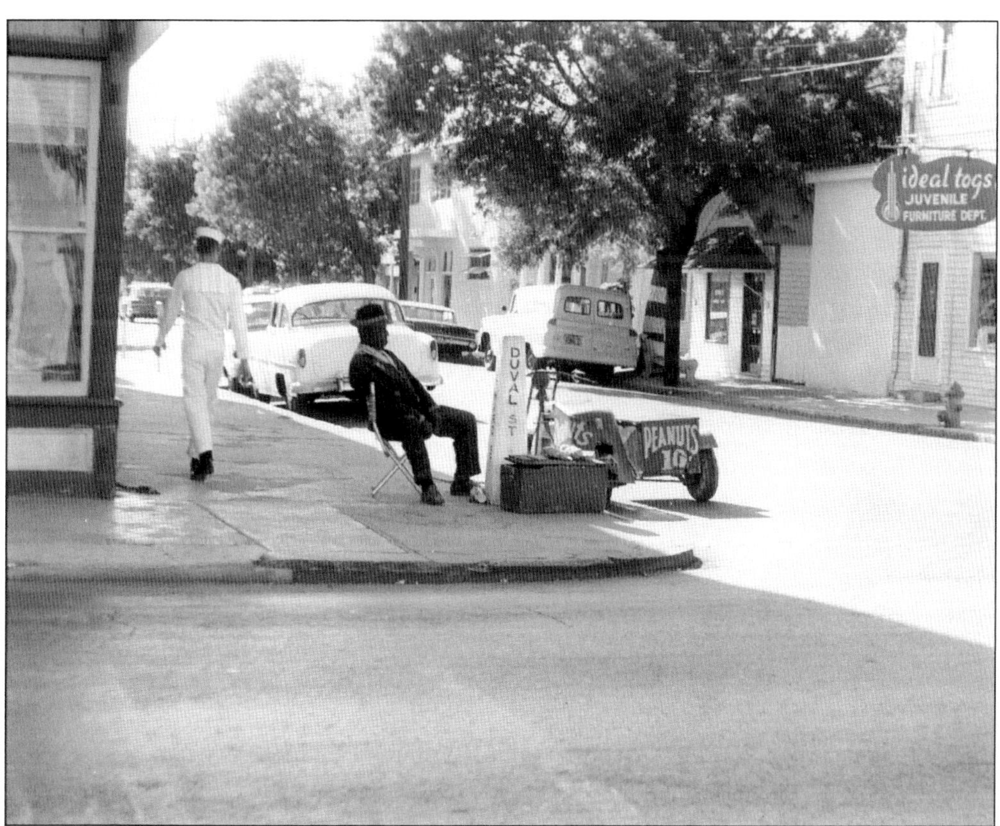

In this 1962 photograph, a sailor passes a peanut seller on the sleepy corner of Duval and Southard Streets. In the 1960s and 1970s, Duval Street had to grapple with profound changes. The *Key West Citizen* reported, "Gone are the harried clerks in two travel agencies that were flush with tourists in pre-Castro days and gone are half a dozen once-prosperous bollo and beer bars." (Courtesy of Monroe County Library, Key West.)

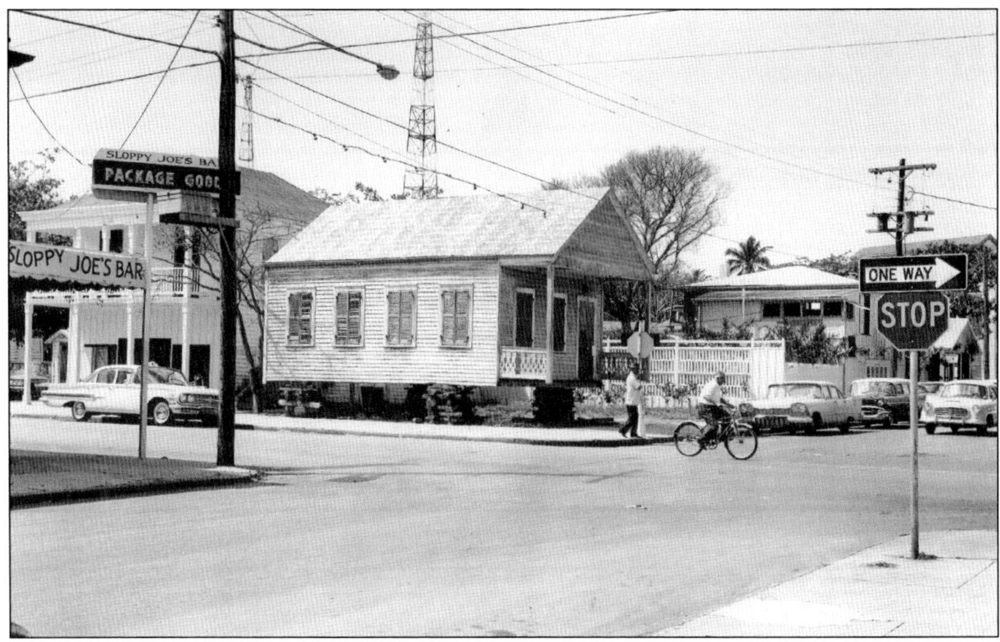

This photograph was taken in 1963, looking from Greene Street toward a very unhurried slice of Duval. As the sign on the left advertises, Sloppy Joe's then sold "Package Goods." The handsome two-story building across the street at 202 Duval Street at one time housed the original Pepe's Café (now found on Caroline Street). (Courtesy of Monroe County Library, Key West.)

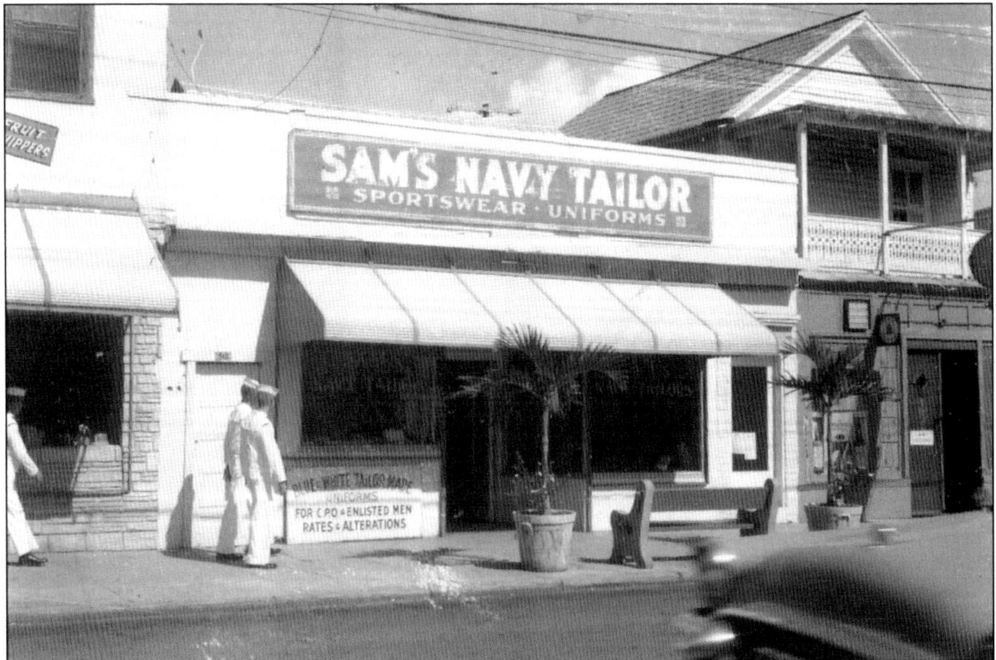

Sailors walk toward Sam's Navy Tailor, a shop that sold uniforms to chief petty officers and enlisted men. Although the Navy remained in Key West, the number of military personnel fell considerably after World War II and the 1950s; Duval Street saw a direct impact on its businesses. (Courtesy of Monroe County Library, Key West.)

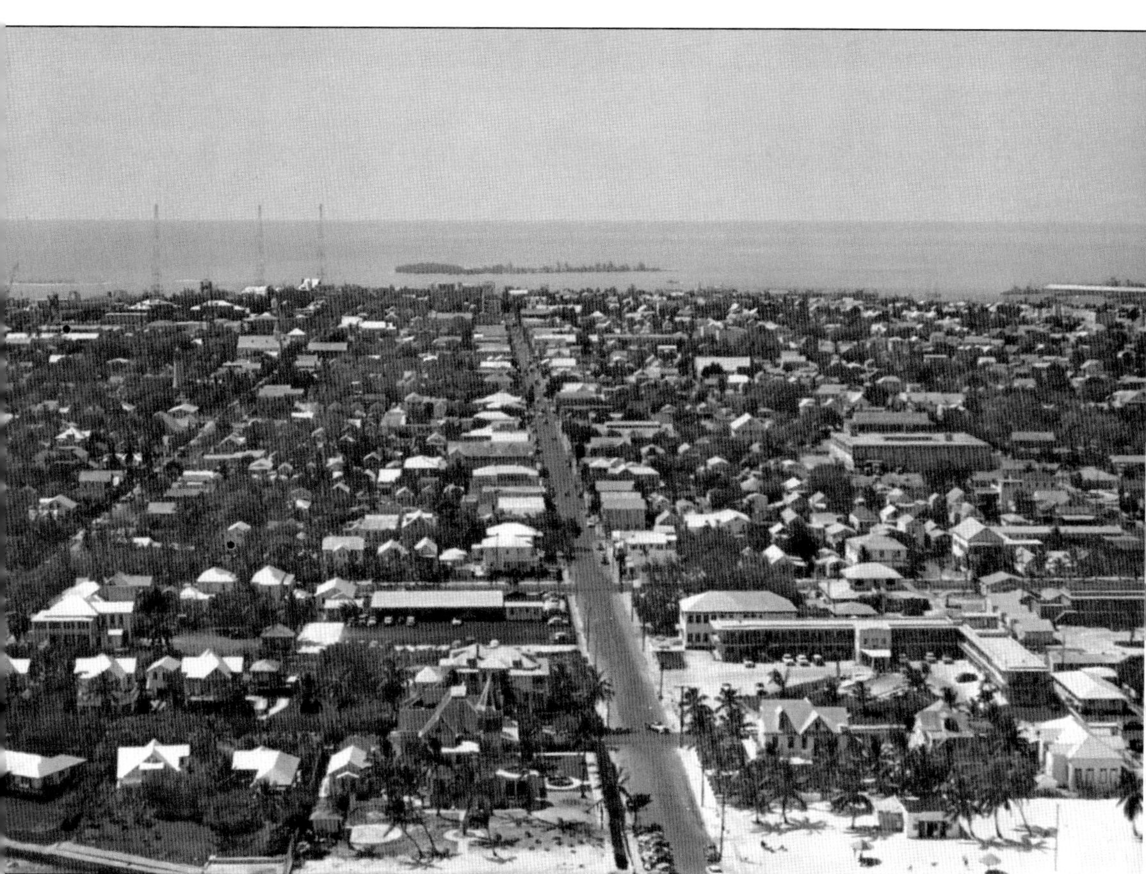

This 1960s postcard captures the entire one-and-a-quarter-mile length of Duval Street, from the Gulf of Mexico to the Atlantic Ocean. In the foreground are the Southernmost House and South Beach, while beyond Duval lies uninhabited Wisteria Island, also known as Christmas Tree Island due to its Australian pines. The previously frenetic pace of Duval Street slowed down, and it exuded a quieter, small-town vibe. Certain aspects of daily life continued as usual, but the economic decline was taking its toll on merchants and the avenue's architectural heritage. In a *Key West Citizen* article dated March 7, 1965, William Appelrouth of the Downtown Business and Property Owners Association remarked, "We are very concerned with the appearance of the street and we would like to see it made more appealing to the public." (Courtesy of Monroe County Library, Key West.)

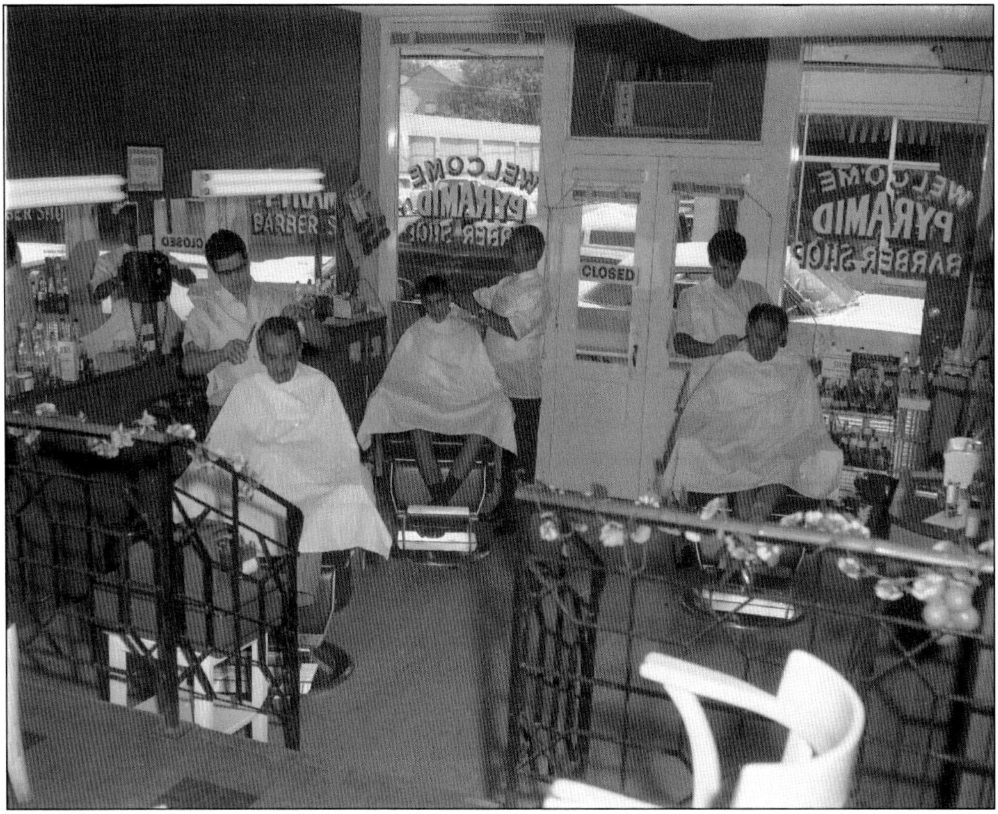

In 1965, Key Westers could get a trim at the Pyramid Barber Shop on Duval Street. Three barbers intently work away trimming their clients' hair into neat, short styles. Later in the 1960s, long-haired hippies started to arrive in Key West, much to the consternation of certain citizens. (Courtesy of Monroe County Library, Key West.)

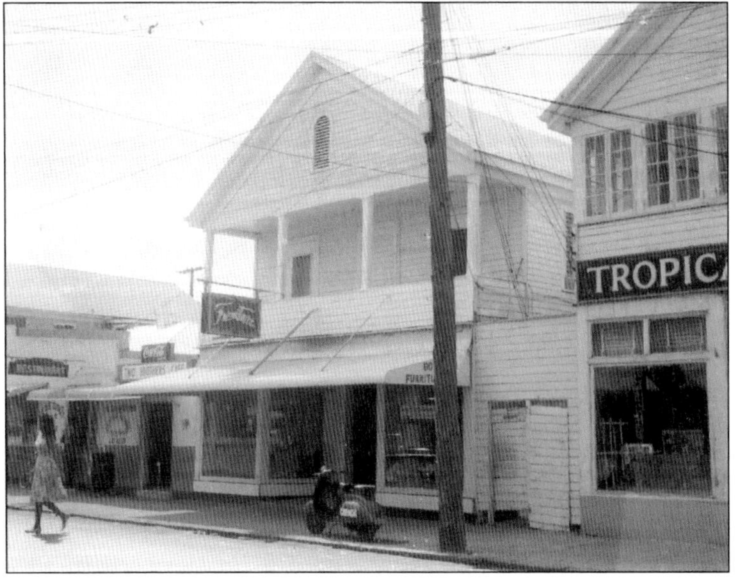

A woman walks across an otherwise empty Duval Street in the mid-1960s, past a furniture store and the Two Brothers Cafe, on the 700 block of the street. The café served customers *café con leche* (strong Cuban coffee with milk) for 15¢, while the furniture shop advertised radios with five-year warranties to Key West locals. (Courtesy of Monroe County Library, Key West.)

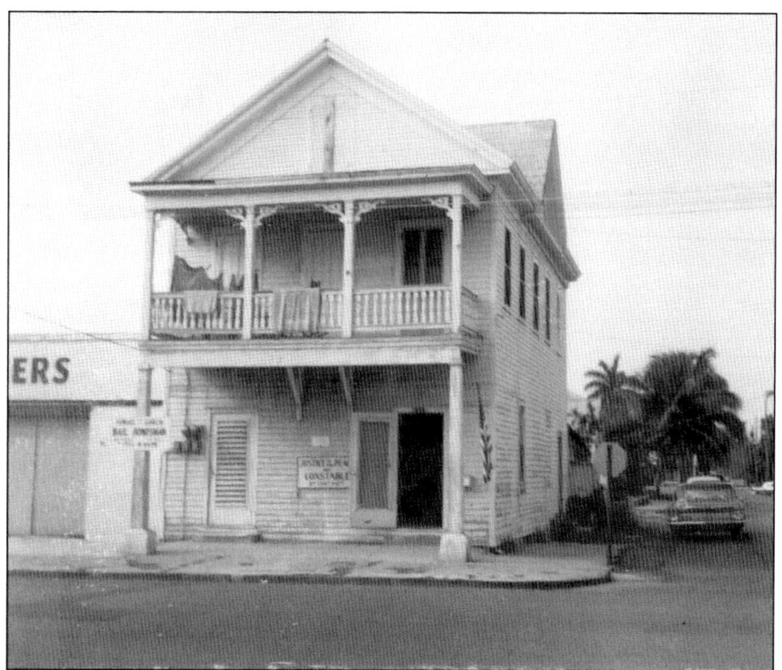

Signs of everyday life are evident at 1100 Duval Street, a building constructed in the 1890s. By the 1960s, it housed the office of native Conch, constable, and justice of the peace Berl R. Pinder. There is also a sign for bail bondsman Ismael Garcia. Upstairs, laundry slowly dries in the humid Key West salt air. (Courtesy of Monroe County Library, Key West.)

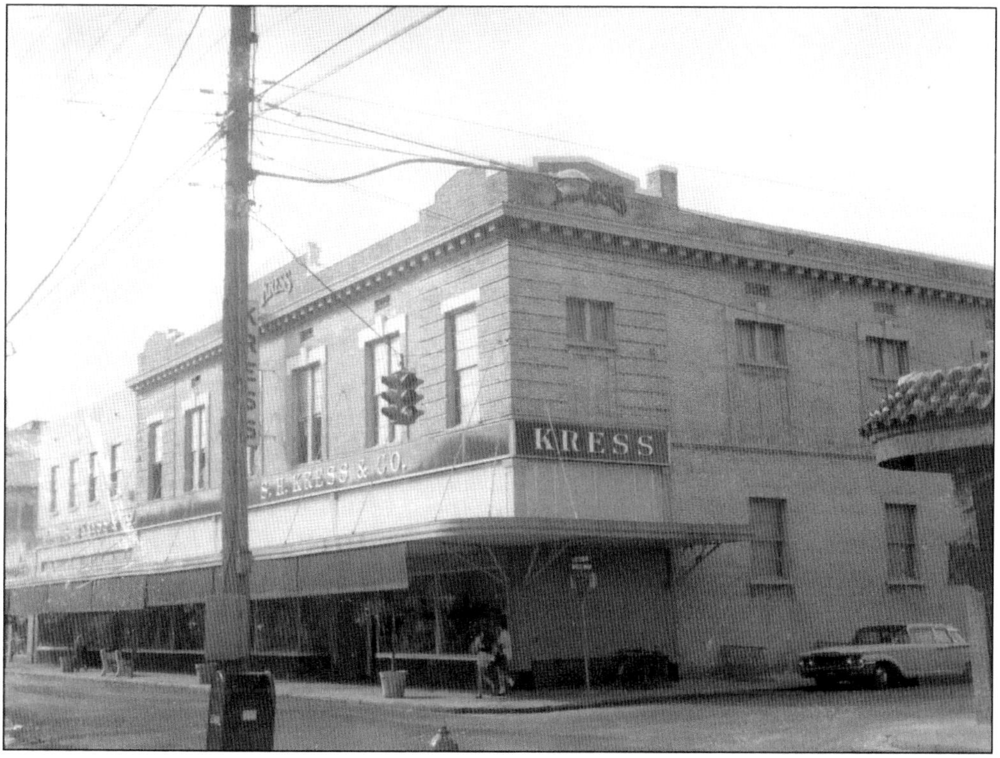

One fixture on Duval Street was the Kress five-and-dime department store, which operated here for decades. Samuel Henry Kress commissioned grand structures for his national chain of stores, and Key West's was no exception. The Kress store stayed in business until the early 1970s; later, it housed Fast Buck Freddie's. (Courtesy of Monroe County Library, Key West.)

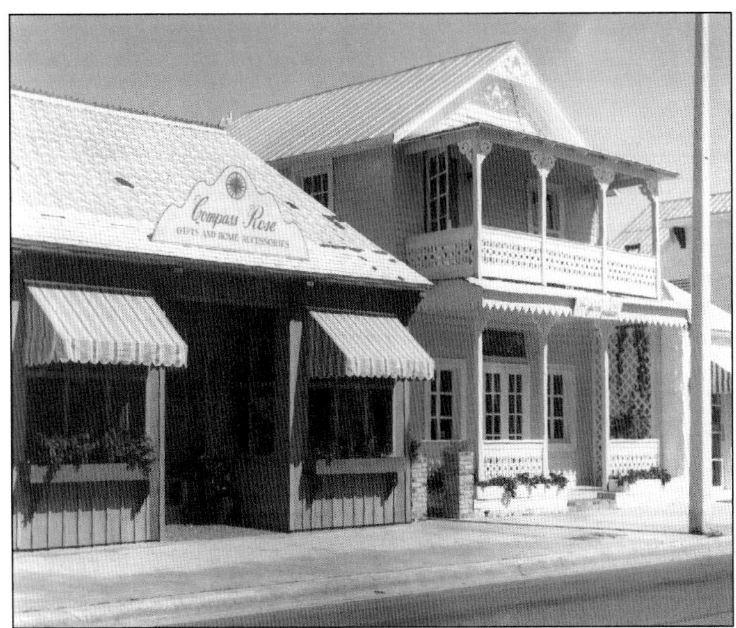

Although retail became an increasingly tough business on Duval Street, merchants worked hard to survive. The neat store Compass Rose, with its matching awnings, sold gifts and home accessories at 611 Duval between Southard and Angela Streets; today, a boutique called Tucker's Provisions carries on the tradition, with gifts and clothing. (Courtesy of Monroe County Library, Key West.)

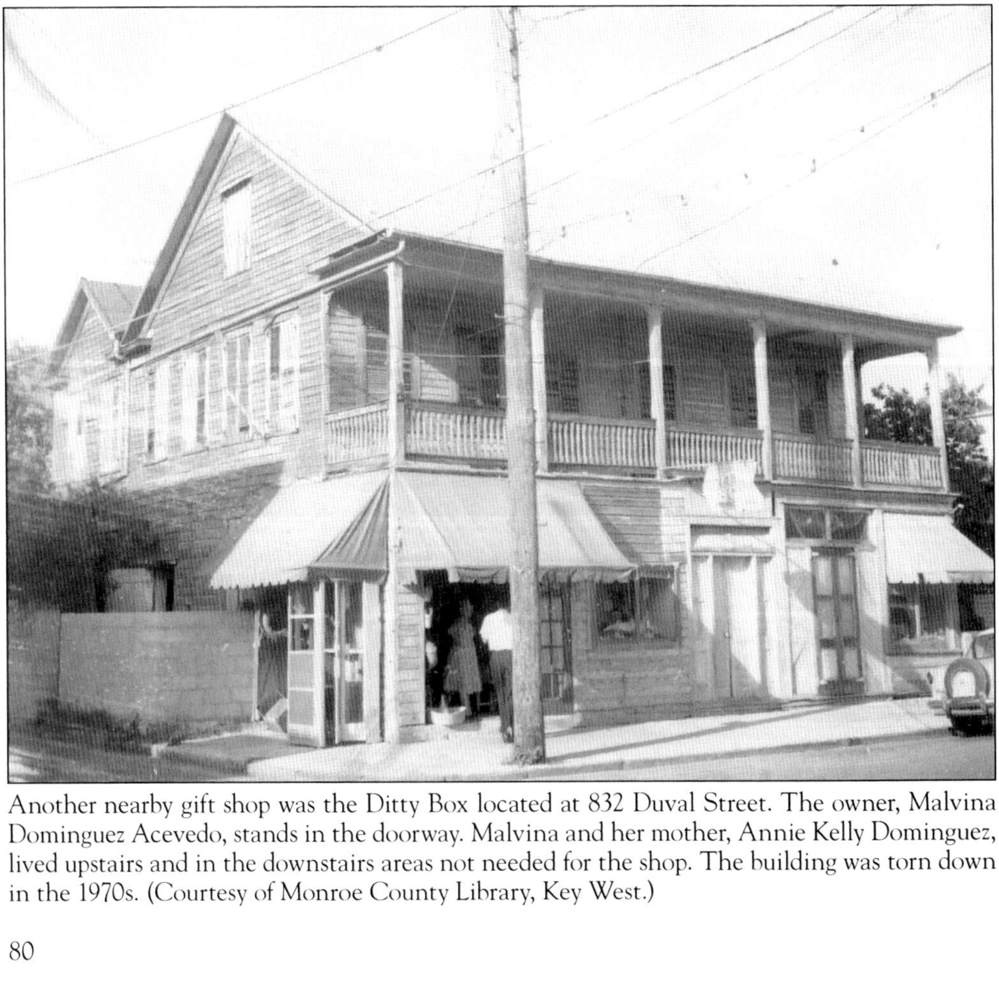

Another nearby gift shop was the Ditty Box located at 832 Duval Street. The owner, Malvina Dominguez Acevedo, stands in the doorway. Malvina and her mother, Annie Kelly Dominguez, lived upstairs and in the downstairs areas not needed for the shop. The building was torn down in the 1970s. (Courtesy of Monroe County Library, Key West.)

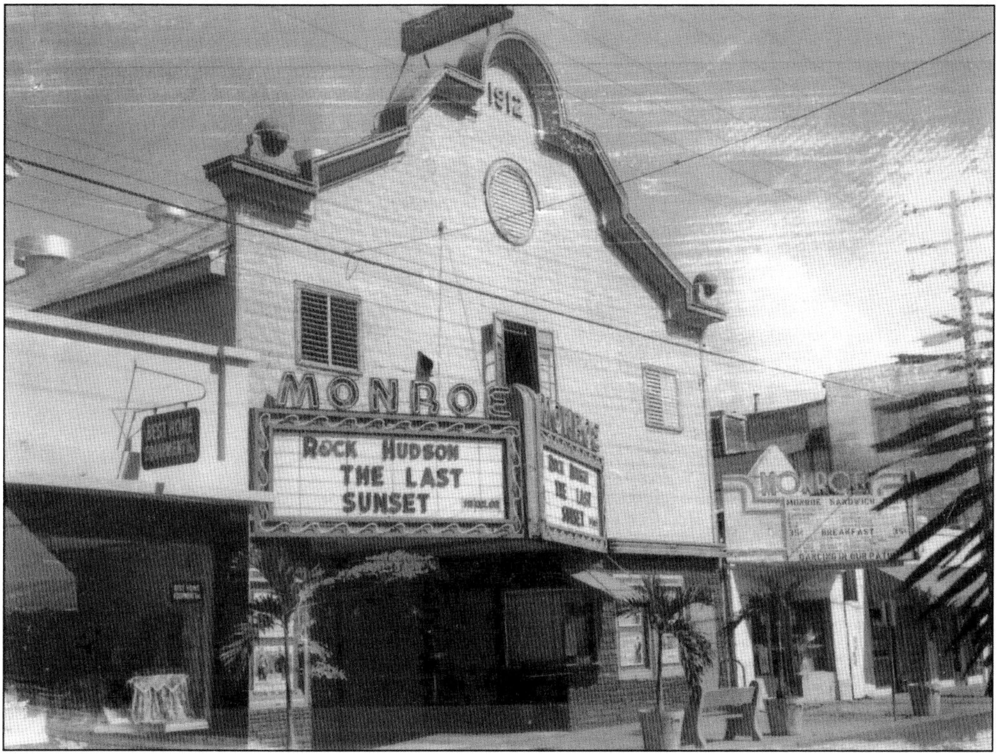

The Monroe Theater was built in 1912 for theater and musical entertainment, and then operated as a movie theater, screening films like Rock Hudson's 1961 picture *The Last Sunset*. By the 1970s, however, the theater showed "adult films." It would be reinvented once more, as the famed Copa nightclub, which brought in acts like Grace Jones and Divine. (Courtesy of Monroe County Library, Key West.)

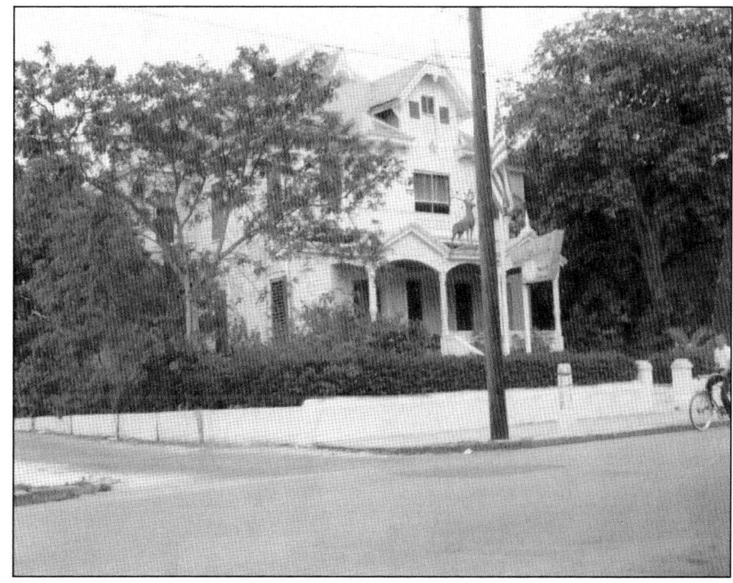

In the 1960s, Duval Street continued to play its part in the life of the community: this grand house at 313 Duval was home to the Elks Lodge, a fraternal order. Note the elk statue on the porch roof. Key West millionaire William Curry built the house for his son Robert in the 19th century, and fortunately, it still survives today. (Courtesy of Monroe County Library, Key West.)

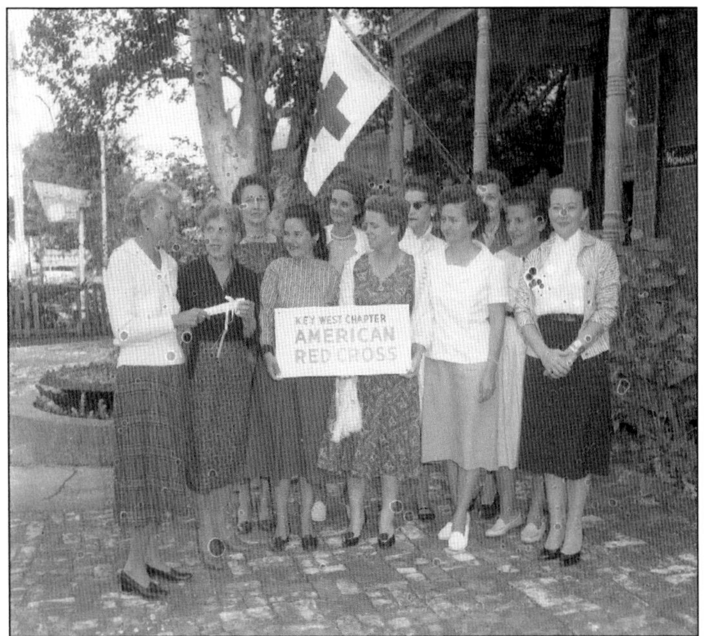

Another community organization headquartered on Duval was the Key West Women's Club. Ladies from the Key West chapter of the American Red Cross pose outside the building in the mid-1960s. The house was commissioned in the 1890s by Capt. Martin Hellings, who married Eleanor Curry, daughter of millionaire William Curry. The Key West Women's Club continues its work from this same home. (Courtesy of Monroe County Library, Key West.)

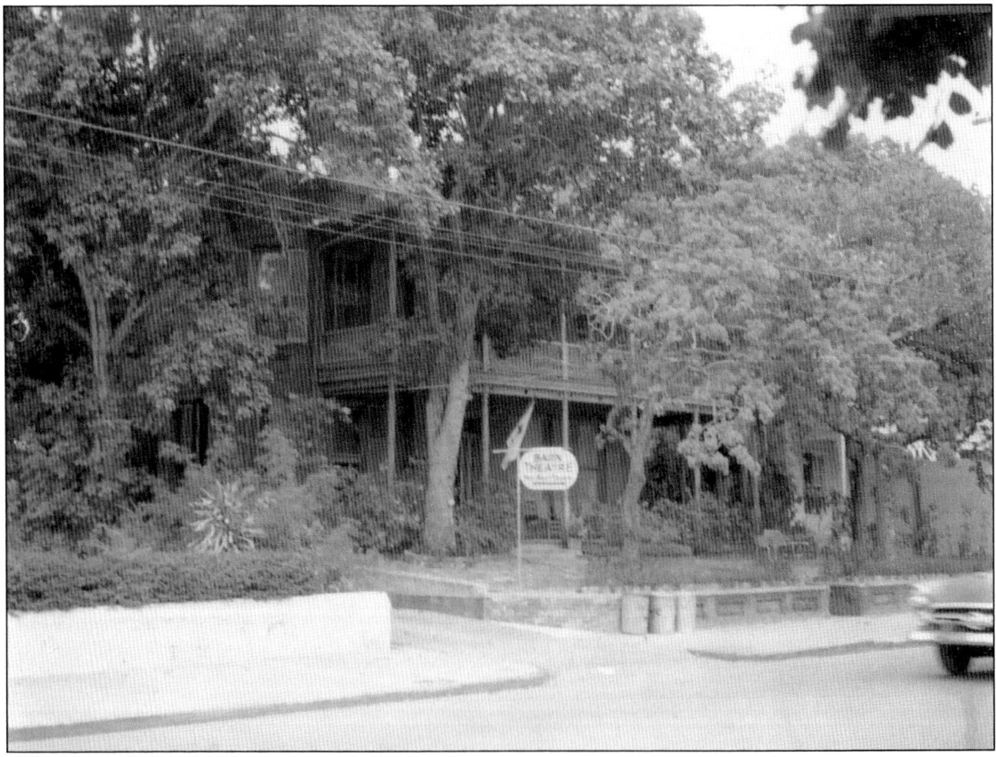

Although businesses struggled, artists, writers, actors, and musicians still found a home on Duval Street. This 1960s sign in front of the Women's Club points to the Barn Theater, located in an 1829 carriage house at the back of the property. The Barn Theater Players performed here in the 1940s, then the building was renovated as a small concert hall. (Courtesy of Monroe County Library, Key West.)

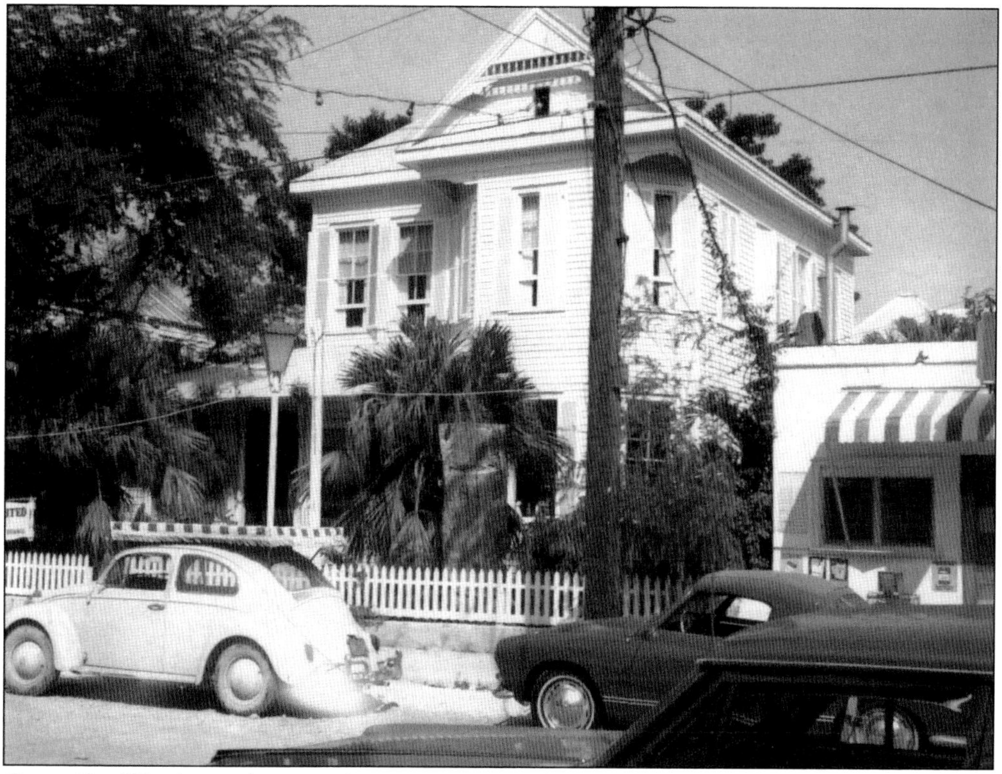

Given Key West's popularity with artists, it was only natural that a number of galleries would open on Key West's "Main Street" over the decades. In the 1960s, this imposing two-story house at 221 Duval was repurposed as the art gallery Artists Unlimited. (Courtesy of Monroe County Library, Key West.)

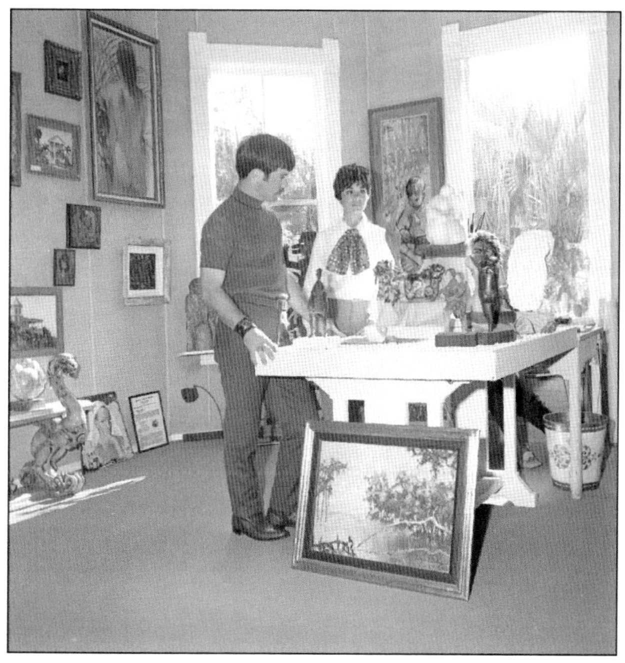

Here, a hip couple browses through the artwork inside the Artists Unlimited gallery at 221 Duval Street. The painting on the floor is by one of Florida's Highwaymen, self-taught African American artists who worked from the 1950s through the 1980s and often sold their works by the side of the road. (Courtesy of the State Archives of Florida.)

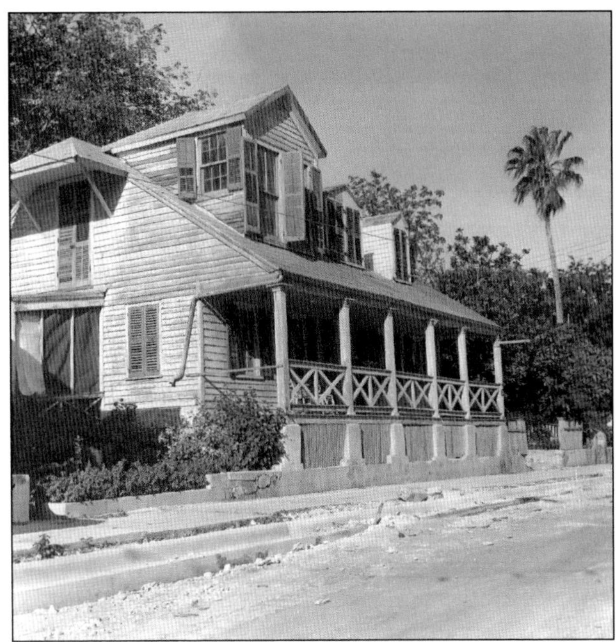

The condition of Key West's Oldest House and the state of the street and sidewalk underline the need for renovation and repairs. *Miami Herald* journalist George Flynn took this photograph of the home in 1965 and wrote an article entitled, "Upper Duval Street: Surgery Required?" about the falloff in the street's business. (Courtesy of Monroe County Library, Key West.)

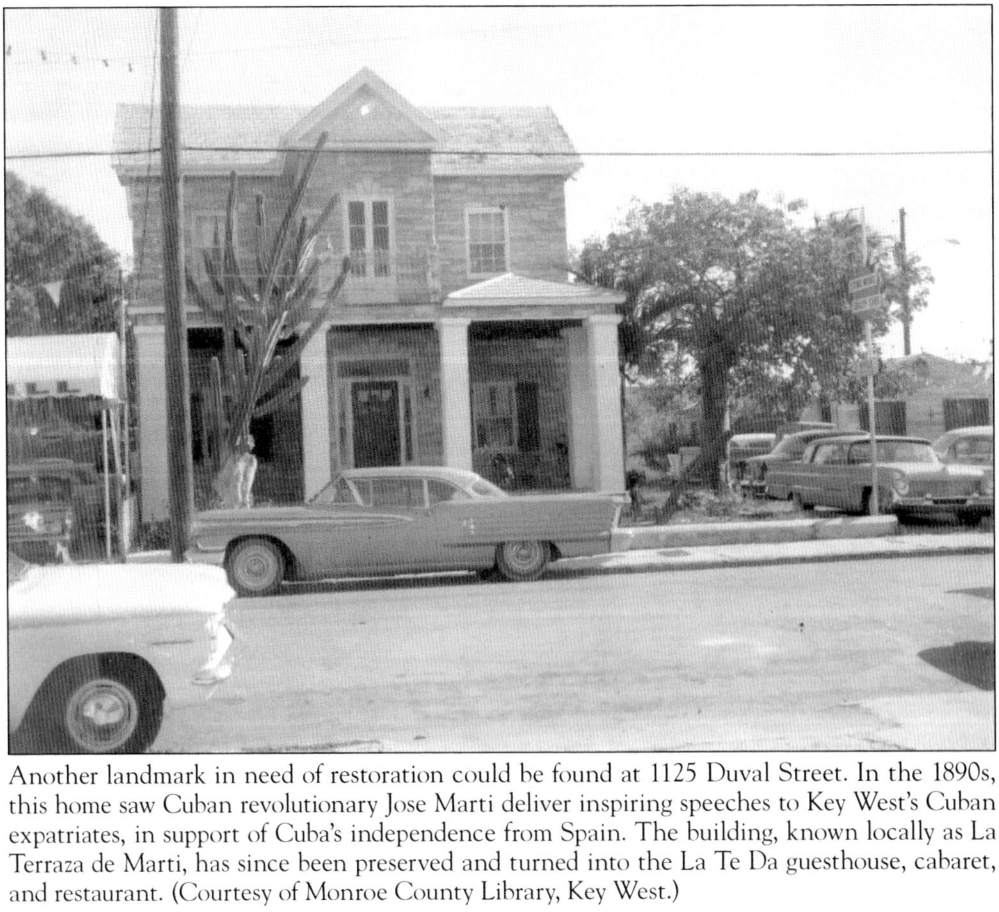

Another landmark in need of restoration could be found at 1125 Duval Street. In the 1890s, this home saw Cuban revolutionary Jose Marti deliver inspiring speeches to Key West's Cuban expatriates, in support of Cuba's independence from Spain. The building, known locally as La Terraza de Marti, has since been preserved and turned into the La Te Da guesthouse, cabaret, and restaurant. (Courtesy of Monroe County Library, Key West.)

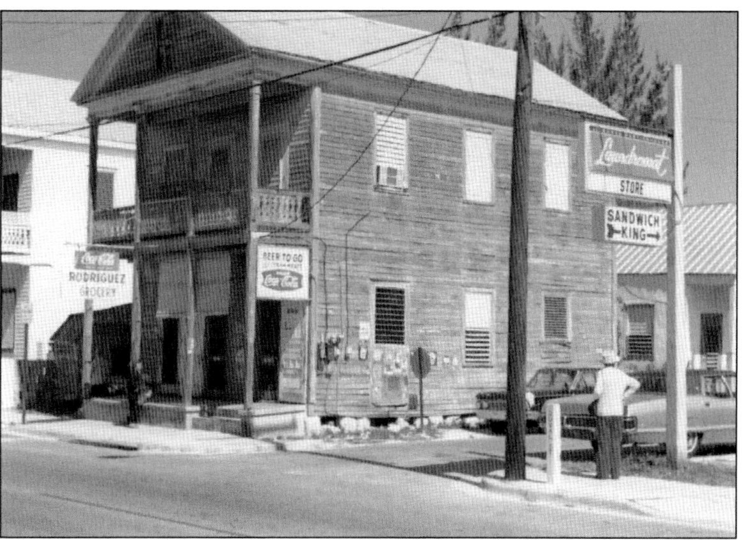

The challenges of maintaining Key West's beautiful wood-frame buildings can be seen in this photograph. The Rodriguez Grocery stood at 1211 Duval at the corner of Louisa Street in the 1970s. Salt air, intense sun, tropical rains, and termites took their toll. (Courtesy of Monroe County Library, Key West.)

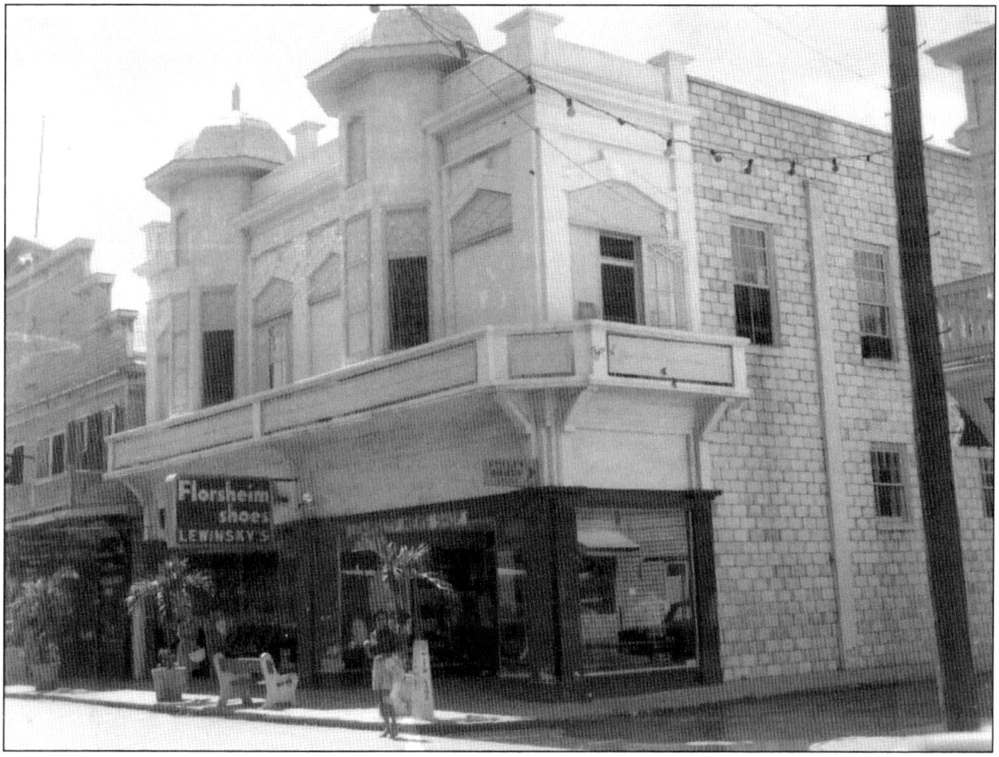

Some business owners began to take action to restore Key West's faded charm. This photograph shows Lewinsky's Men's Shop at 526 Duval Street, a fantastical building with its grand towers, next to William Gamble's store. The *Miami Herald* reported, "The first step in a proposed facelift of Duval St. is nearing completion this week with an Old Island style addition to Gamble's Jewelry Store." (Courtesy of Monroe County Library, Key West.)

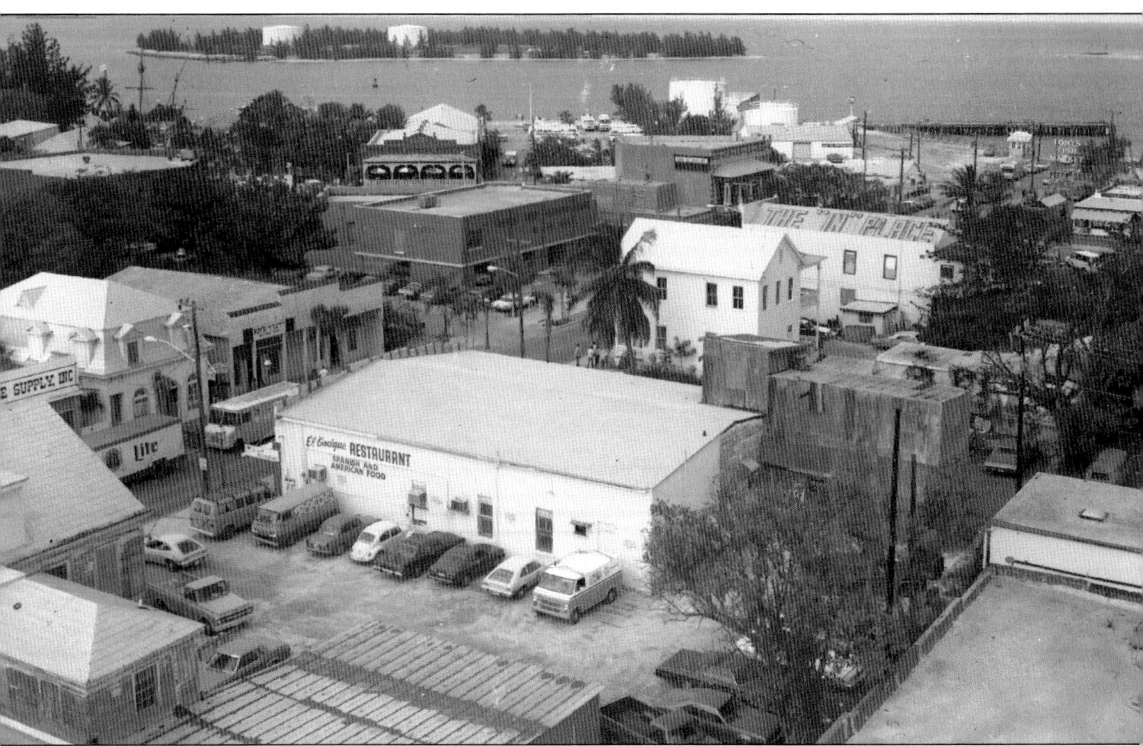

Taken from the Old City Hall, this photograph captures the 100 block of Duval Street, with El Cacique restaurant and the Old Customs House in the frame. For some years, the new shopping centers on Roosevelt Boulevard lured locals away from Duval. Navy reductions also had an economic impact. More businesses were shuttered, as the street sunk into further decline and seeming irrelevance. In one letter to the *Key West Citizen*, a resident wrote, "Beautifying Duval Street is not an impractical dream; it's a dream which could not only help beautify this island, but, in addition, accelerate the cash registers of Duval Street. This has been discussed with them time and time again, when word went around that 'business is bad.' " Another letter writer suggested that "some face lifting of some of the buildings on this street would add greatly to the looks of this street." (Courtesy of Monroe County Library, Key West.)

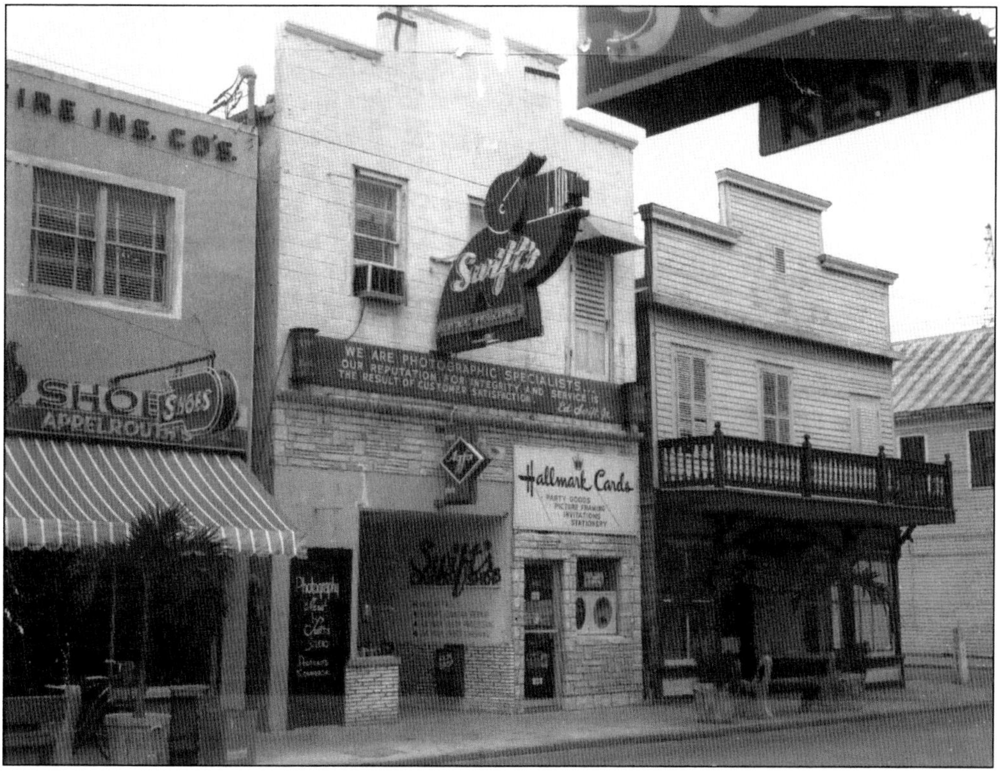

This photograph of Swift's camera shop at 602 Duval Street was taken in the 1960s. Edwin O. Swift II was a nationally-known photographer; his son Edwin Swift III operated this shop on Duval for years and saw firsthand the need to preserve a number of historic buildings. (Courtesy of Monroe County Library, Key West.)

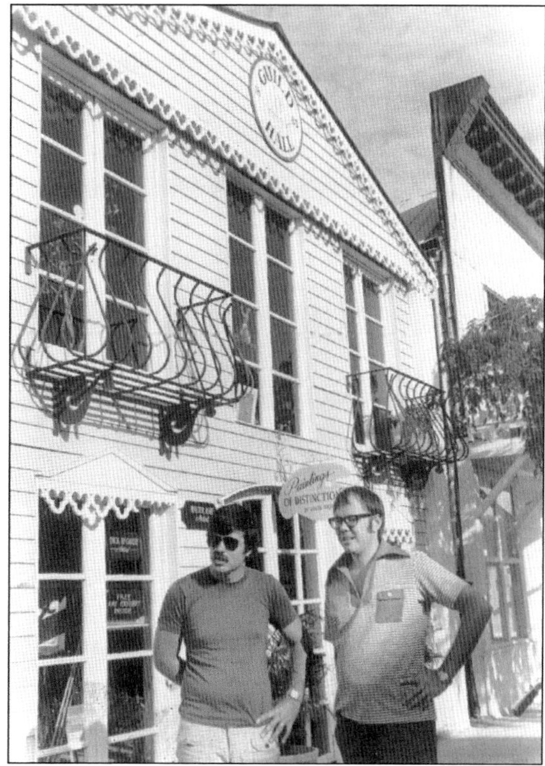

Key Westers Ed Swift (right) and Chris Belland, pictured here in front of the Guild Hall at 614 Duval Street, grew concerned about the state of Duval Street and the island's architectural heritage. Along with other businesspeople including Moe Mosher, they formed the Old Town Key West Development Company, a driving force in the fledgling restoration movement. (Courtesy of Monroe County Library, Key West.)

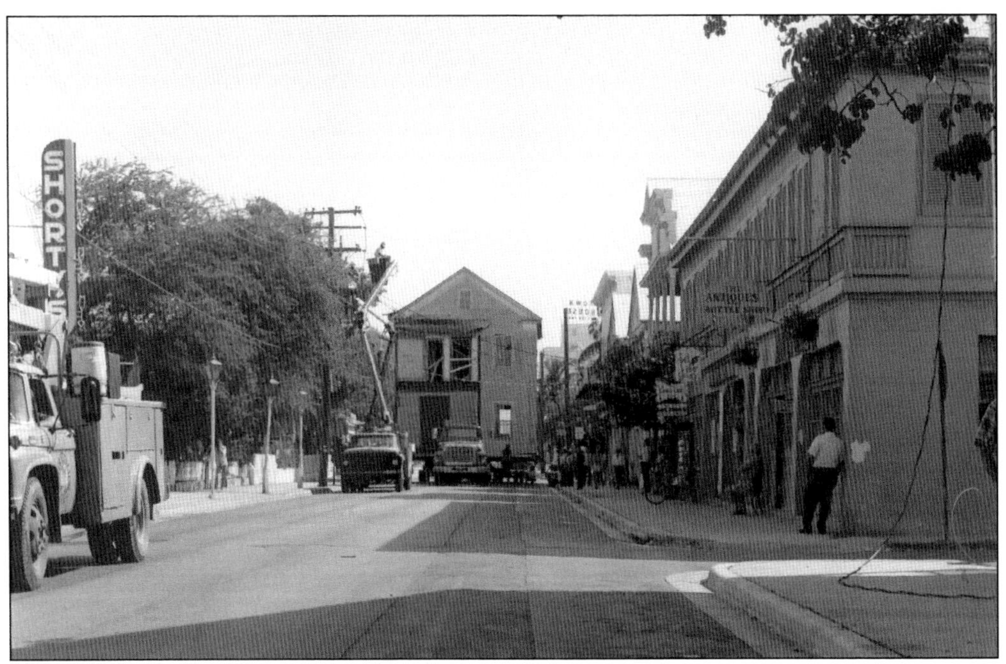

Sometimes historic buildings could survive only if they were moved. This house, which originally stood at 716 Fleming Street, is being transported to 115 Duval Street in 1974. The workman in the "bucket" on the left ensures that the house does not tear into any wiring. (Courtesy of Monroe County Library, Key West.)

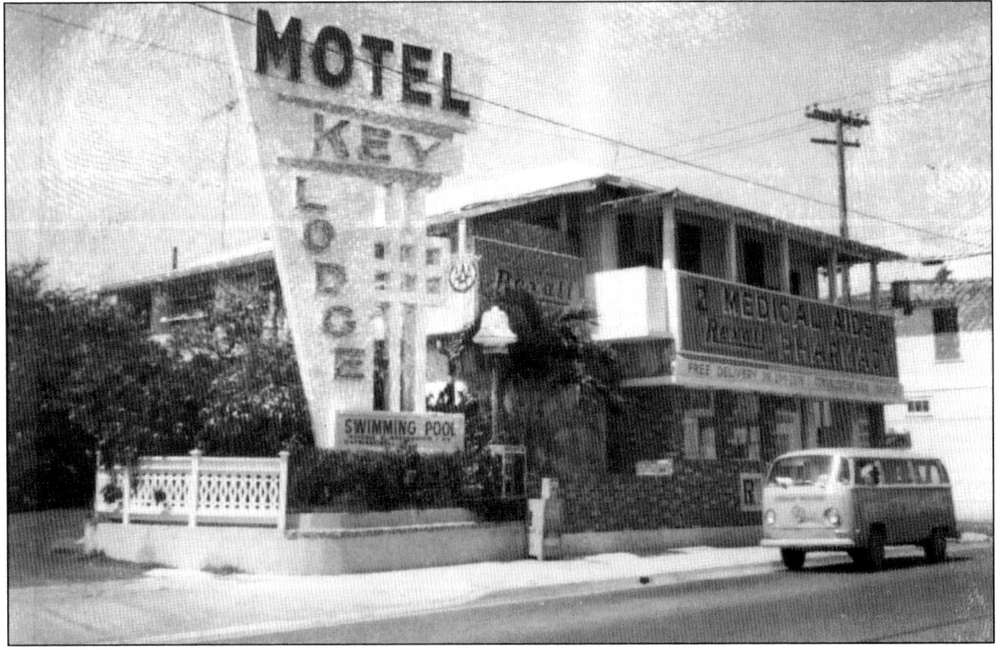

In addition to Bahamian, Classical Revival, "Conch," and Queen Anne, new types of architecture gradually appeared on Duval Street. The Motel Key Lodge at 1000 Duval Street epitomized mid-century modern style and would eventually become a Duval Street icon in its own right. Today, it operates as the Orchid Key Inn. (Courtesy of Monroe County Library, Key West.)

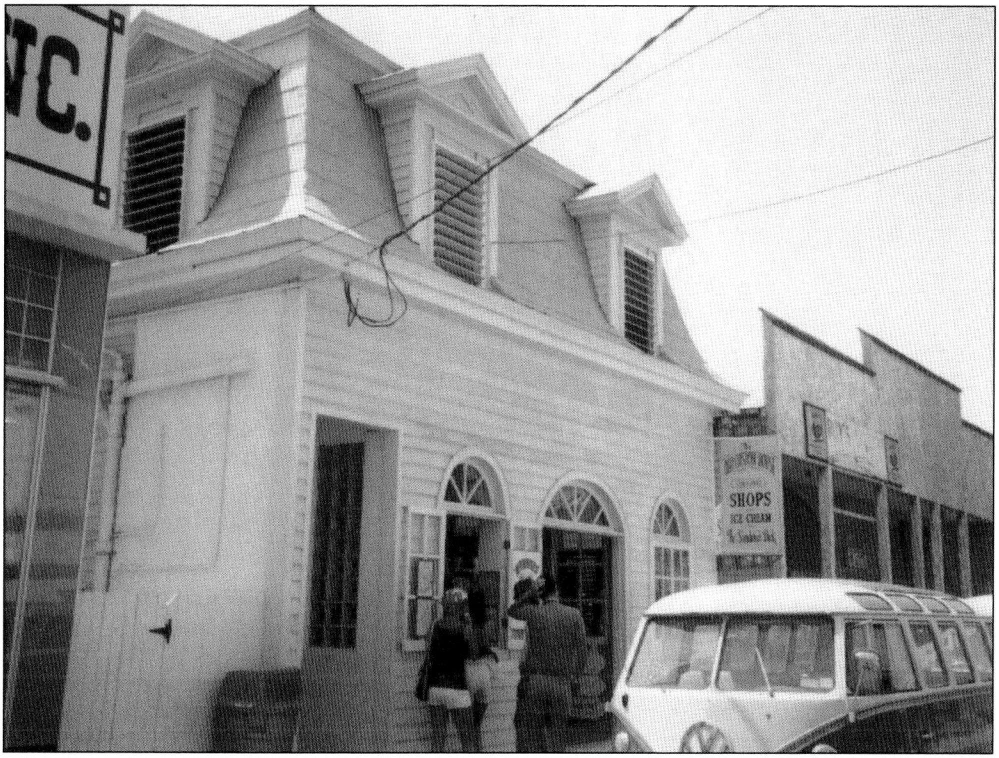

The 19th-century Old Customs House is another historic building that survived on Duval, thanks to maintenance and refurbishment. As Key West's preservation movement gained momentum, Mayor Charles "Sonny" McCoy helped secure federal funds to revitalize Duval Street. The project was named Downtown '76, in honor of America's bicentennial. Duval Street received much-needed repaving and sewer repairs. (Courtesy of Monroe County Library, Key West.)

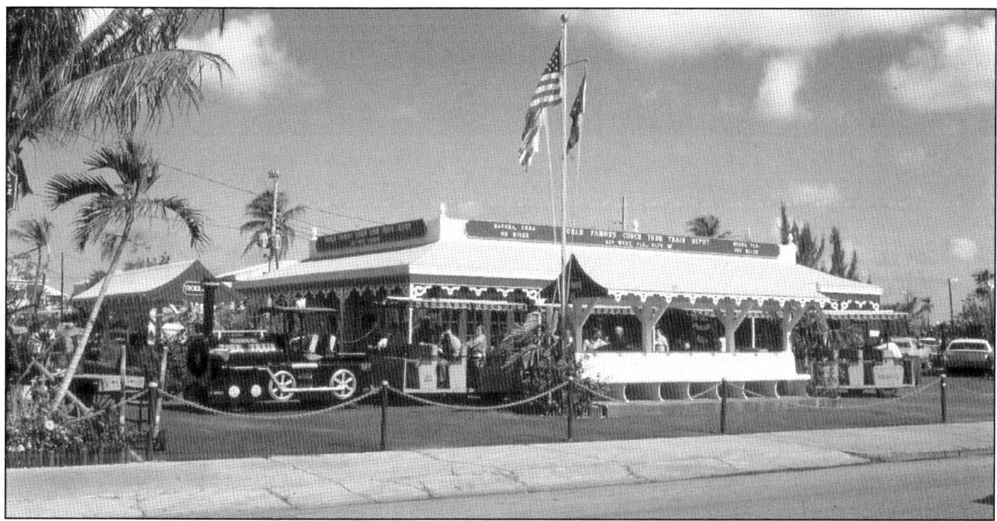

While Duval Street's buildings underwent restoration, tourism got a boost. Here is the Conch Train station, situated on the corner of Front and Duval Streets, in 1976. Today, Conch Trains continue to roll down Duval Street as their guides describe the history of this famous avenue. (Courtesy of Monroe County Library, Key West.)

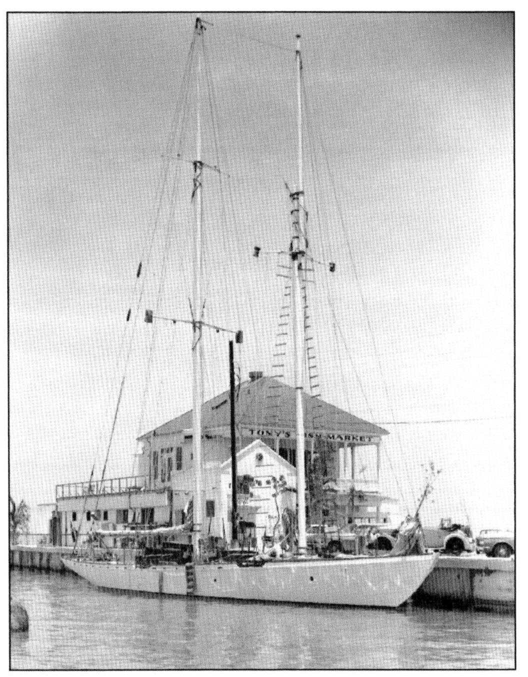

In the 1960s, third-generation Key Wester David Wolkowsky had the former P&O steamship office moved and repurposed as the upper story of Tony's Fish Market, a restaurant and cocktail lounge at 1 Duval Street. In the 1960s and 1970s, individual and group initiatives, including those of the Old Island Restoration Foundation, gradually fostered a renewed pride in the island's architectural heritage. (Courtesy of Monroe County Library, Key West.)

In 1967, Wolkowsky built a motel around his restaurant, and called the complex the Pier House. By 1980, it had become the place to see and be seen. With new trees and widened sidewalks, Duval itself was also making a comeback. As the *Key West Citizen* observed, "No longer is Duval Street a run-down conglomerate of garish store fronts and plastic neon signs." (Courtesy of Monroe County Library, Key West.)

Six

WATERING HOLES

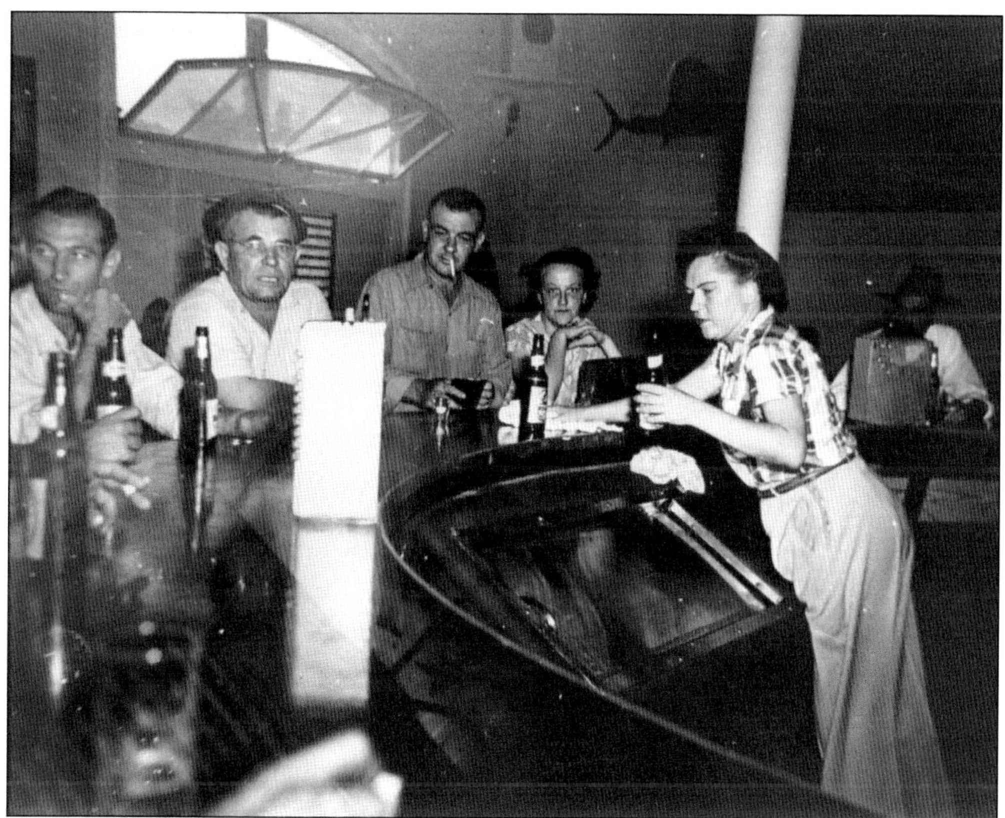

Drinking is not so much a pastime on Duval Street as a religion. Some folks have a particular establishment they favor, while others are more democratic in their devotions. Even in 1834, however, people complained about grog shops opening on the Sabbath: "These places encourage the idle and the profligate, and the same are highly destructive to the morals and order of good society." (Courtesy of Monroe County Library, Key West.)

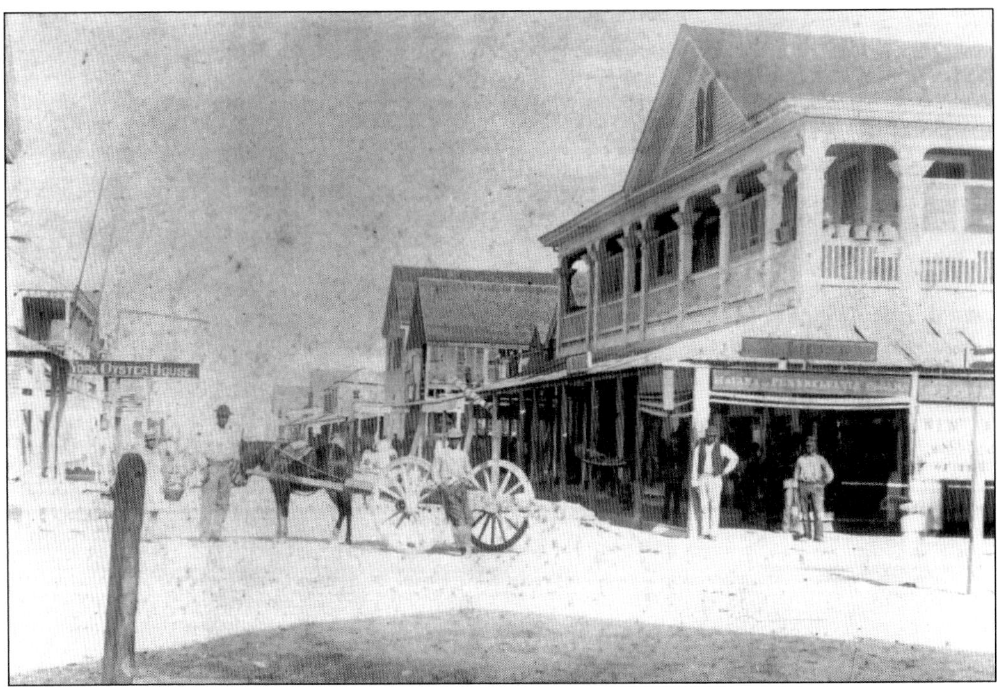

In this 1884 image, a Duval Street saloon operates on the second floor of the building on the left. According to Key West chronicler Jefferson Browne, one of the earliest Duval Street bars was "the 'Gem' saloon, presided over by 'Captain Jack,' . . . an Englishman, and once a sailor [who] could neither read nor write." By 1907, a total of 38 legal saloons served patrons in Key West. (Courtesy of Monroe County Library, Key West.)

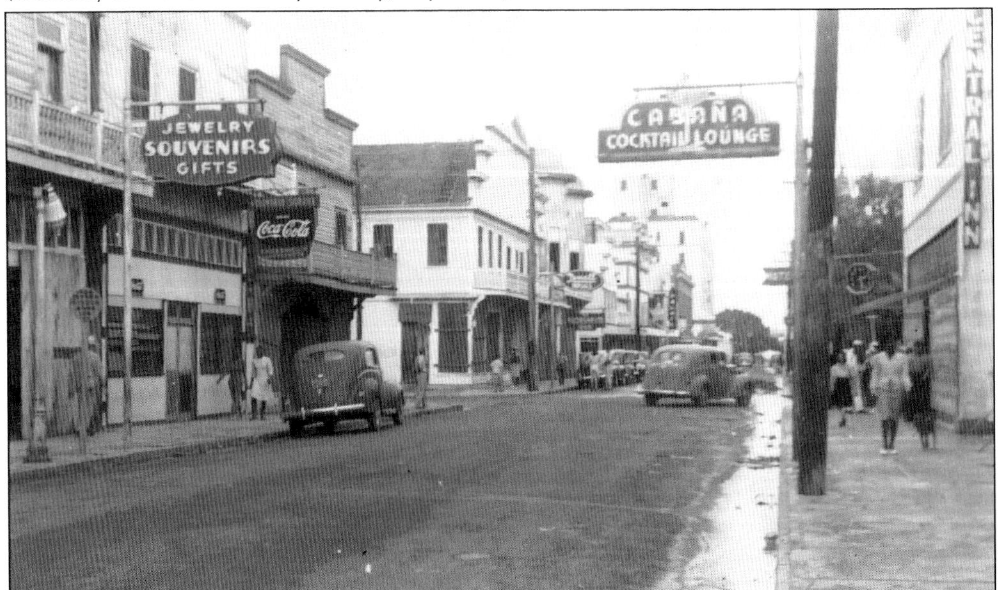

This photograph shows the popular Cabaña Cocktail Lounge, located on Duval near Southard Street. After the repressive years of Prohibition, Key West was in the mood to celebrate. Duval Street's watering holes flung open their doors once again in the 1930s and seemingly have never closed since. (Courtesy of Monroe County Library, Key West.)

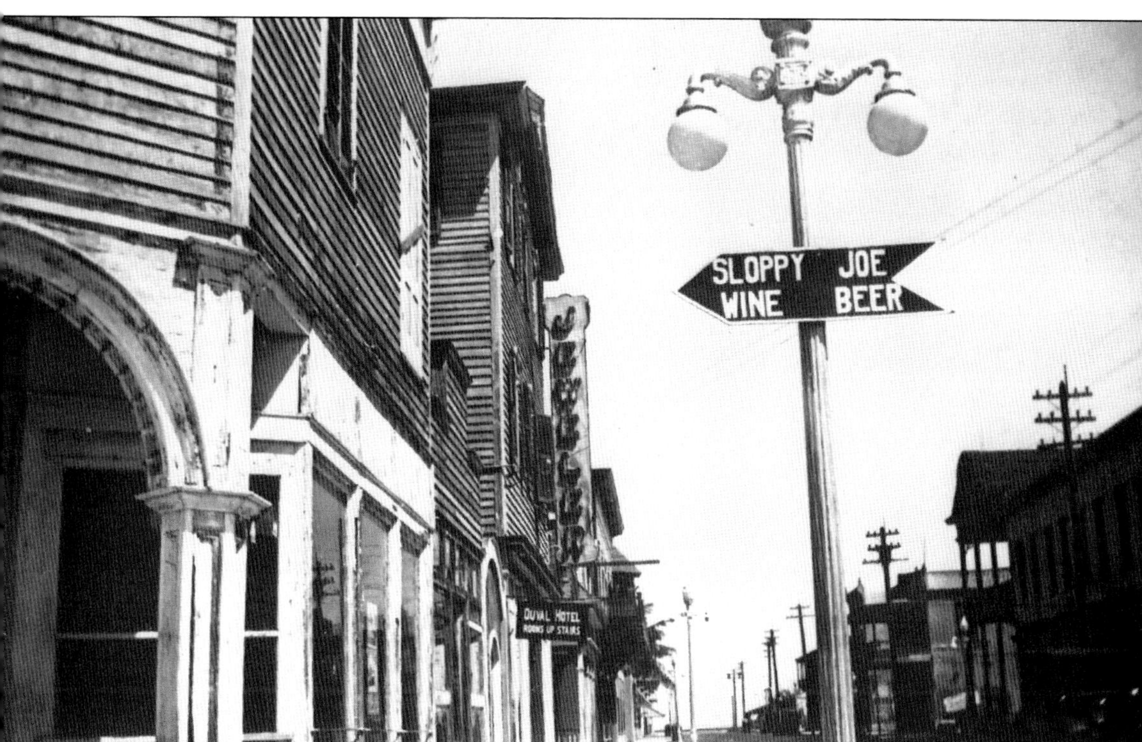

A sign for Sloppy Joe's bar hangs from a street lamp on Duval Street. The year was 1935, when Sloppy Joe's still poured drinks on Greene Street: only this lone advertisement existed on Duval. Former rumrunner Joe Russell opened his joint after Prohibition, first with the name "the Blind Pig" (a nickname for a speakeasy) and then the Silver Slipper. In 1937, infuriated by a $1 rise in his rent, Russell decided to relocate to the former Victoria Restaurant just down the block. The impressively solid building had been constructed by Juan Farto in 1917 for his Spanish-themed establishment and cost Joe $2,500 (or $42,000 today). The story goes that on May 5, Russell and his customers moved the tables, the chairs, and apparently, all the liquor to the new Duval digs overnight. Historian Sharon Wells chronicles Joe's son as saying, "We never closed. Everybody just picked up their drinks and walked down the street." (Courtesy of Monroe County Library, Key West.)

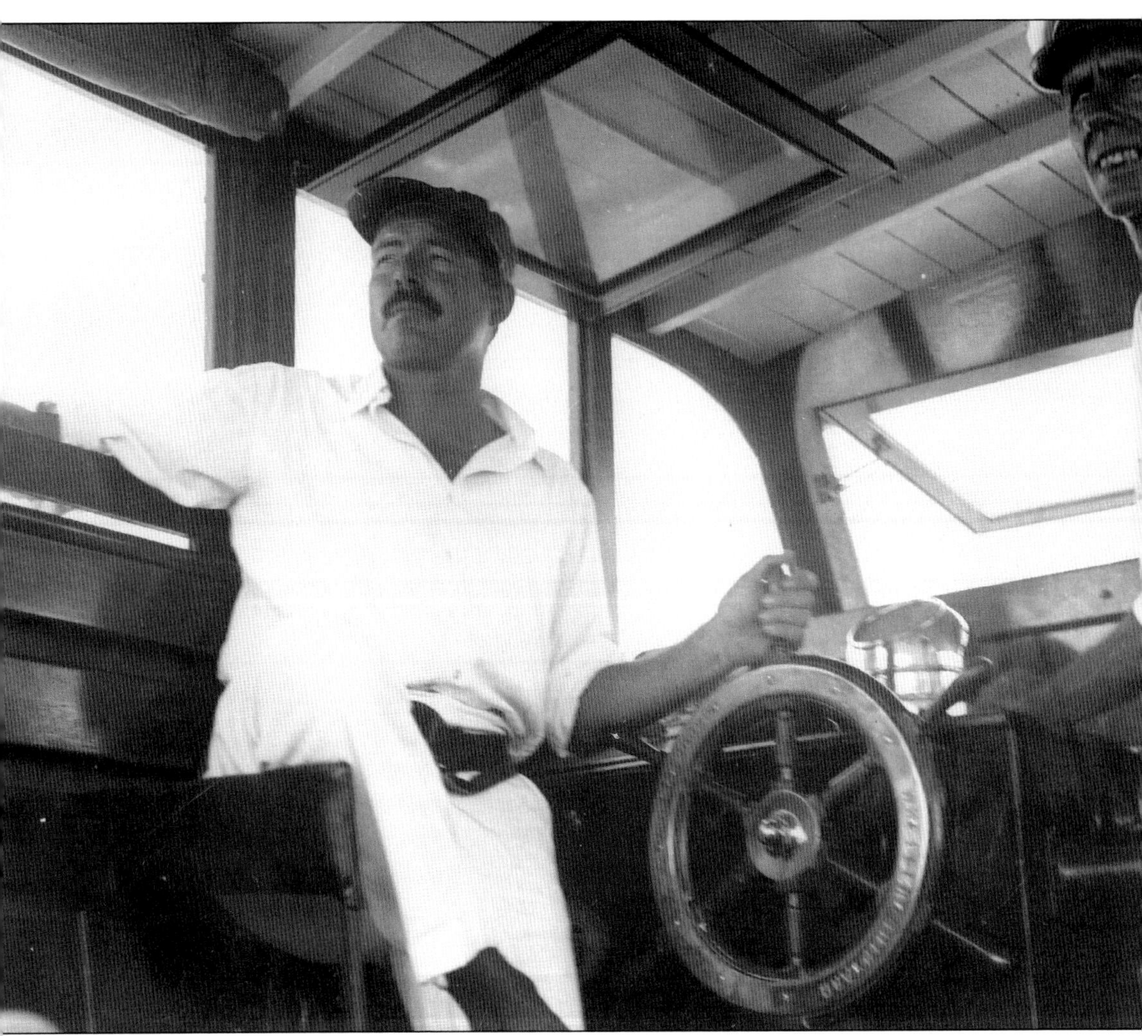

In Key West, Joe Russell (right) became friends with the famous writer, Ernest Hemingway (left, on his boat *Pilar*). They bonded over drinking and fishing. Hemingway allegedly took a liking to Russell when the bar owner agreed to cash a royalty check for him; he is also credited with convincing Russell to name his bar "Sloppy Joe's." With his "mob" of friends and fellow drinkers, including the writer John Dos Passos, Hemingway spent innumerable hours here savoring rum and conversation. One afternoon at Sloppy Joe's, the great man met a young journalist named Martha Gellhorn; this encounter sparked an affair that would end in Hemingway's divorce from his second wife, Pauline Pfeiffer, and his marriage to Martha. After he moved away from Key West in 1939, his ex-wife Pauline continued to frequent Sloppy Joe's and dance there on rumba nights. (Courtesy of Monroe County Library, Key West.)

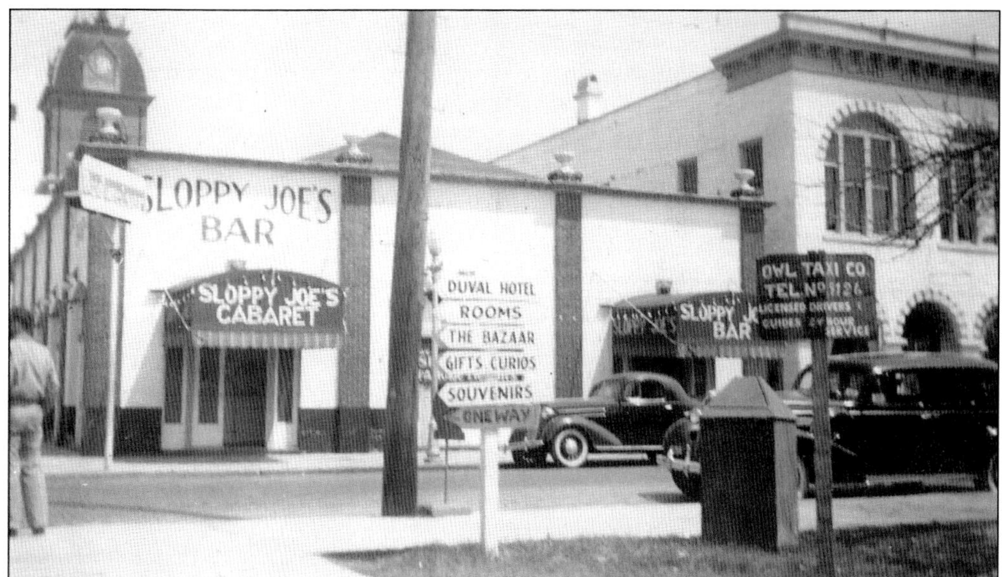

From 1937 onwards, Sloppy Joe's became a fixture on Duval Street. The awning pictured here advertises its musical cabaret. One of the most recognizable characters at the bar was African American bartender "Big" Al Skinner, who weighed about 300 pounds and had a personality just as large. During the Depression, WPA artist Erik Smith painted a mural of Big Skinner, Ernest Hemingway, and Joe Russell. (Courtesy of Monroe County Library, Key West.)

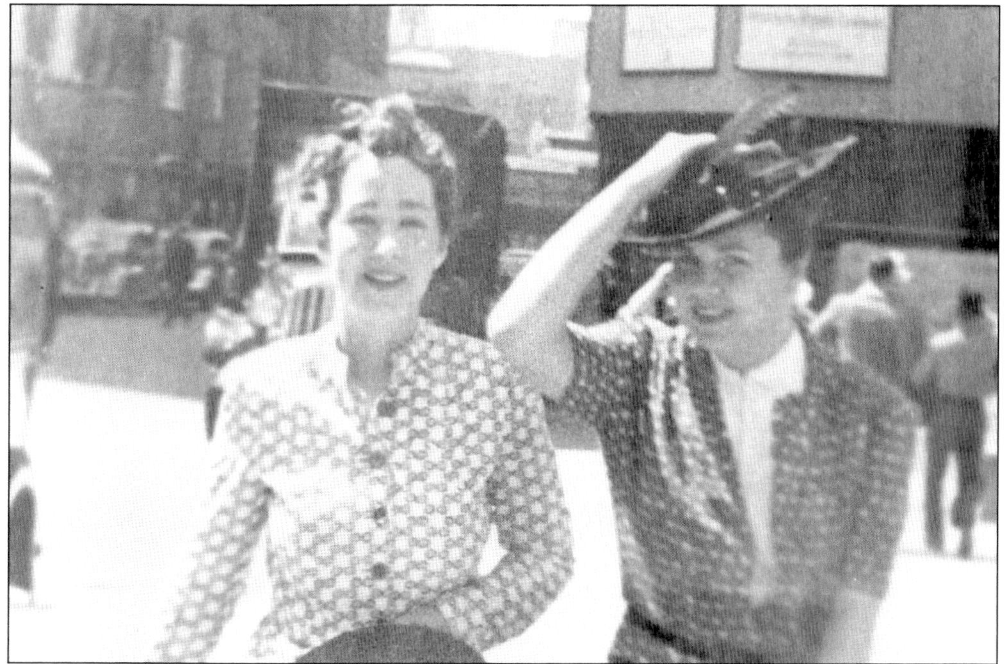

In the late 1930s, writer Elizabeth Bishop (right) also sipped cocktails at Sloppy Joe's. The poet would wear "a tight white satin evening dress" to the bar on rumba nights, to dance with her partner, Louise Crane (left), along with Pauline Hemingway and her friends. The Pulitzer prize–winning poet's striking poem "Full Moon, Key West" describes the streets coming alive at night. (Courtesy of Vassar College Libraries.)

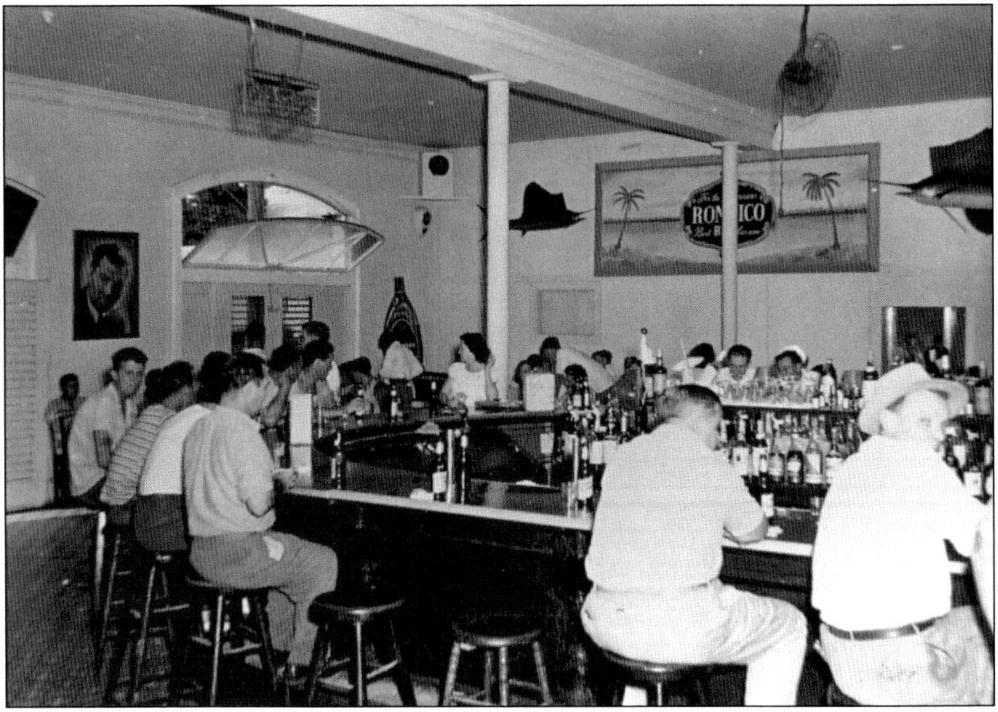

This photograph was taken inside Sloppy Joe's. Yet another writer to pass time at this fabled watering hole was Tennessee Williams, famous playwright and Key West resident for several years. In 1941, he wrote to his friend Josephine Healy, "Friday morning I was in Miami and Saturday night I was in Sloppy Joe's bar in Key West." (Courtesy of Monroe County Library, Key West.)

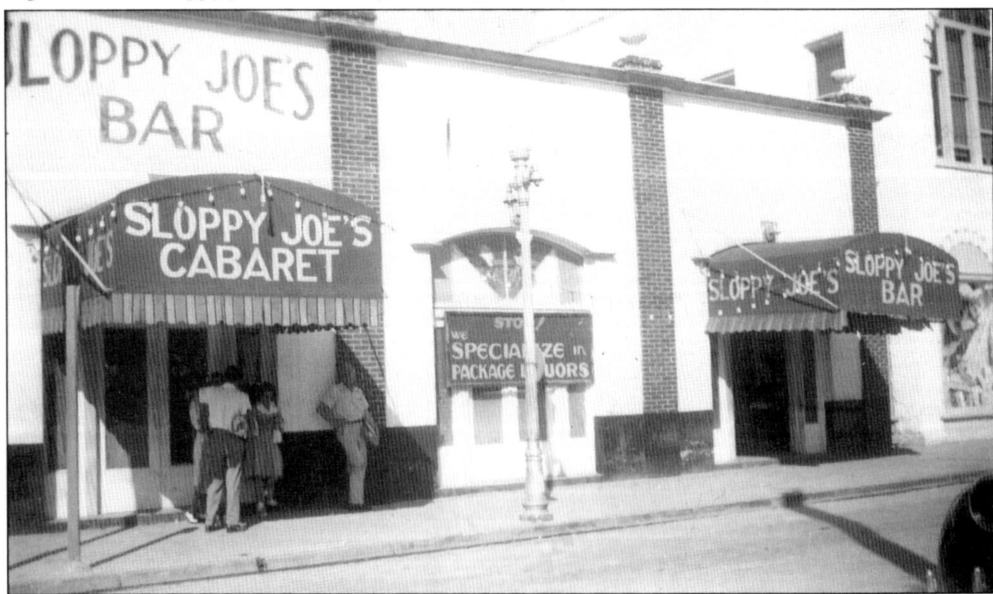

While Sloppy Joe's bar did a healthy business, Joe Russell himself—whom Ernest Hemingway nicknamed "Josie Grunts"—fared worse. The fisherman and bar owner died of a heart attack in 1941 at the age of 53. Despite his early death, the famous bar bearing his name lived on. (Courtesy of Monroe County Library, Key West.)

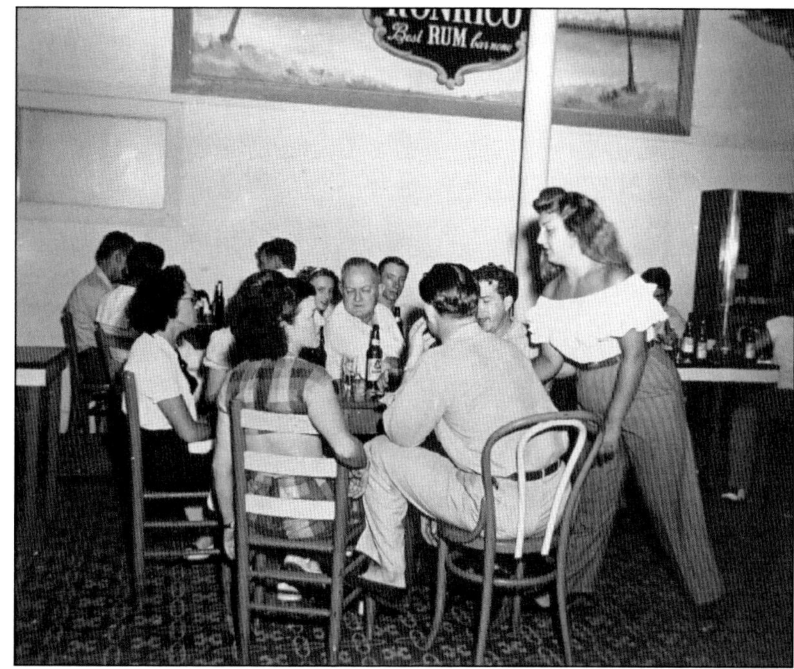

Men and women gather around tables as a waitress delivers drinks at Sloppy Joe's in the 1950s. Decorating the floor are cement Cuban tiles that original owner Juan Farto had laid in 1917. On the wall hangs a sign touting the virtues of Ronrico rum. (Courtesy of Monroe County Library, Key West.)

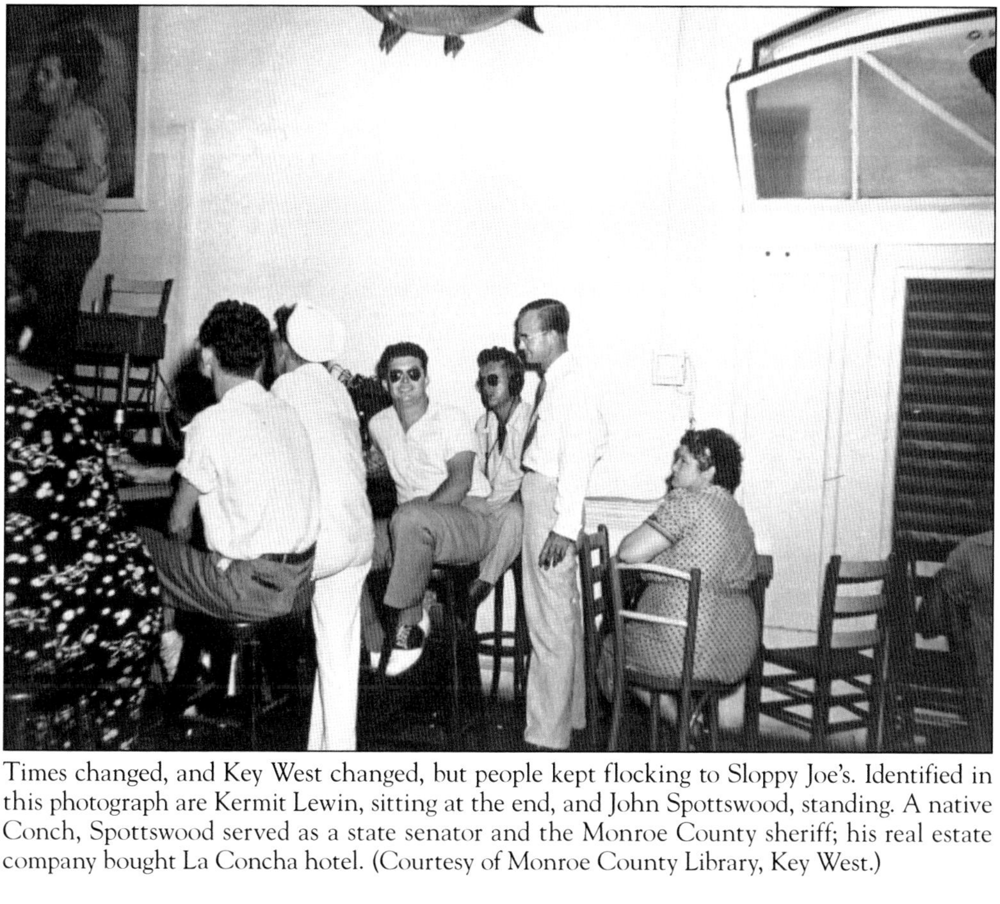

Times changed, and Key West changed, but people kept flocking to Sloppy Joe's. Identified in this photograph are Kermit Lewin, sitting at the end, and John Spottswood, standing. A native Conch, Spottswood served as a state senator and the Monroe County sheriff; his real estate company bought La Concha hotel. (Courtesy of Monroe County Library, Key West.)

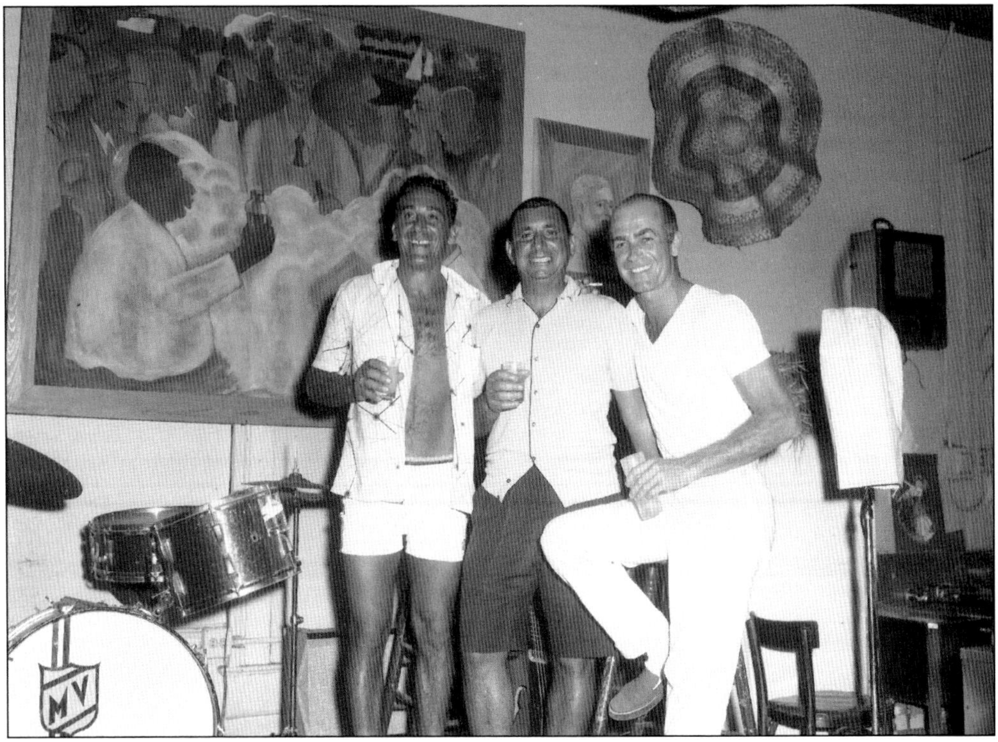

Three very relaxed-looking men, dressed for the tropical heat, pose at the bandstand inside Sloppy Joe's bar. In the background is the Depression-era mural of Big Skinner, Ernest Hemingway, and Joe Russell himself; on the right is a portrait of "Papa" Hemingway. (Courtesy of Monroe County Library, Key West.)

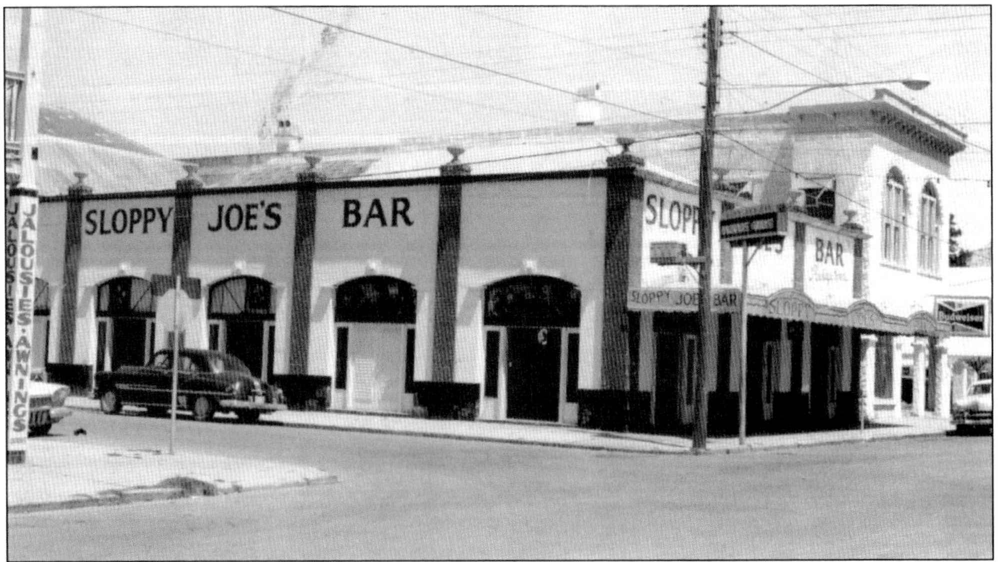

This image captures Sloppy Joe's in the 1960s. Hidden in a back room was a treasure trove of Ernest Hemingway memorabilia, including partial manuscripts that the writer had left in Joe Russell's care. These papers were rediscovered by his widow, Mary, after Hemingway's death in 1961. (Courtesy of Monroe County Library, Key West.)

The elk head on the wall hints that this photograph was taken inside the Elks Lodge bar at 313 Duval Street. It is the 1940s, and the place is packed with civilians and sailors. In the foreground, a bartender prepares to concoct cocktails for the waiting crowd. (Courtesy of Monroe County Library, Key West.)

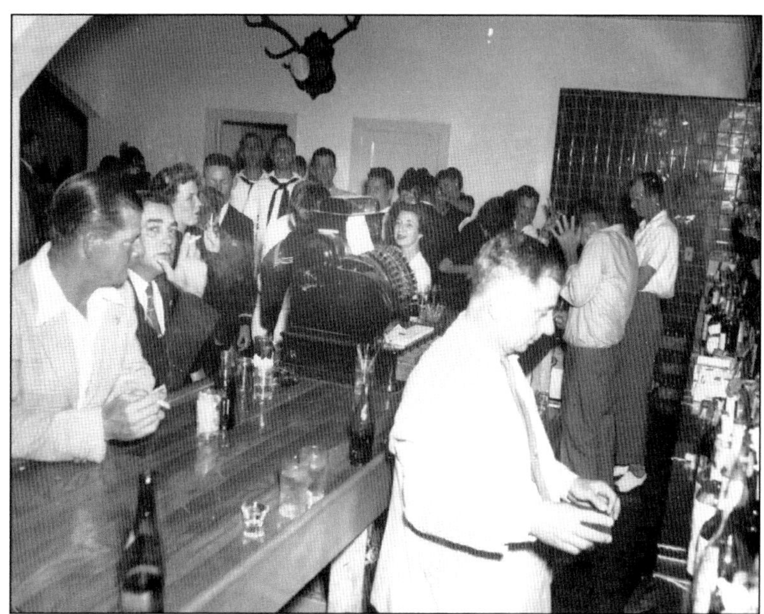

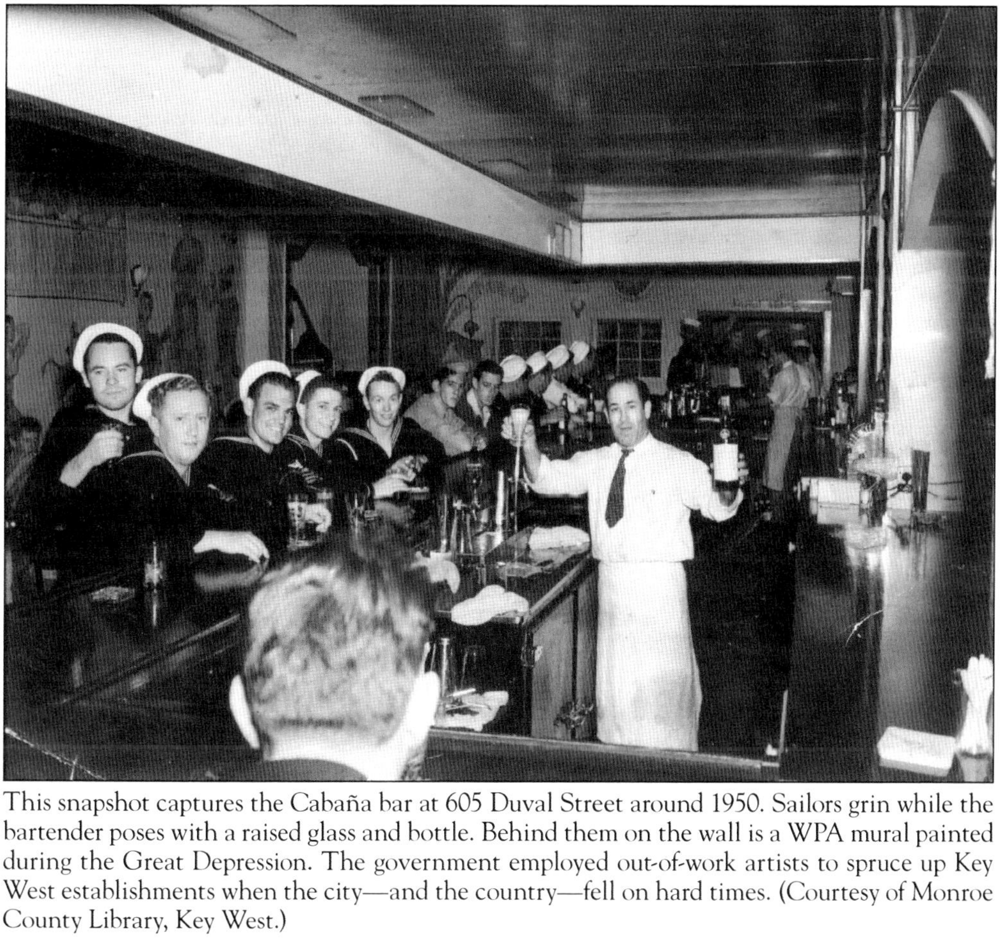

This snapshot captures the Cabaña bar at 605 Duval Street around 1950. Sailors grin while the bartender poses with a raised glass and bottle. Behind them on the wall is a WPA mural painted during the Great Depression. The government employed out-of-work artists to spruce up Key West establishments when the city—and the country—fell on hard times. (Courtesy of Monroe County Library, Key West.)

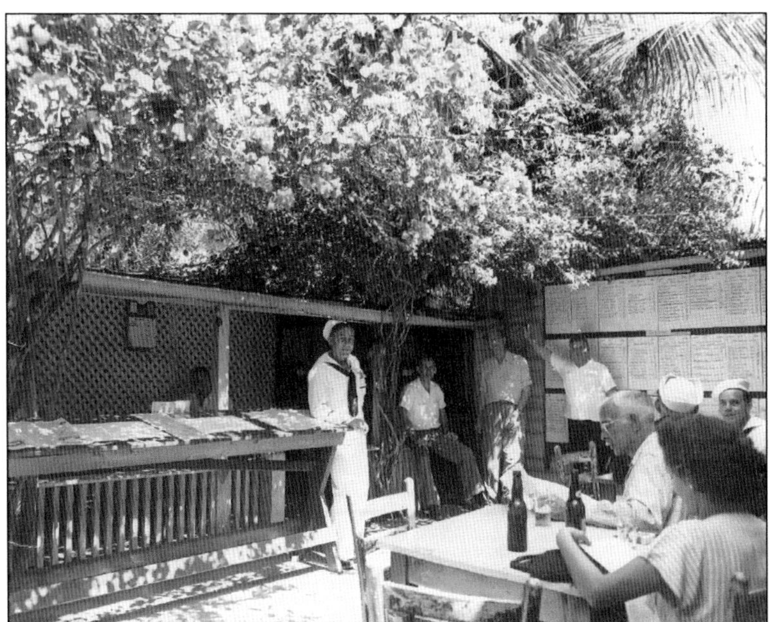

The Cabaña Cocktail Lounge not only provided customers with many varieties of alcoholic refreshment, it also gave folks a chance to gamble out back. The boards on the right list two racetracks, Bowie and Gulfstream, with horses and their odds. (Courtesy of Monroe County Library, Key West.)

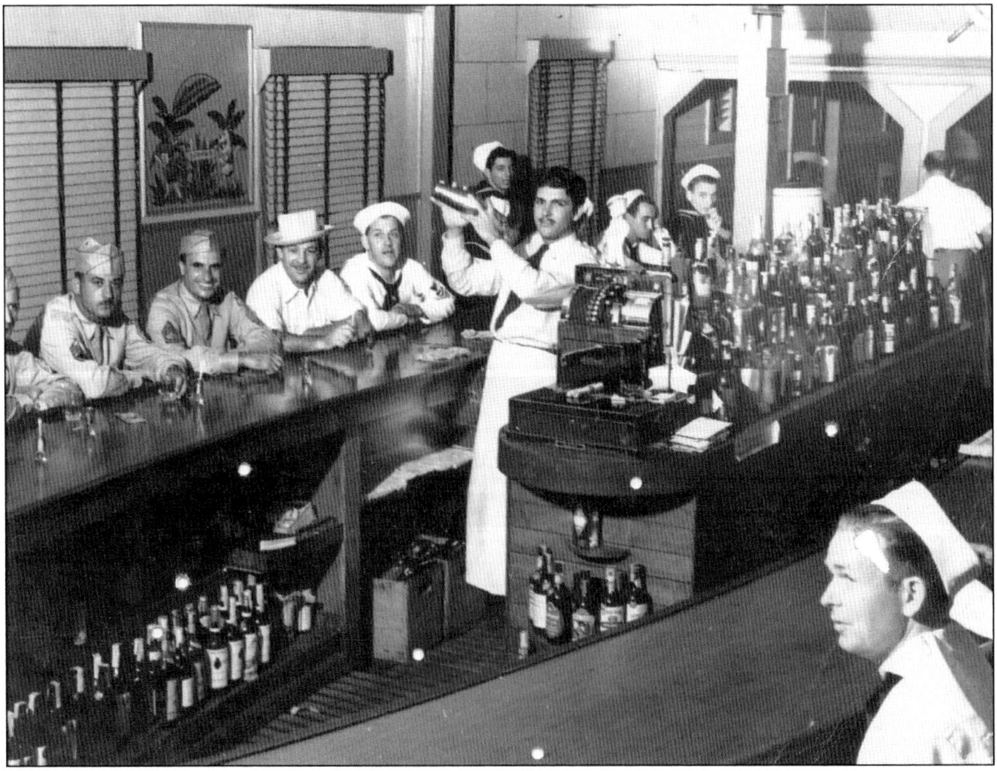

Bartender Pete Sanchez hoists a cocktail shaker at the Boat Bar around 1950. Located at 503 Duval Street, this watering hole featured a handsome wooden bar designed to look like a boat's hull. Servicemen, like the ones pictured here, ensured the Boat Bar had plenty of business. Judging from the number of bottles, thirsty patrons could order almost any kind of cocktail imaginable. (Courtesy of Monroe County Library, Key West.)

This 1965 photograph shows the exterior of the Boat Bar. The front windows advertise beer on tap and package goods to go. The historic house with its gingerbread-trimmed balcony was built in approximately 1889; the building survives today, although it no longer houses a bar. (Courtesy of Monroe County Library, Key West.)

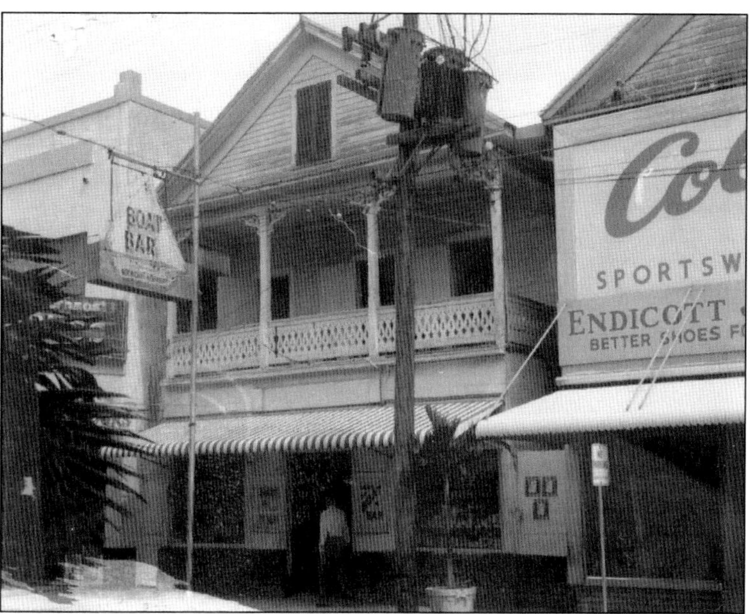

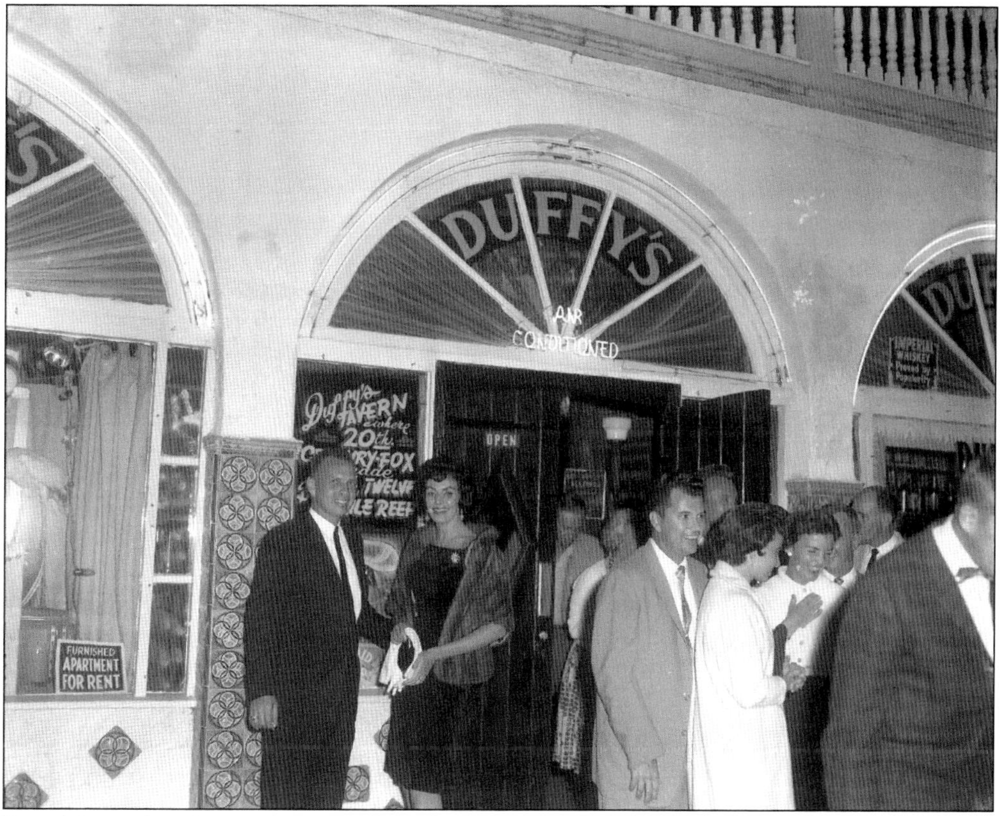

Duval Street bars have seen more than their share of parties over the decades. Here, at Duffy's Tavern, the cast, crew, and other guests celebrate the 1953 release of 20th Century Fox's picture *Beneath the 12-Mile Reef*, filmed partially in Key West. Glamorous actress Terry Moore is pictured at center. (Courtesy of Monroe County Library, Key West.)

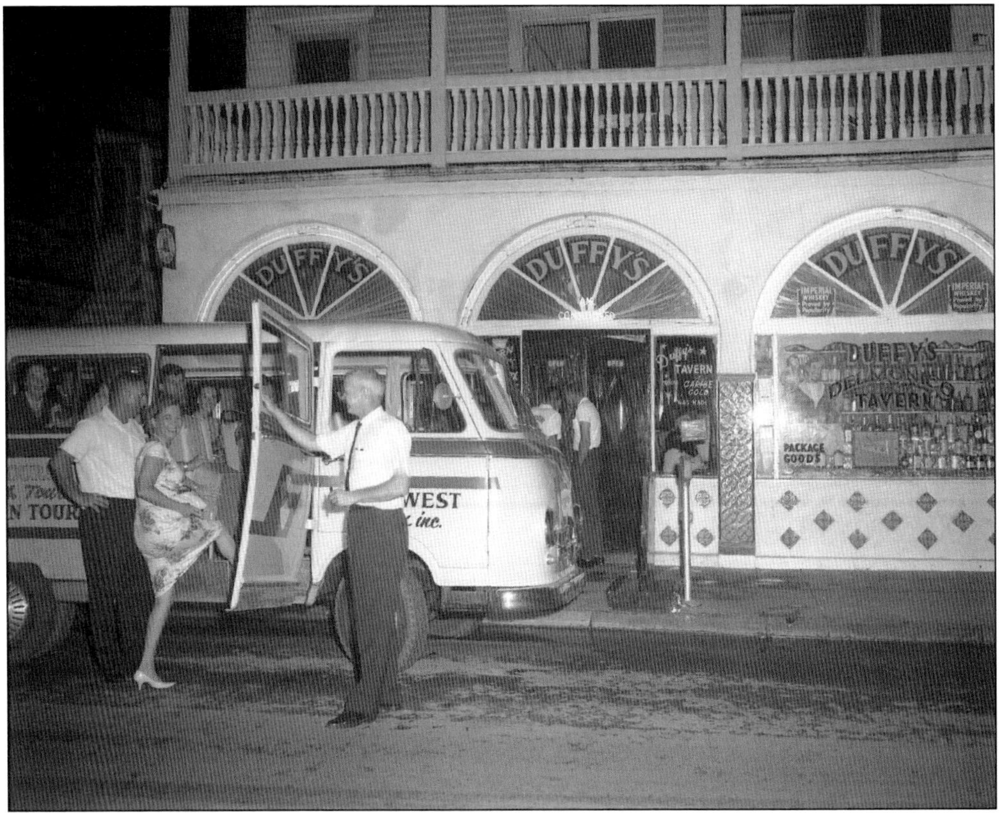

Duffy's Tavern was located at 218 Duval Street, just north of Caroline Street. Here, revelers climb aboard the Honky Tonk bus to continue onwards to the next bar. The women, dressed up for a night on the town, wear strands of pearls and cocktail dresses. (Courtesy of Monroe County Library, Key West.)

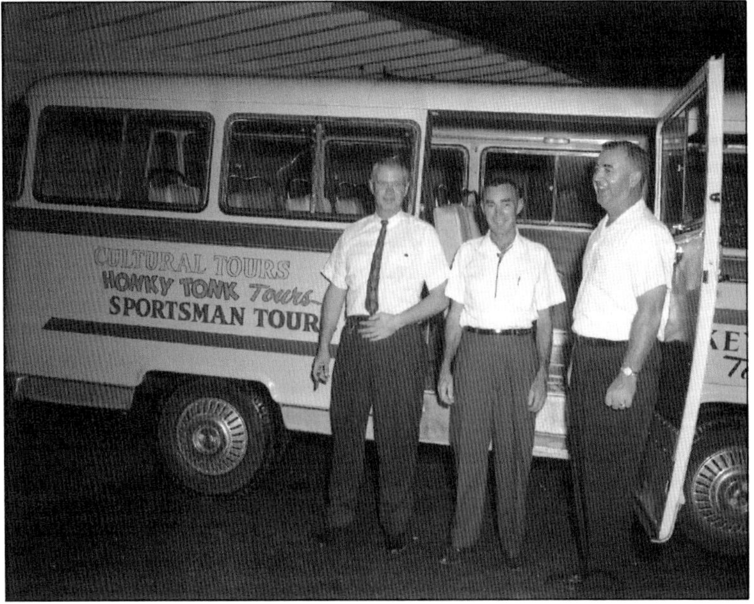

Three smiling men pose in front of the Honky Tonk bar bus in the 1950s. Rather than doing the Duval Street scene on foot, guests of the Honky Tonk tour could ride to watering holes in comfort and save their energy for drinking and possibly dancing. (Courtesy of Monroe County Library, Key West.)

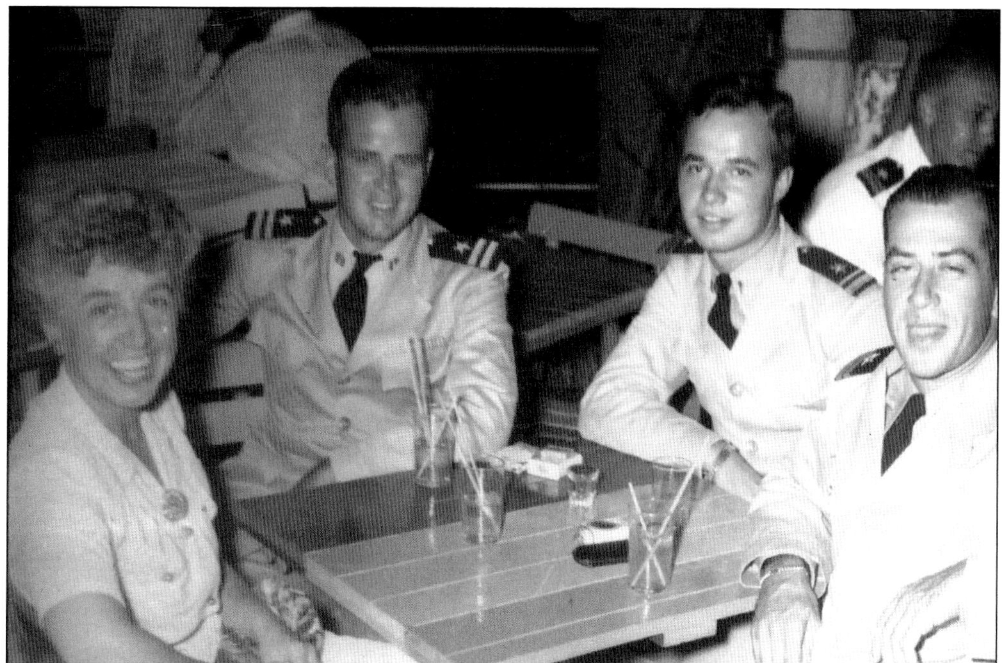

Fifth-generation Key Wester Jessie Porter enjoys drinks with some Navy officers at Sally Rand's nightclub, located at the end of Duval Street, in the 1950s. Sally Rand was a well-known exotic fan dancer. "Miss Jessie," as people called her, collected WPA artwork, helped Key West's historic preservation movement get off the ground, and befriended visiting writers such as Robert Frost, Wallace Stevens, and Archibald MacLeish. (Courtesy of Monroe County Library, Key West.)

Duval Street celebrates New Year's Eve with gusto and wild abandon. This 1950 photograph was taken on January 31 inside the Musical Bar at 627 Duval, between Southard and Angela Streets. Party hats are donned, and noise makers are ready as everyone squeezes closer to the action. (Courtesy of Monroe County Library, Key West.)

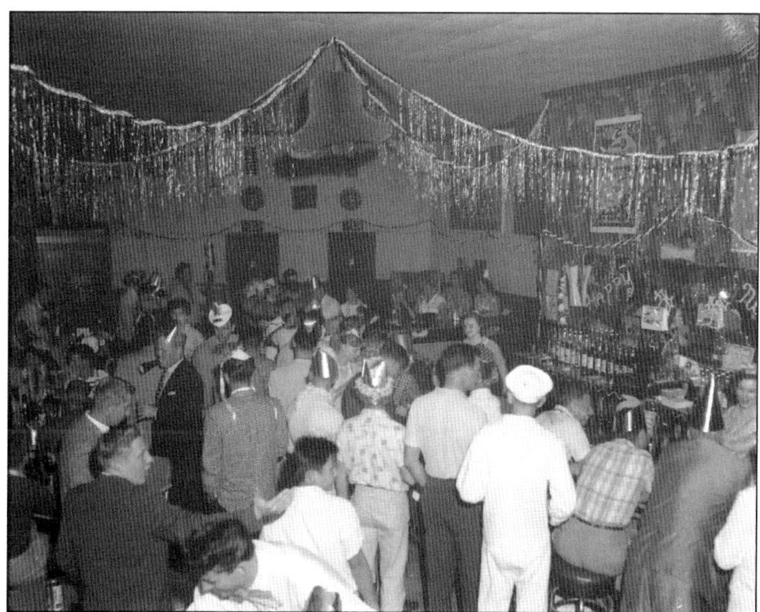

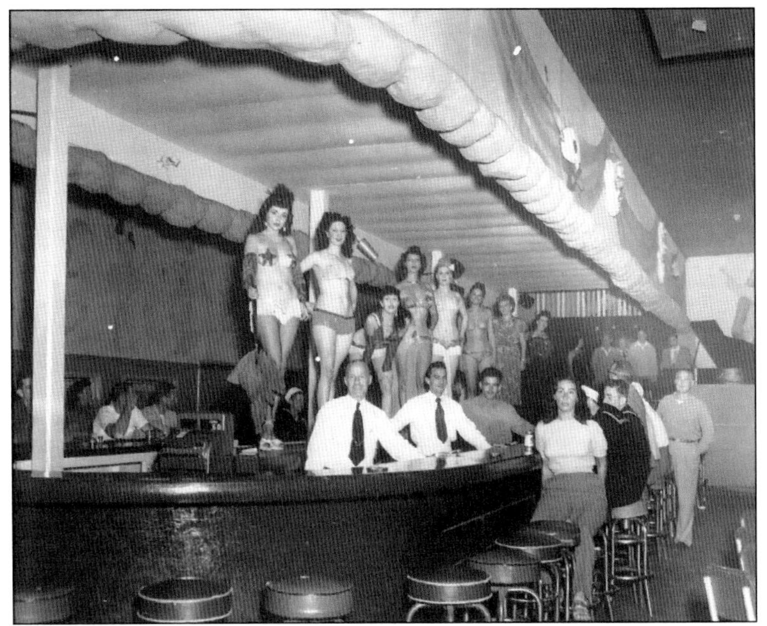

The Mardi Gras Club advertised "Floor Shows Nitely" along with air conditioning and "Continuous Entertainment" at 92 Duval Street. Posing on top of the bar in this 1960 photograph are some of the dancers who performed to live music, played on the baby grand piano in the background. A major fire erupted at the nightclub in 1963. (Courtesy of Monroe County Library, Key West.)

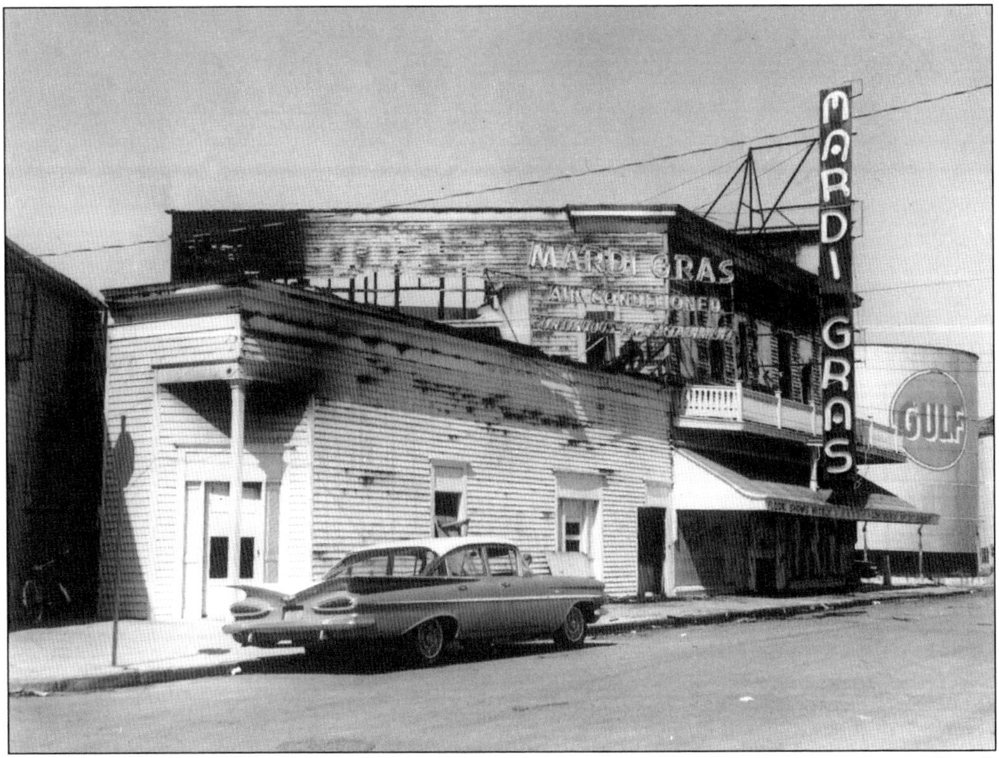

The Mardi Gras Club, where scenes from Tennessee Williams's *The Rose Tattoo* were filmed, appears devastated by a 1963 fire. Over the years, a number of Duval Street bars fell victim to fires, including the Trade Winds Bar in 1956 and the famous Copa nightclub in 1995. (Courtesy of Monroe County Library, Key West.)

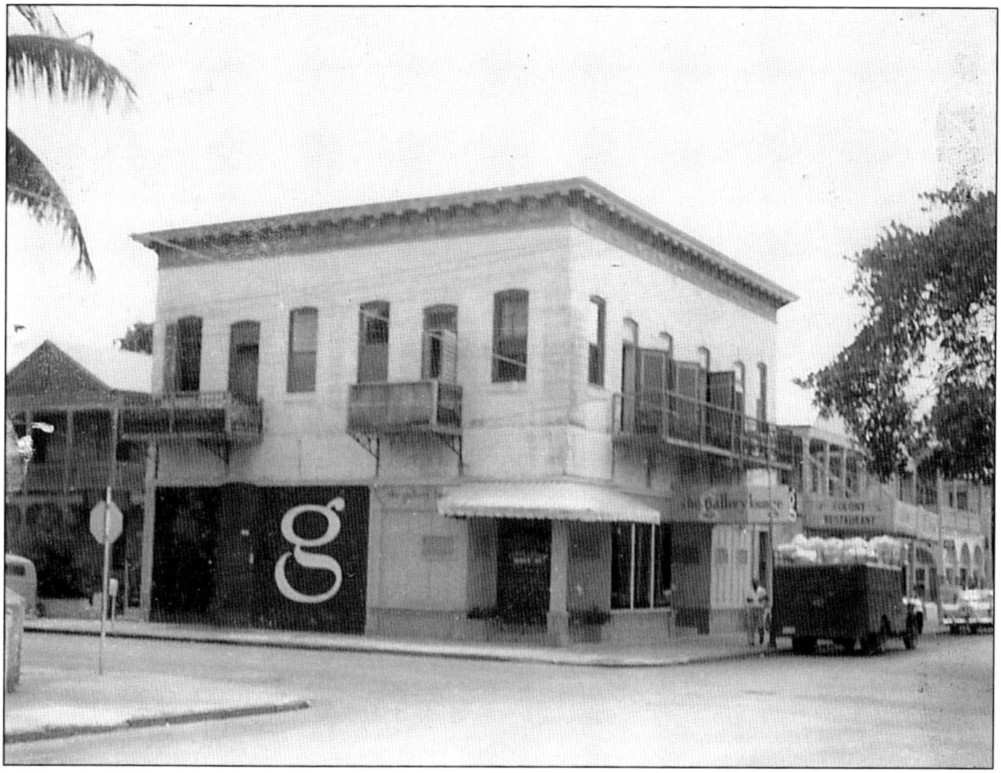

Duval Street and its bars have evolved for close to two centuries. This 1960s photograph shows the Gallery Lounge, housed in a 1912 building located next door to the Colony Restaurant. Today, it houses three bars: the Bull, the Whistle Bar, and the clothing-optional Garden of Eden. (Courtesy of Monroe County Library, Key West.)

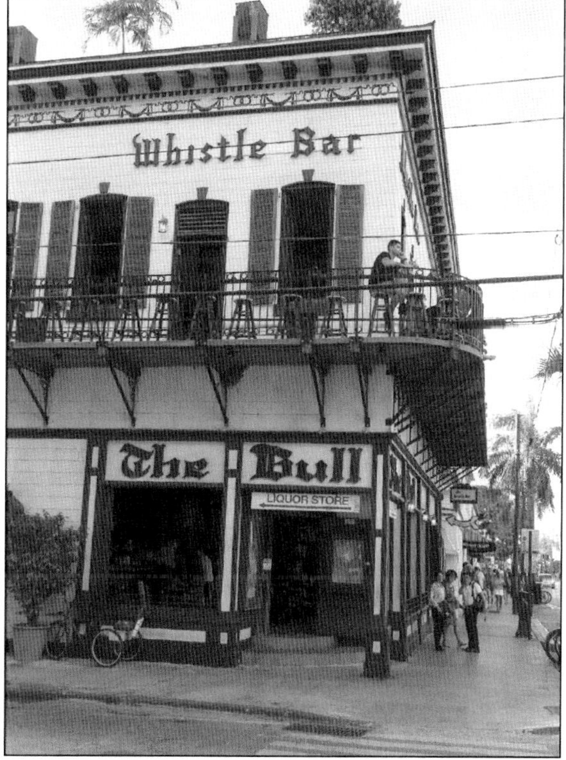

The Bull and Whistle Bar, along with the rooftop Garden of Eden, have become Duval Street icons. Inside the Bull are murals of important figures from Key West history, such as Henry Flagler and Mel Fisher. Since the days of the Gallery Lounge, the upstairs balcony has been expanded so that it gives patrons a front-row view onto Duval Street. (Courtesy of Zickie Allgrove.)

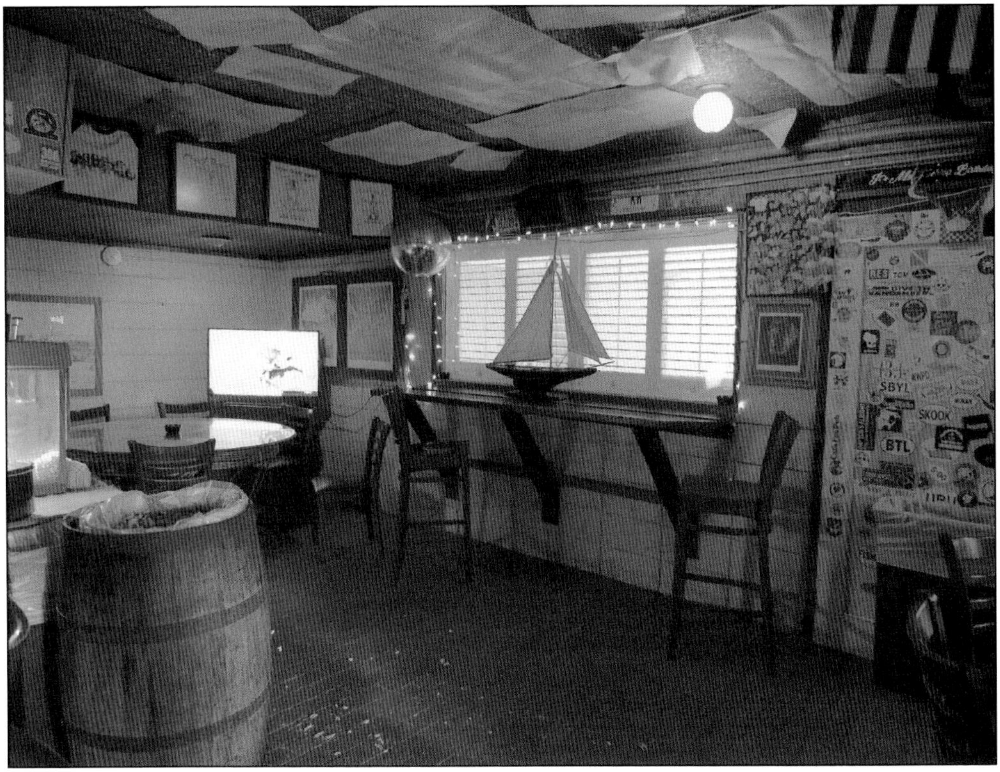

Inside the Pier House hotel at 1 Duval Street is the legendary Chart Room bar. Here, treasure salvor Mel Fisher and his crew dreamed of finding the Atocha treasure, and Jimmy Buffett played some of his very first gigs in Key West. Some patrons were so devoted that they had their ashes installed in the wooden countertop. (Courtesy of Zickie Allgrove.)

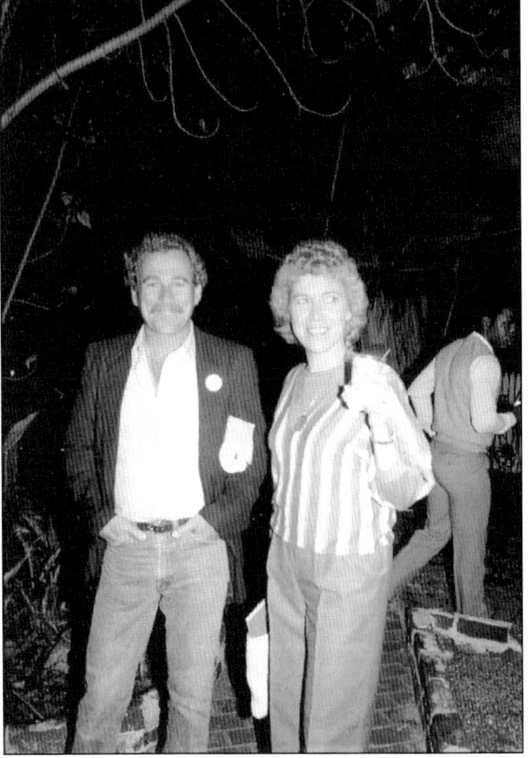

Musician and songwriter Jimmy Buffett (pictured here around 1980 with *Key West Citizen* editor Betty Williams) would make Duval Street even more famous. In his song, "My Head Hurts, My Feet Stink, and I Don't Love Jesus," he sings about recovering from an especially rough night that included Duval Street festivities. (Courtesy of Monroe County Library, Key West.)

Not only did Jimmy Buffett celebrate Key West's allure in song, he also founded one of Duval Street's most iconic and enduring destinations. Buffett himself opened the original Margaritaville at 500 Duval Street in 1985. This island institution takes its name from one of his most successful tunes. (Courtesy of Zickie Allgrove.)

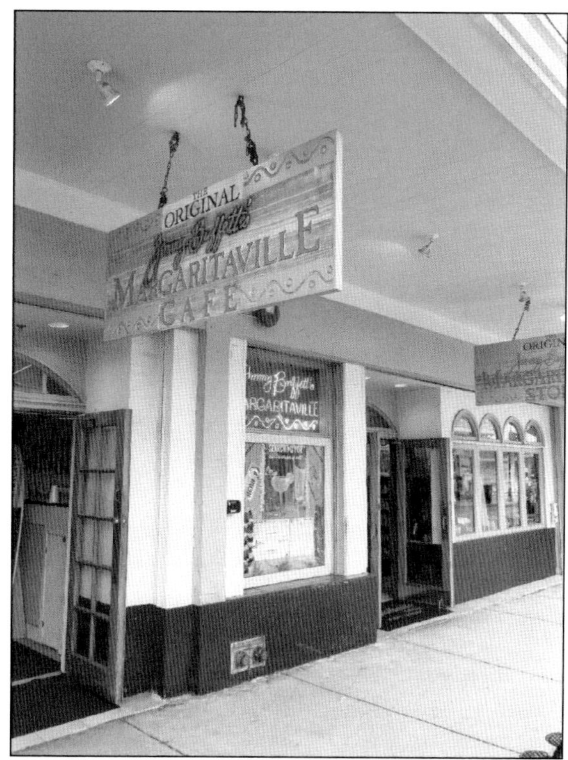

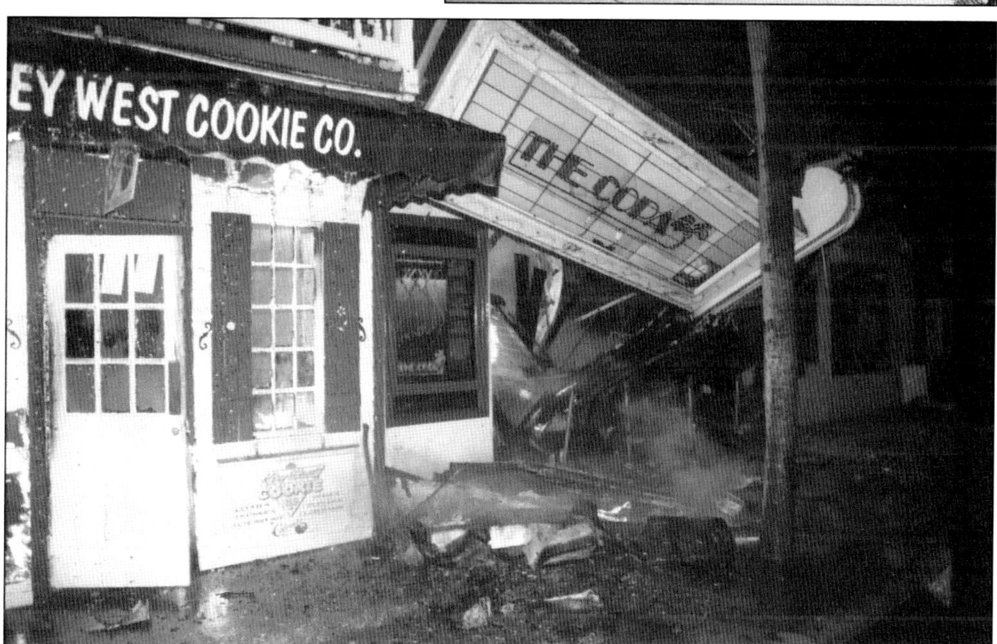

This picture shows the Copa nightclub on the 600 block of Duval Street after a fire. In the 1980s, the Copa boasted one of wildest gay bar scenes around. Grace Jones, Divine, and Sylvester—the disco star with hits like "You Make Me Feel (Mighty Real)"—performed here. These days, Duval's 801 Bourbon Street and Aqua carry on the tradition with exuberant drag shows. (Photograph by Dale McDonald, courtesy of the State Archives of Florida.)

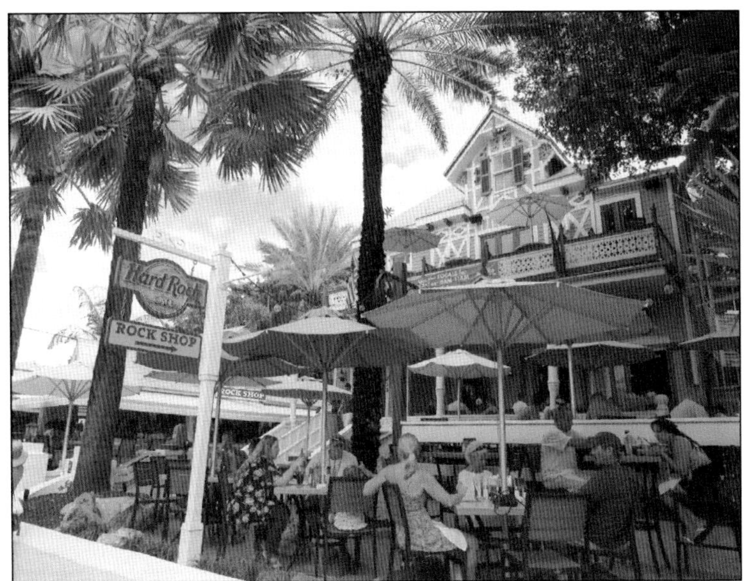

Another popular watering hole appeared on Duval in 1996. The Hard Rock Café, part of the international rock-and-roll chain, opened at 313 Duval Street in the mansion that Key West millionaire William Curry commissioned for his son Robert. Robert later committed suicide here; some report that his ghost still haunts the house. (Courtesy of Zickie Allgrove.)

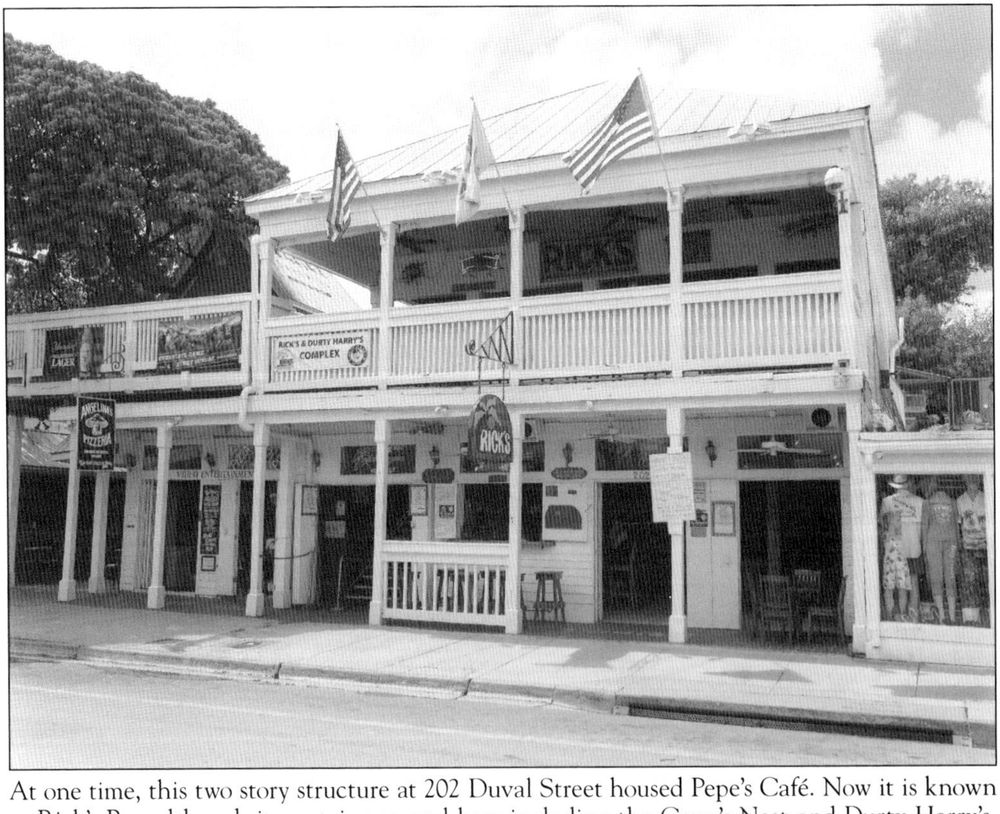

At one time, this two story structure at 202 Duval Street housed Pepe's Café. Now it is known as Rick's Bar, although it contains several bars including the Crow's Nest and Durty Harry's. For over 150 years—since before the Civil War—Duval Street's saloons, bars, and nightclubs have enticed residents and visitors alike with live music, dancing, and generously poured drinks. (Courtesy of Zickie Allgrove.)

Seven

The Cuba Connection

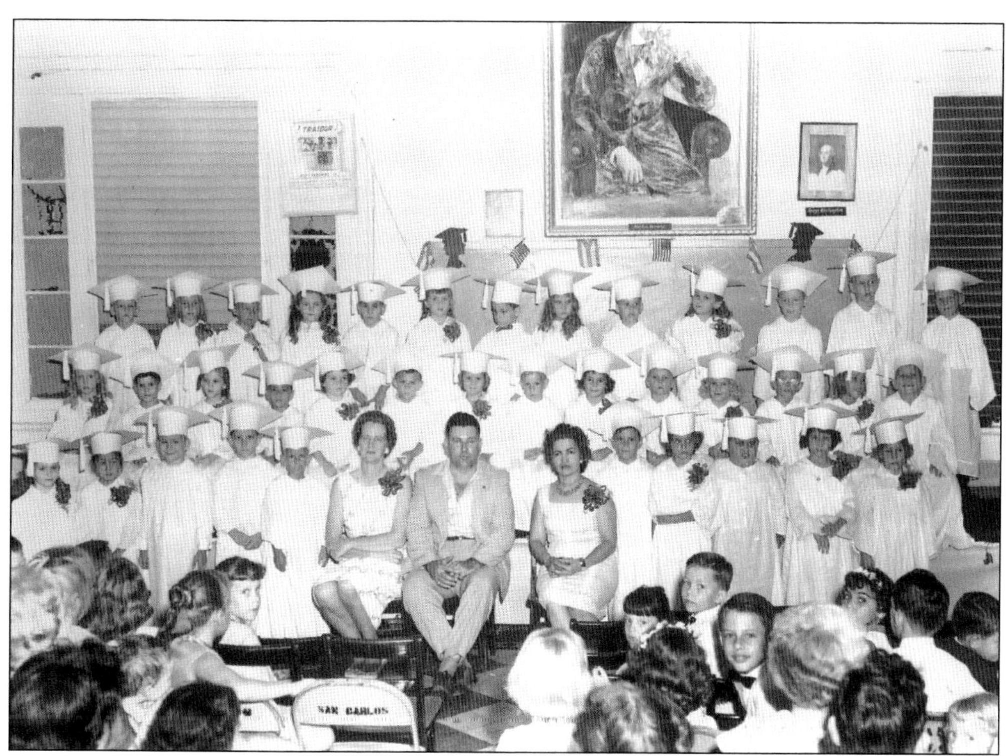

Starting in the 19th century, Cubans have enriched Duval Street with their culture, social clubs, political struggles, and institutions. Here, Cuban and Cuban American schoolchildren pose at the San Carlos Institute at 516 Duval Street on their graduation day. For decades, Cuban immigrants sent their children to school at the San Carlos. (Courtesy of Monroe County Library, Key West.)

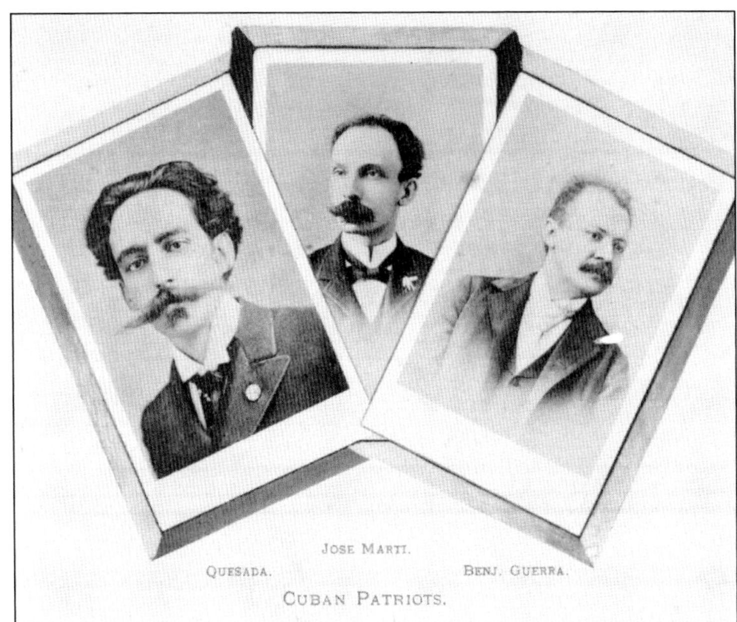

As Cubans endeavored to win freedom from Spain, Jose Marti (center) emerged as one of the movement's great orators and leaders. Marti stayed at 1125 Duval Street at the home of cigar factory owner Teodoro Perez, and in 1892, gave speeches there and at the San Carlos in support of the cause. (Courtesy of Monroe County Library, Key West.)

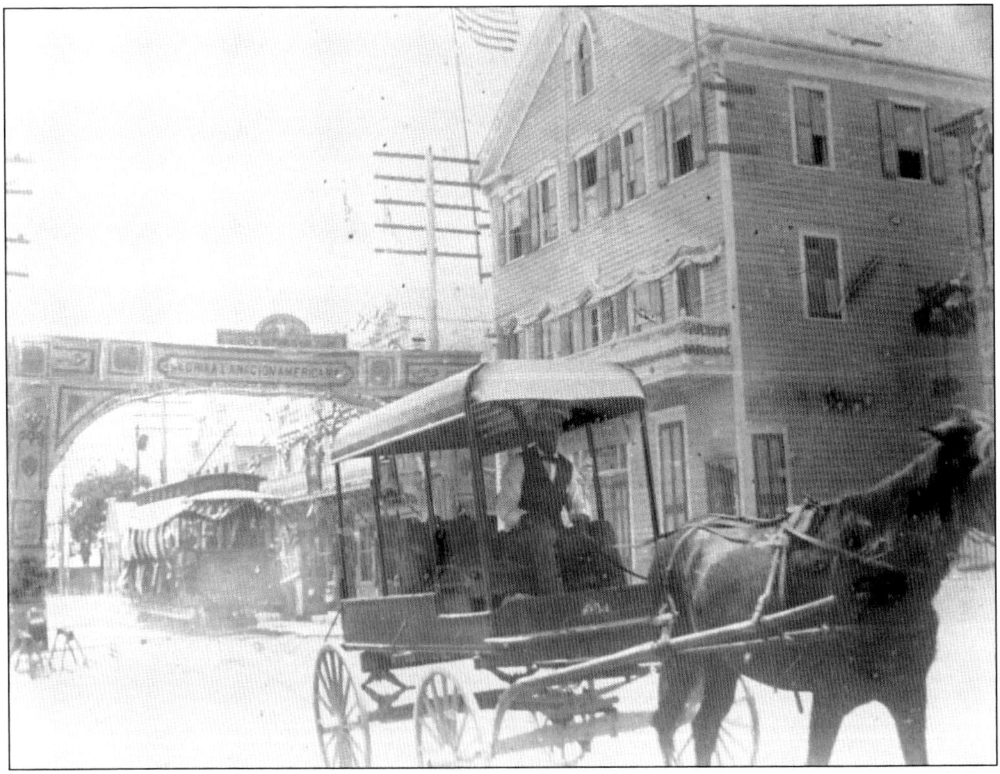

In 1905, a horse and buggy ride past the San Carlos Institute (right). Cuban exiles opened this cultural and educational institution in 1871, first on Anne Street and then on Fleming Street; the Great Fire of 1886 started at that second building. In 1890, a new San Carlos opened on Duval. This one survived until a hurricane struck Key West in 1919. (Courtesy of Monroe County Library, Key West.)

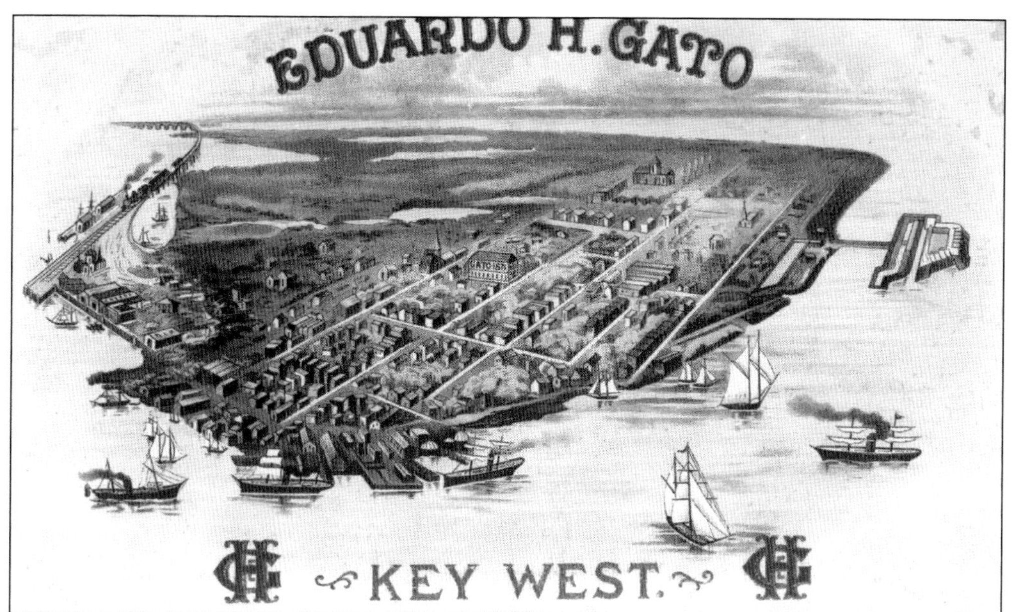

As Cubans struggled to win independence from the Spanish in the 1800s, many cigar manufacturers relocated from Cuba to Key West and opened factories. One of those to immigrate to Key West was Eduardo Hidalgo Gato. This cigar box label shows the island, including what appears to be Duval Street. (Courtesy of Monroe County Library, Key West.)

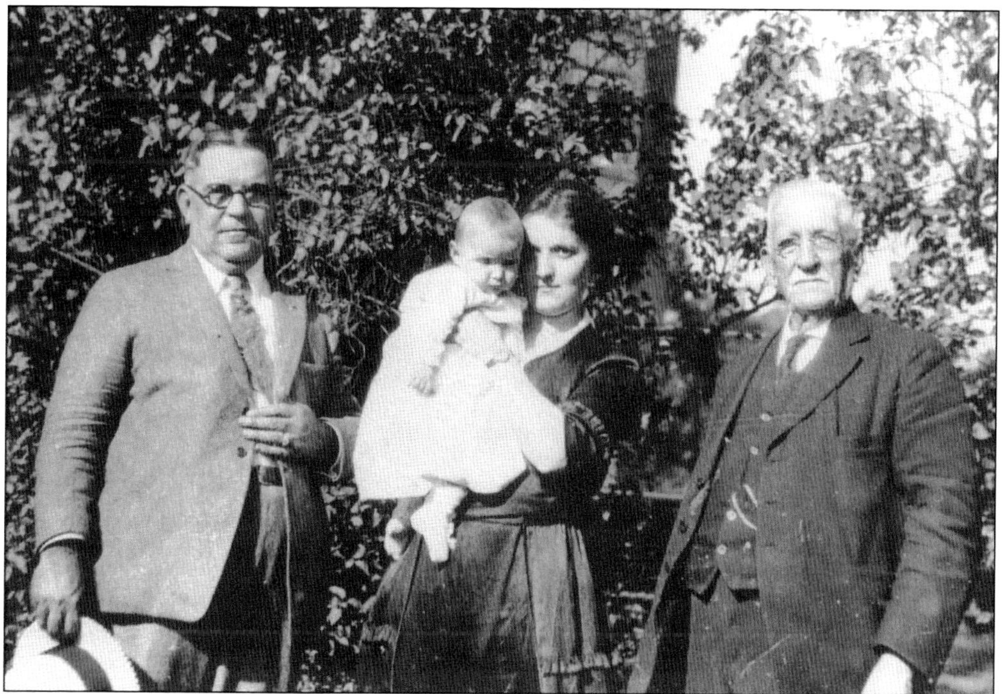

Here, Eduardo Gato Sr. poses with his son Eduardo Gato Jr., his daughter-in-law Nettie Weatherford Gato, and his grandchild in the early 20th century. Eduardo Sr. founded the streetcar line that ran along certain Key West streets, including Duval Street, so his workers had transportation to his cigar factory. (Courtesy of Monroe County Library, Key West.)

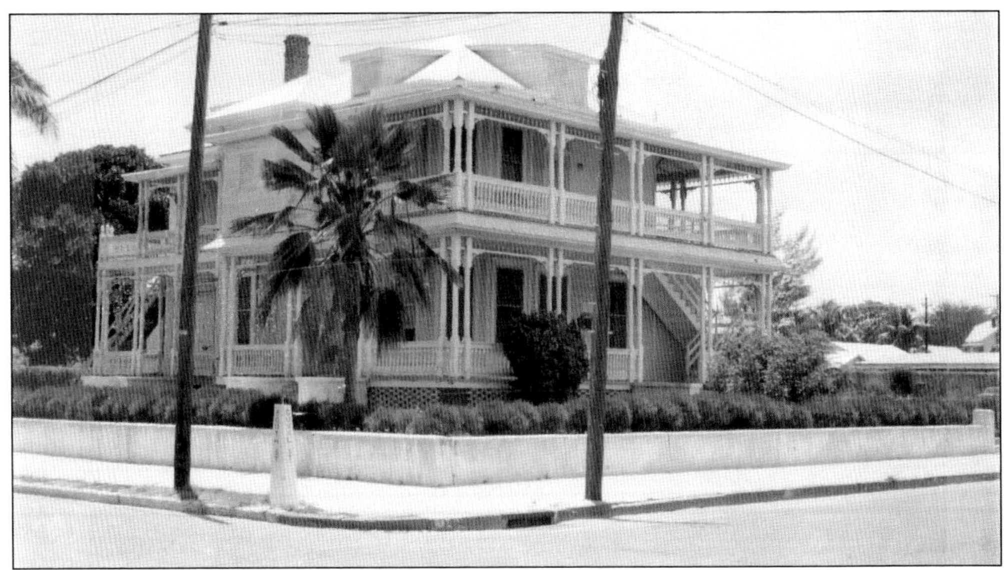

In 1894, Eduardo Gato Sr. commissioned a stately mansion for his family at 1327 Duval Street. After its construction, he was not happy with the way the sun struck the home in the afternoon, so he had the sizable house moved across the street. It kept its street number and is the only odd-numbered residence on that side of Duval Street today. (Courtesy of Monroe County Library, Key West.)

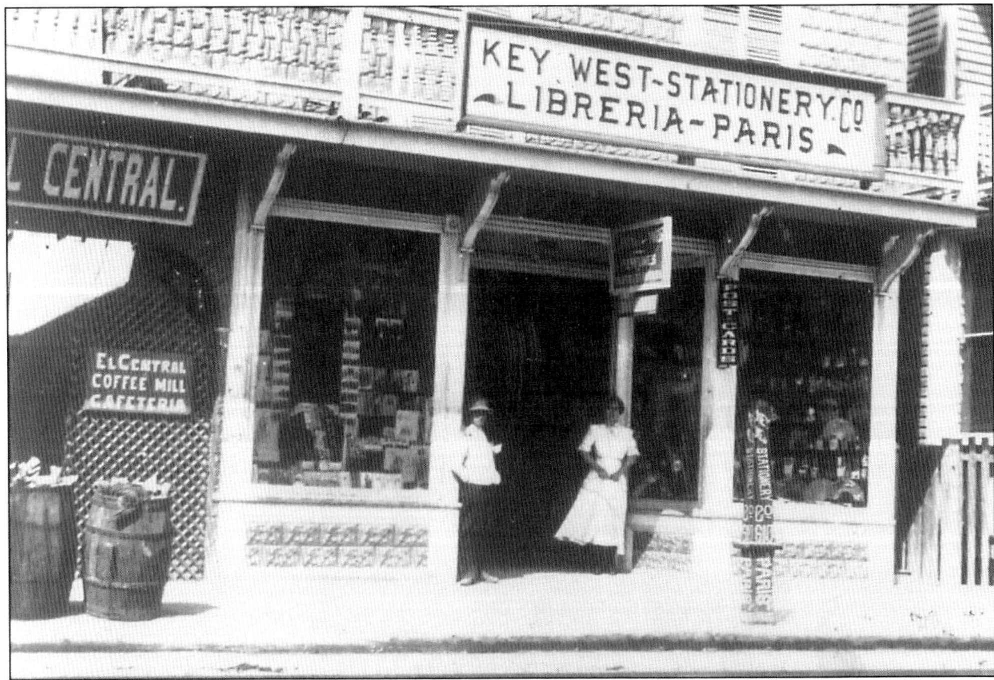

The majority of Cuban cigar factories relocated to Ybor City in Tampa, due in part to its new railroad line and also plentiful fresh water. But many Cuban Key Westers remained. The Key West Stationery Company at 610 Duval Street, pictured here around 1920, was owned by Alberto L. Villar. The sign advertises a "librería," or Spanish-language bookstore. (Courtesy of Monroe County Library, Key West.)

After the third San Carlos building was destroyed in a 1919 hurricane, Cuban Key Westers rallied to erect a new, studier building at 516 Duval Street. The Cuban government donated $80,000, and well-known Cuban architect Francisco Centurion designed this magnificent two-story structure, which opened in 1924. (Courtesy of Monroe County Library, Key West.)

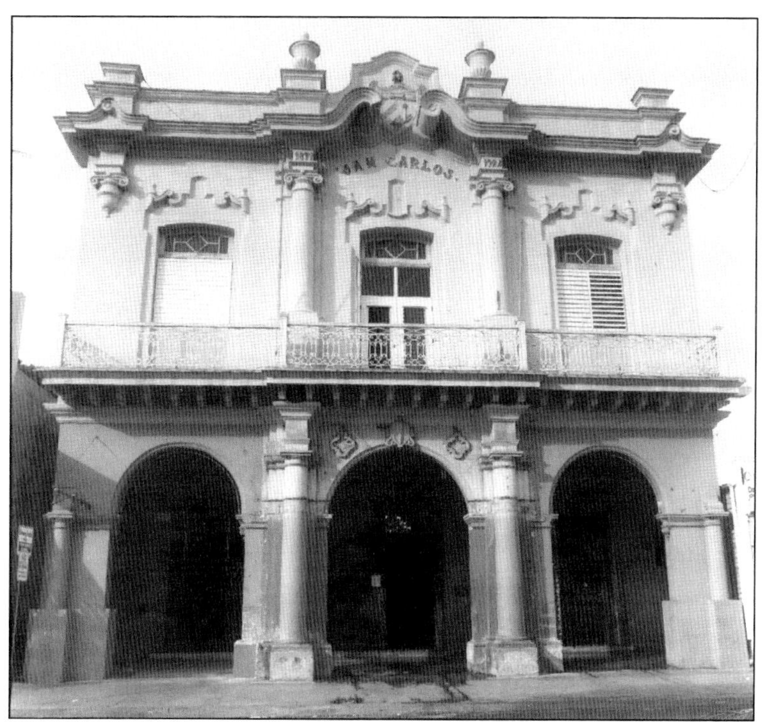

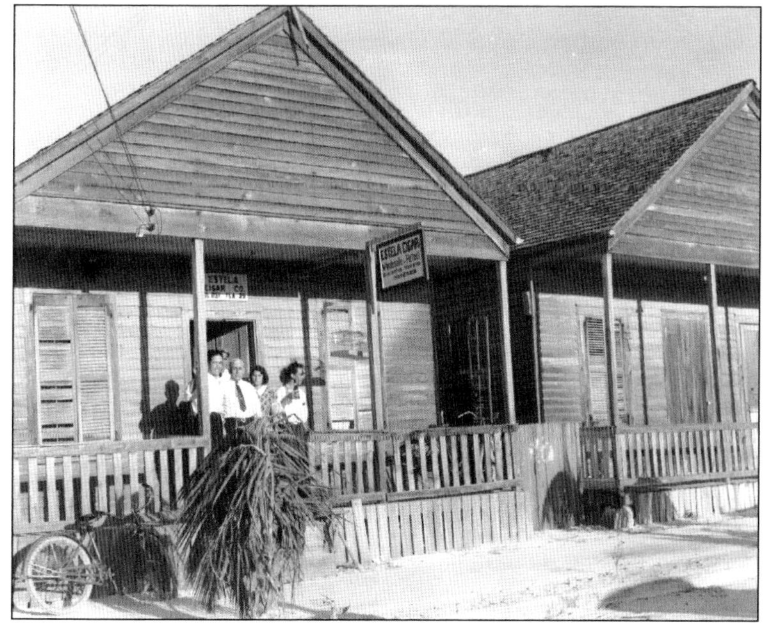

Although cigar making dramatically decreased on the island, a few operations remained, such as the Estela Cigar Shop. According to the book *Grits and Grunts*, this small shop on Duval Street was one of the *chichares*, or "one-man factories," that continued to produce cigars into the 1930s and 1940s. (Courtesy of Monroe County Library, Key West.)

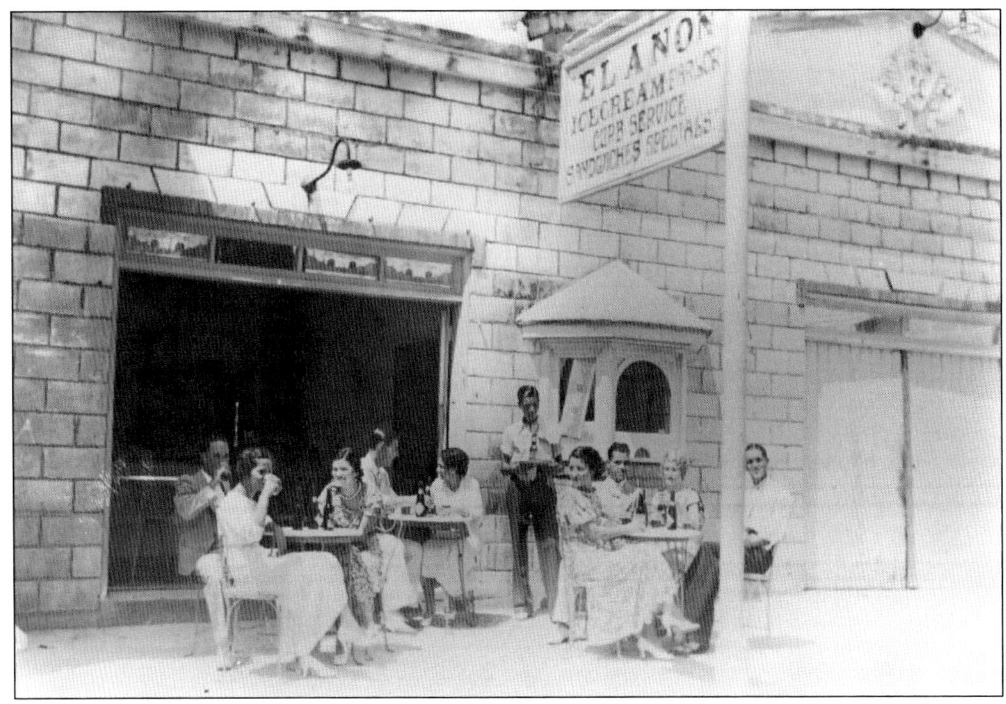

In the 1930s, Jesus Carmona stands outside his ice cream parlor, El Anon, at 1114 Duval Street. Seated at the table on the right are Consuela Carmona, Fifi Diaz, Virginia Perez, and Nene Armayor. At the middle table are ? Armayor and Margaret Loudinia. El Anon (which means "sugar apple" in Spanish) served delicious sherbets and ice creams made from tropical fruits. (Courtesy of Monroe County Library, Key West.)

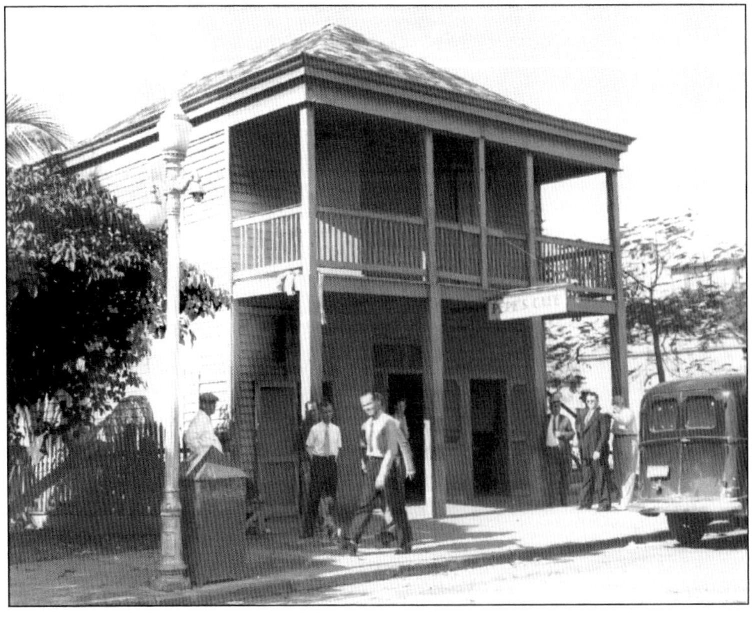

Jose "Pepe" Palaez opened Pepe's Café at 202 Duval Street in 1909. By the 1930s, it was one of *the* places to meet in Key West. Officials of Key West and Monroe County would gather here to hash out policy and strategize. Another customer who stopped in was writer and local celebrity Ernest Hemingway. (Courtesy of Monroe County Library, Key West.)

Photographer Arthur Rothstein captured this image of coffee being prepared inside Pepe's Café in 1938. Customers usually breakfasted over café con leche and Cuban toast. In the afternoons, Pepe's wife, Ellie, cooked delicious dishes. Pepe sold the café to Henrique Henriquez; when the Duval Street café eventually closed, its cook Eduardo "Curi" Garcia reopened Pepe's on Caroline Street. (Courtesy of Monroe County Library, Key West.)

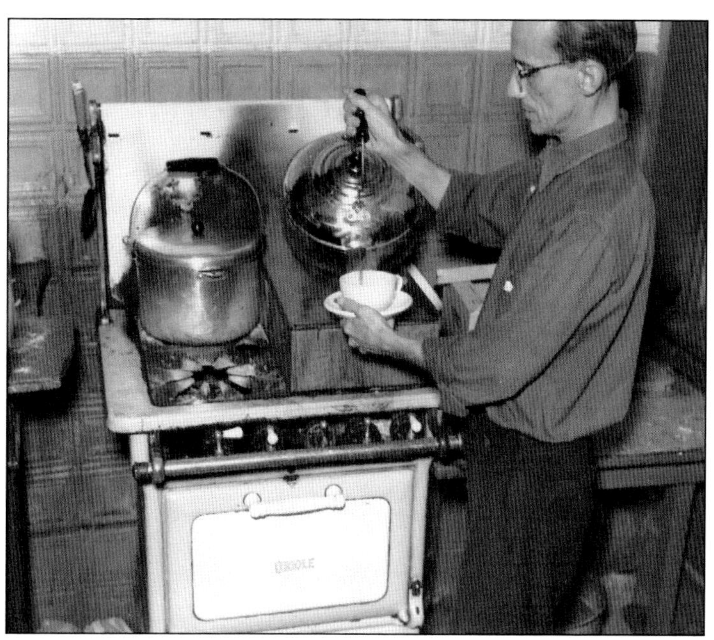

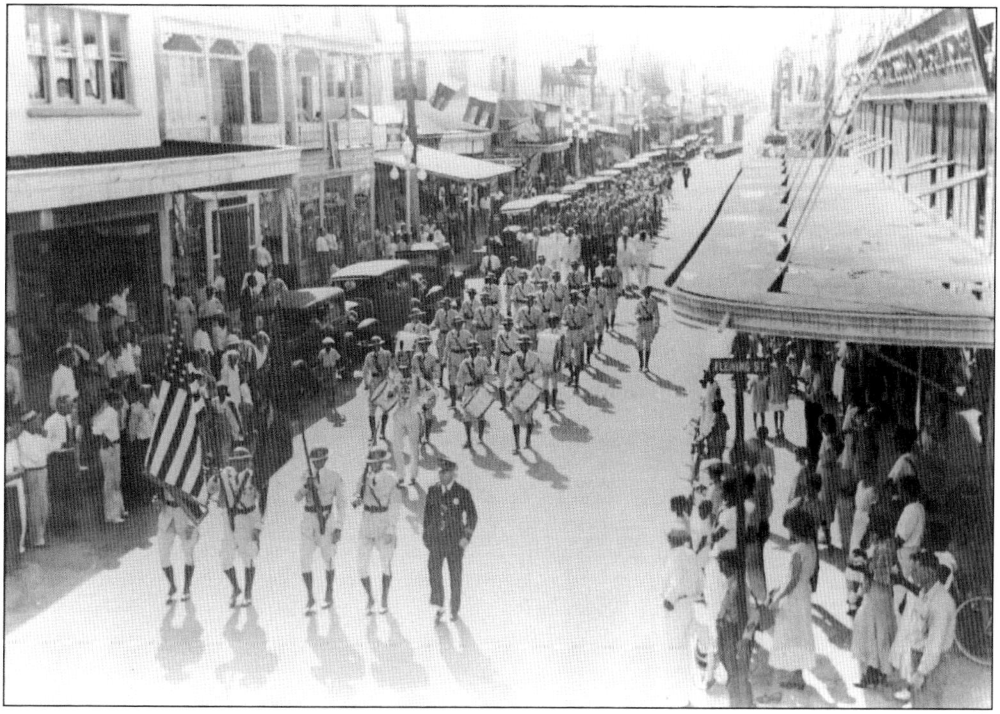

Drummers and flag bearers parade past Duval's 500 block during El Grito de Yara celebrations on October 10, 1934. This parade commemorated Carlos Manuel de Cespedes's call to arms on October 10, 1868, which marked the start of the Ten Years' War in the ongoing struggle to win Cuban independence from Spain. (Courtesy of Monroe County Library, Key West.)

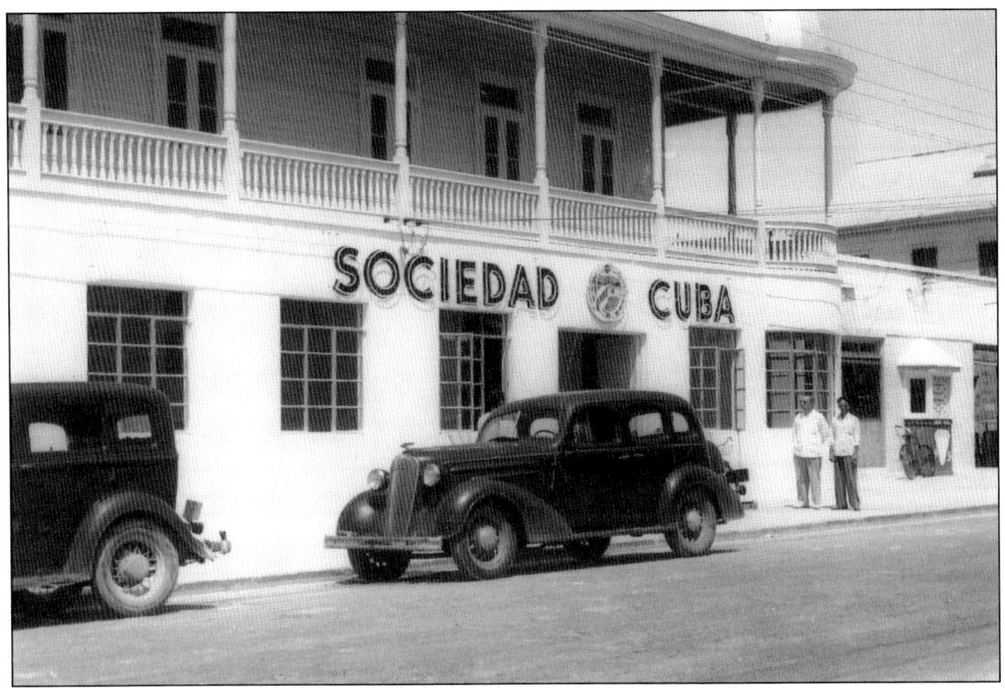

Two men, one of whom wears a traditional Cuban *guayabera* shirt, stand outside the Sociedad de Cuba (also known as the Cuban Club) at 1108 Duval Street. In 1900, Cubans in Key West constructed this building to house a social club. Here, members could read, play chess and dominoes, and socialize. There were also dances and parties in the second-floor ballroom. (Courtesy of Monroe County Library, Key West.)

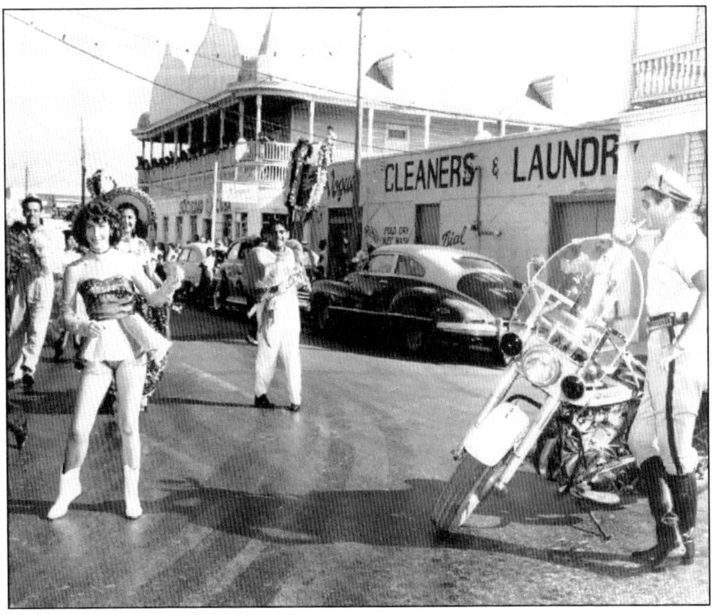

Comparsa dancers whirl jubilantly down Duval Street, with the Cuban Club in the background. Key West's first comparsa dance troupe, Los Dandys de Boza, was organized in 1938 by Abelardo Boza and performed for over five decades. The traditional Cuban comparsa dance usually takes place in a long conga-like line to Afro-Cuban tunes and beating drums, bongos, congas, timbales, and cowbells. (Courtesy of Monroe County Library, Key West.)

Eight

Parades

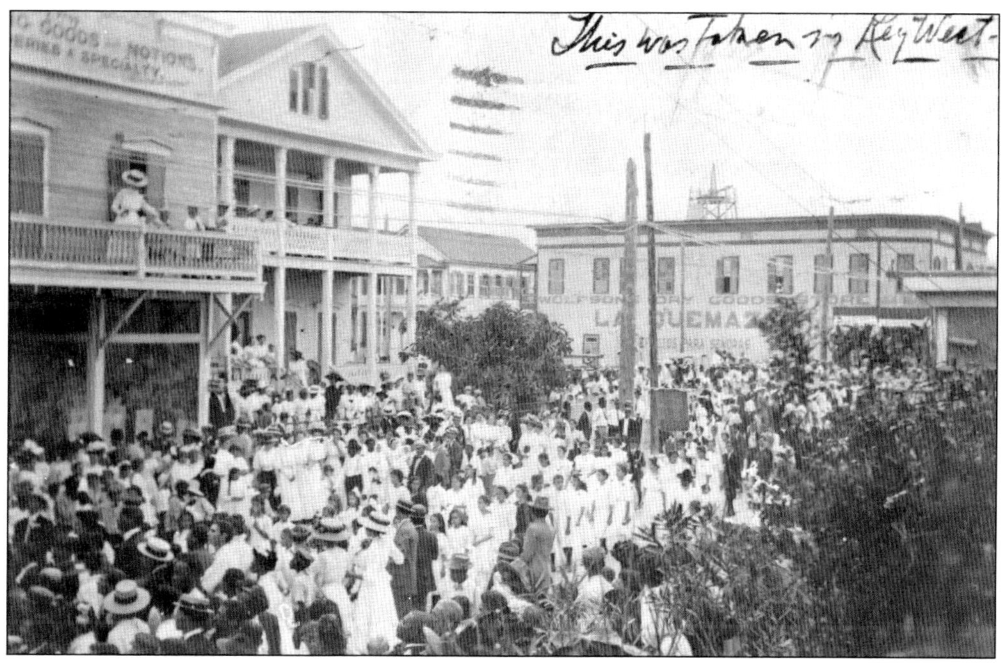

Since the 19th century, residents and visitors have been turning out in droves to see military personnel, beauty queens, school bands, and revelers of every kind make their way down Key West's central avenue. From presidential processions to fantastical bacchanals, Duval Street loves its parades. In this early 20th century image, Key Westers jam the street and its balconies for an unidentified occasion. (Courtesy of Monroe County Library, Key West.)

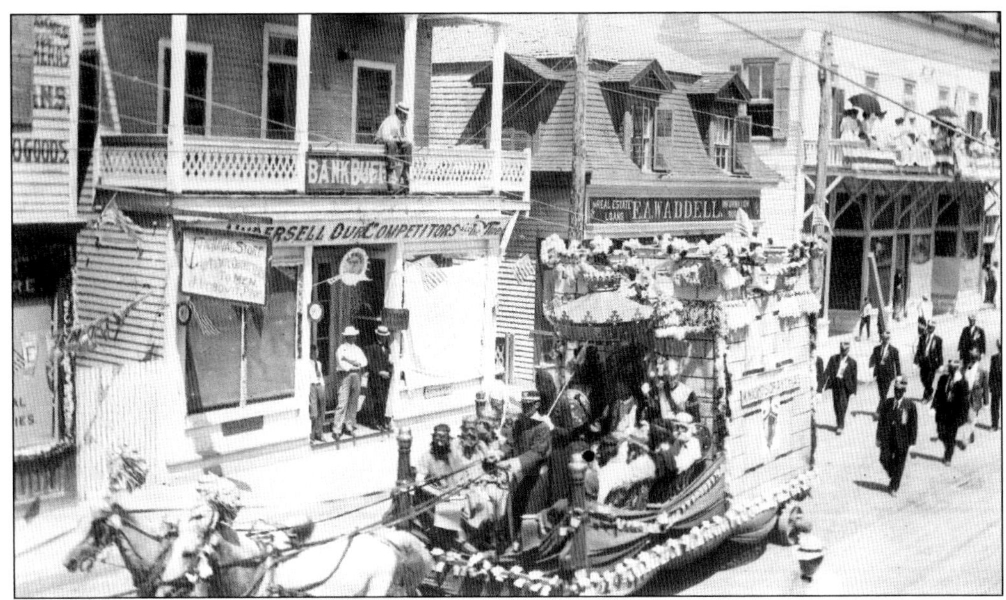

In the early 1900s, costumed Knights of Pythias process past the 100 block of Duval Street in a cart pulled by two horses. Founded in 1864, the fraternal order of the Knights of Pythias focuses on the values of friendship, charity, and benevolence. In the background, the Old Customs House can be seen; at the time, it housed Waddell's real estate office. (Courtesy of Monroe County Library, Key West.)

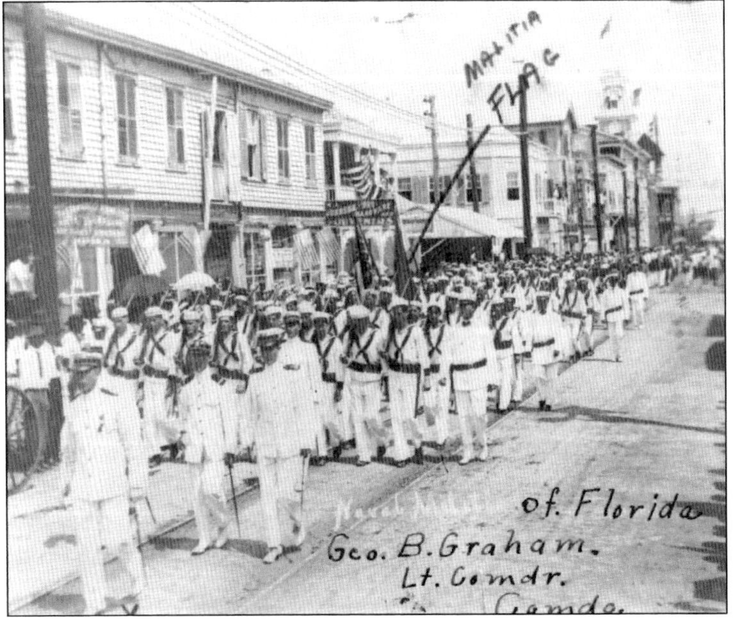

The Naval Militia of Florida marches down Duval Street in January 1912. This parade celebrated the arrival of the Florida East Coast Railway's first train. Finally, the island had a direct transportation link to the mainland. The sailors are coming from the direction of Front Street heading south-southeast. Beneath their polished shoes are the rails for Key West's electric streetcars. (Courtesy of Monroe County Library, Key West.)

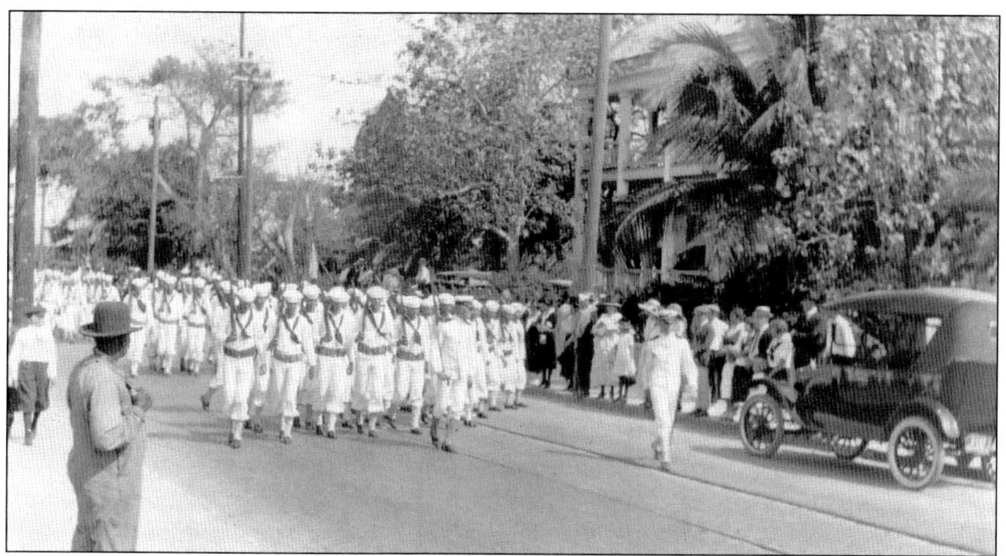

On November 11, 1918, bystanders watch the Victory Day parade, which celebrated the end of World War I. The war began in 1914; the United States entered the fray in April 1917. A total of 110,000 Americans perished, and the declaration of peace led to celebrations throughout the country. (Courtesy of Monroe County Library, Key West.)

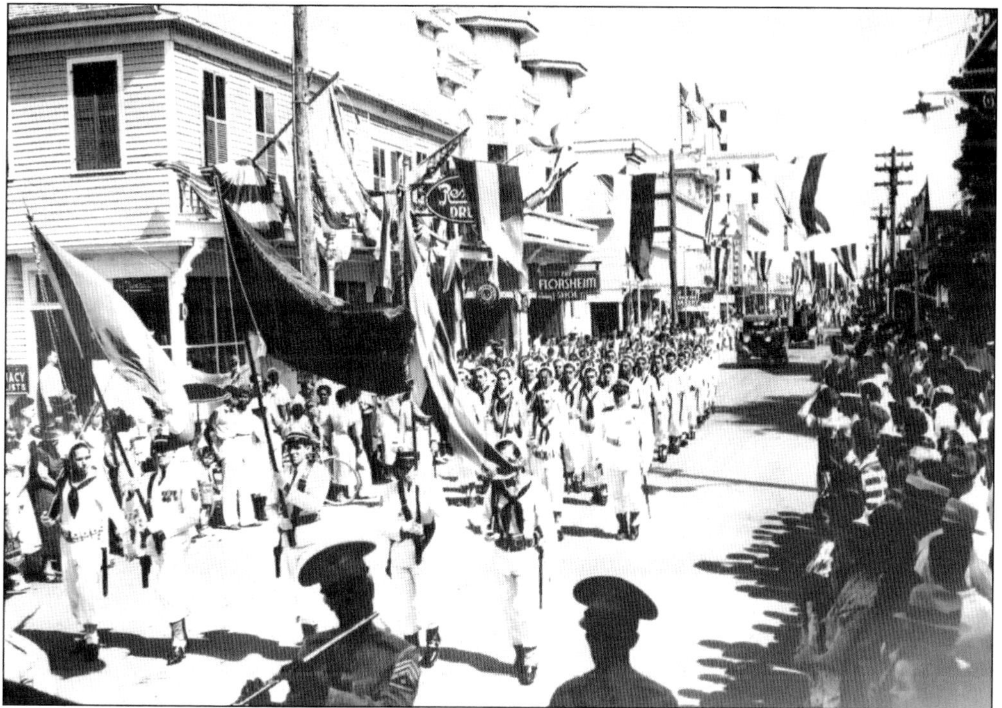

In this 1924 photograph, the Cuban navy parades by Duval's 500 block to celebrate the new San Carlos Institute building. Located at 516 Duval Street, the San Carlos was (and continues to be) an important establishment devoted to Cuban culture and heritage. On this sunny day, Key Westers have turned out in full force to be part of the excitement. (Courtesy of Monroe County Library, Key West.)

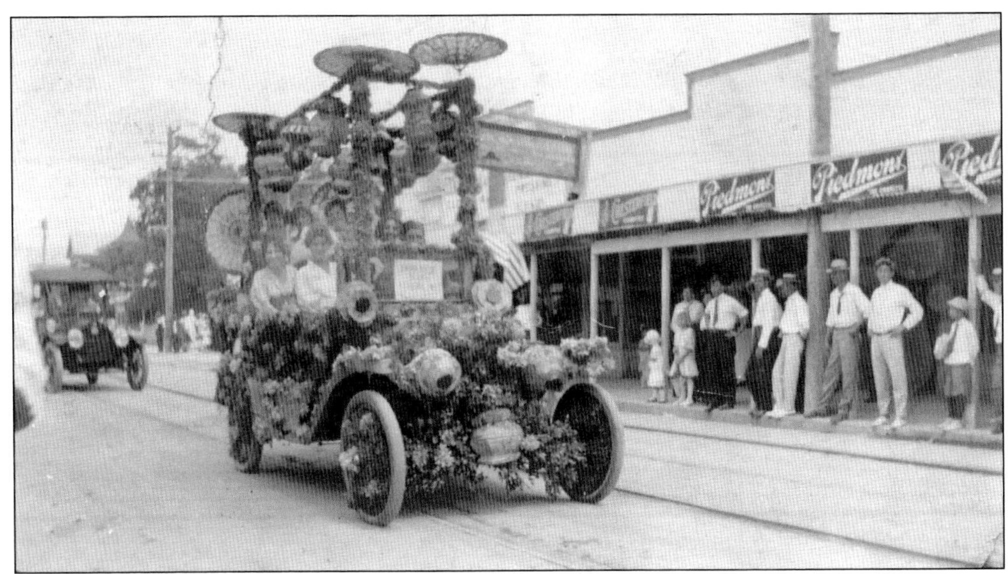

On Wednesday, August 18, 1926, citizens line Duval to watch as automobiles process down the street. This car has been lavishly decorated in a Japanese theme, with greenery, paper umbrellas, and lanterns. A sign attached to the front of the car reads "Japanese Booth/Athletic Meet," which gives a clue about the occasion. The smiling young women are dressed in kimonos. (Courtesy of Monroe County Library, Key West.)

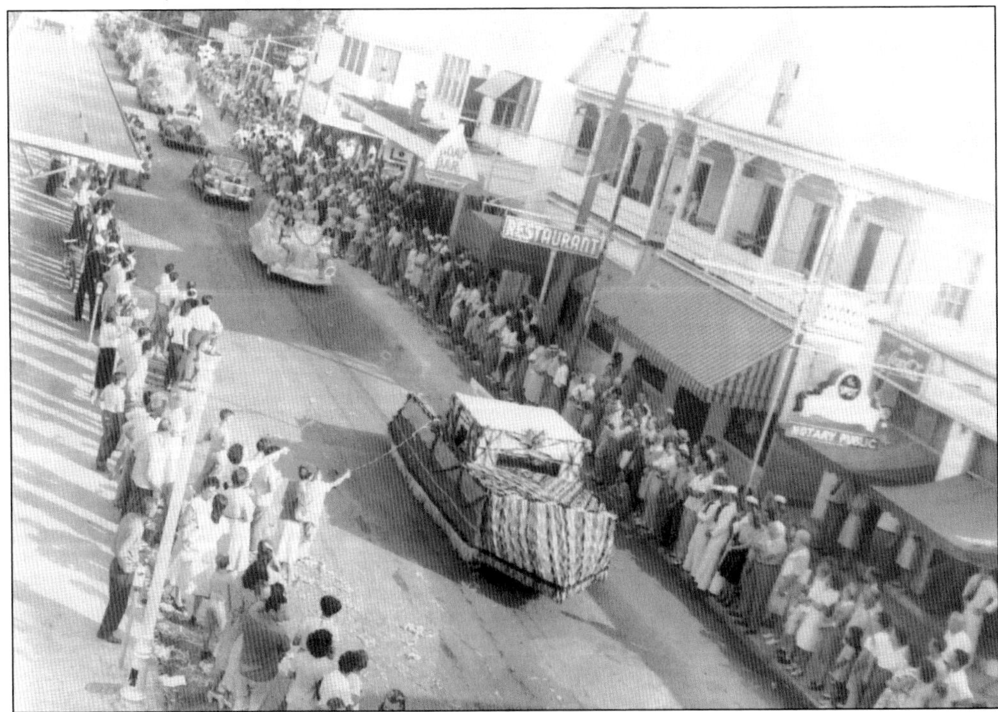

Floats roll through the 500 block of Duval Street during the American Legion parade of 1946. Key West had played an important role as a Navy base during World War II; memories of war and its losses were still very fresh. On the right is the Boat Bar, a popular hangout for sailors and civilians. (Courtesy of Monroe County Library, Key West.)

These young musicians are playing their trumpets, drums, and oboes in an American Legion parade. To the right is the Kress building, a department store built in 1912. Judging from the reindeer banner strung across the street, this parade probably took place in December. (Courtesy of Monroe County Library, Key West.)

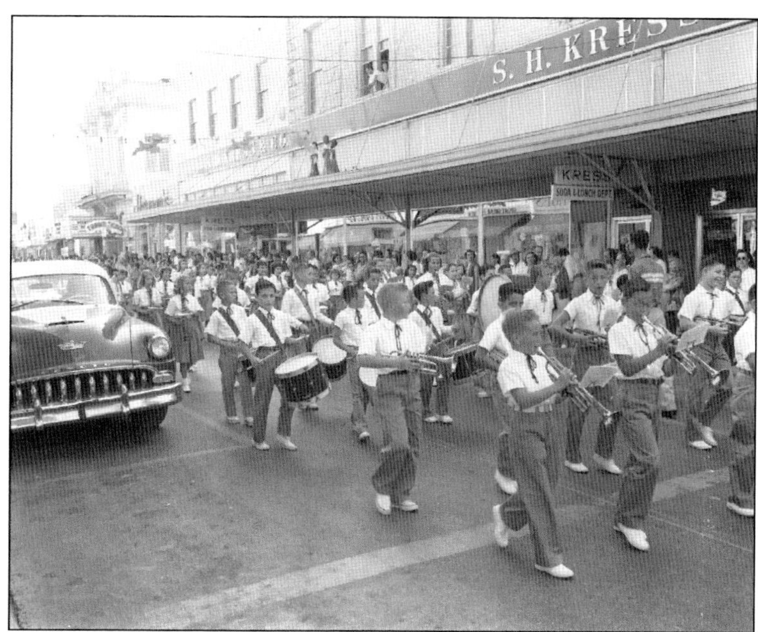

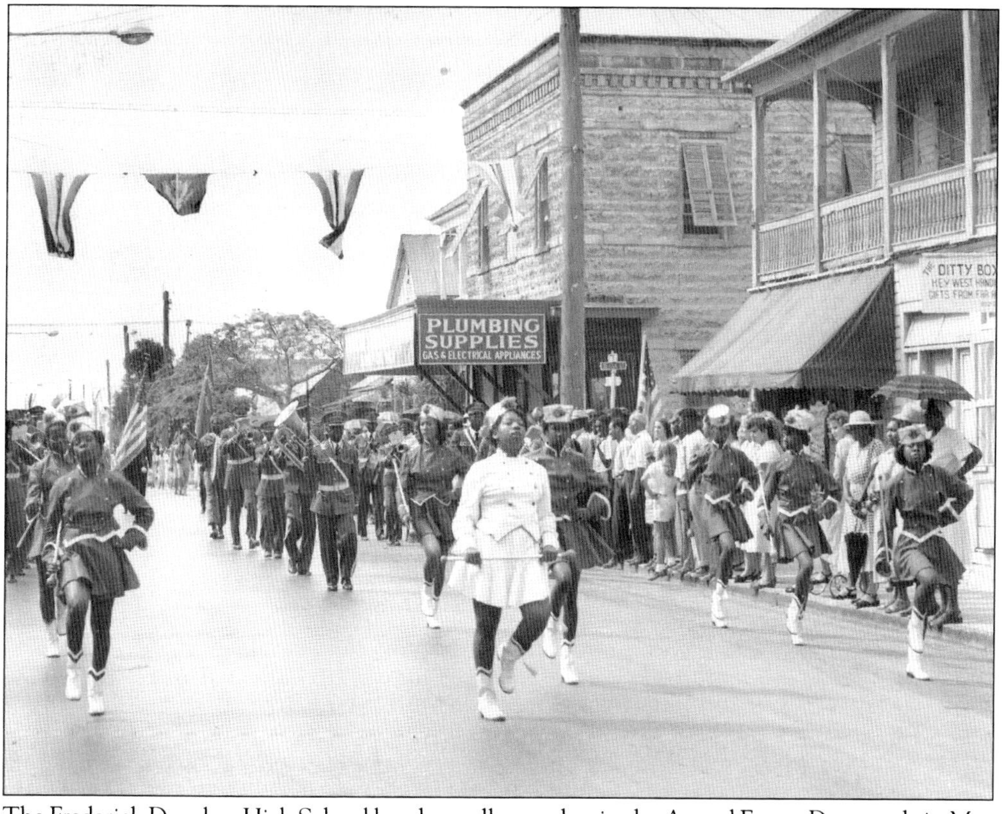

The Frederick Douglass High School band proudly marches in the Armed Forces Day parade in May 1950. With hand-me-down textbooks and limited resources, Douglass High School was attended by African American students in the days of segregation. The original Douglass School opened for Key West's children of color around 1870. (Courtesy of Monroe County Library, Key West.)

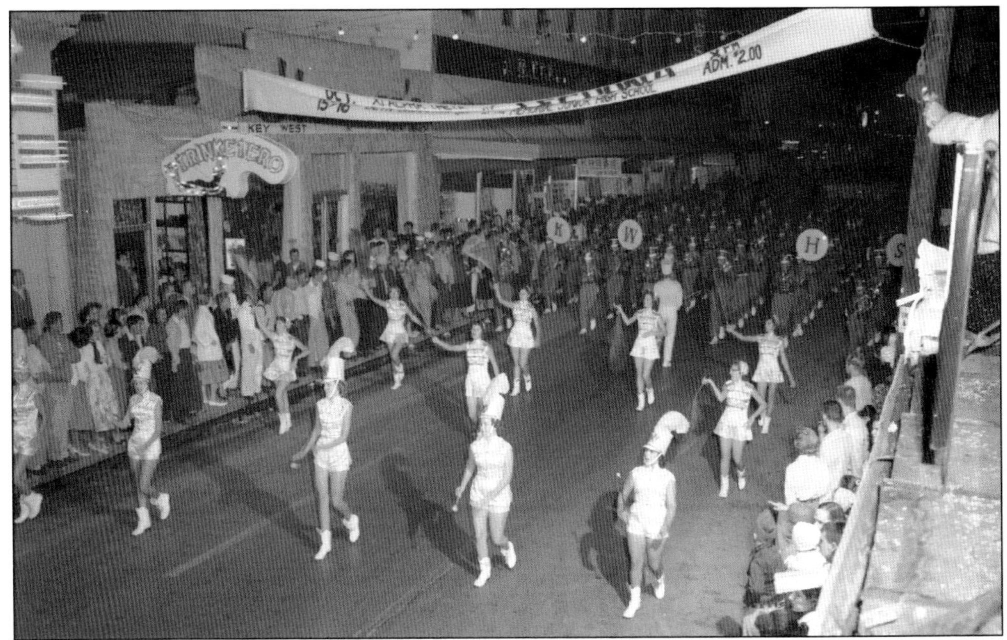

The sidewalks on Duval Street are packed on either side as the Key West High School majorettes in white satin uniforms and hats with plumes parade by. The school band marches just behind them. Key West High School first opened in 1906 and has an especially fitting, tropical mascot: the conch. (Courtesy of Monroe County Library, Key West.)

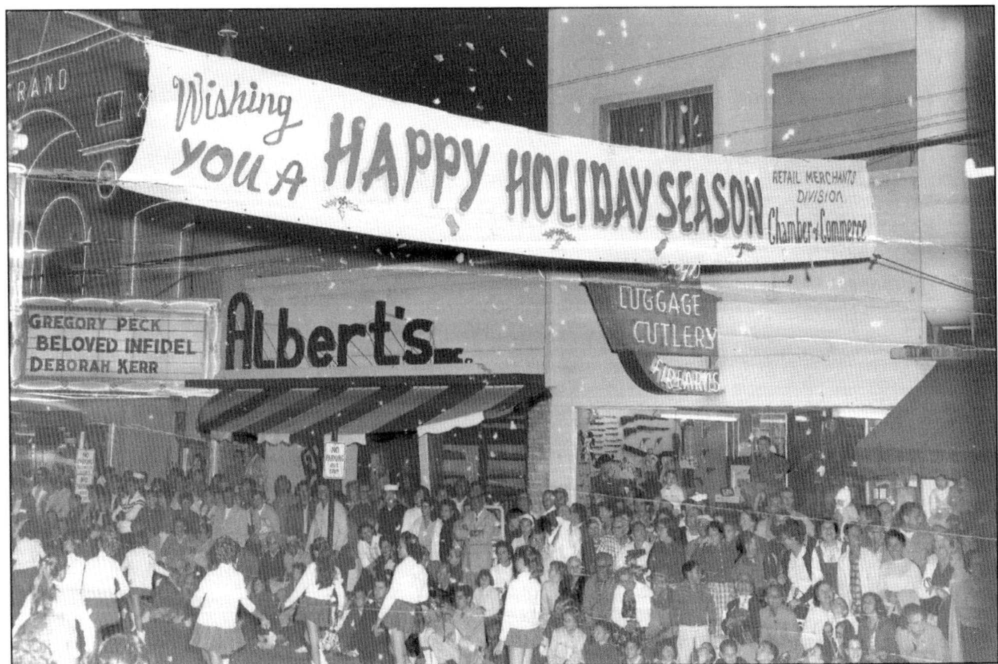

Another big crowd turns out for a parade during the holidays. Confetti floats through the air as girls perform their well-rehearsed moves. The movie marquee on the left advertises *Beloved Infidel*, a Gregory Peck and Deborah Kerr film released in 1959. (Courtesy of Monroe County Library, Key West.)

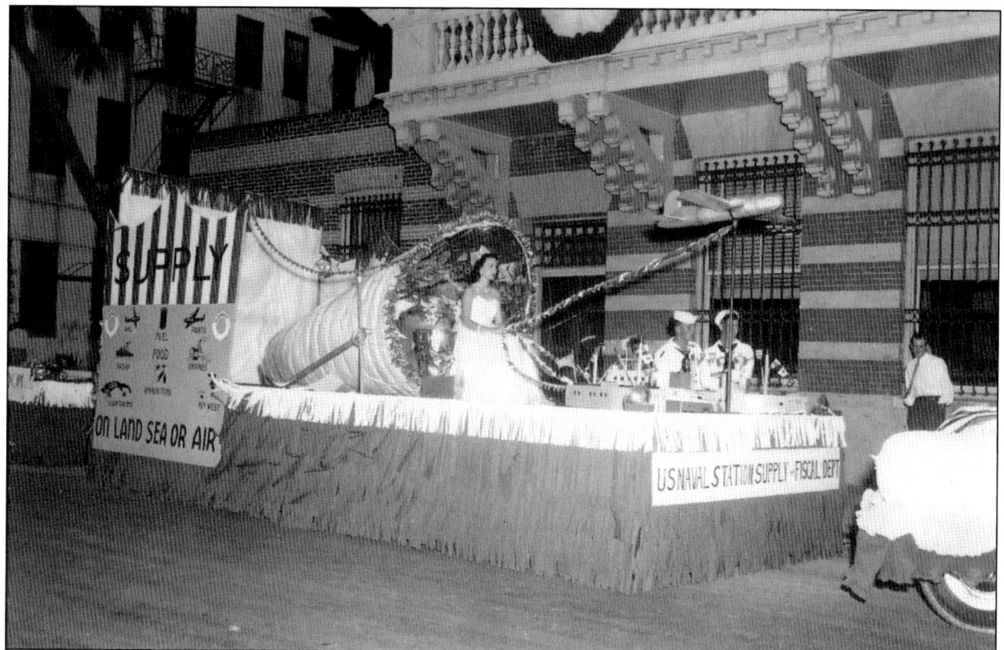

In 1960, a young woman in an elegant gown rides atop a fairly elaborate float celebrating the naval supply station. Models of ships and an airplane have been added to the float for effect. In the background, the distinctive striped brickwork of the First National Bank building can be seen at 94 Duval Street. (Courtesy of Monroe County Library, Key West.)

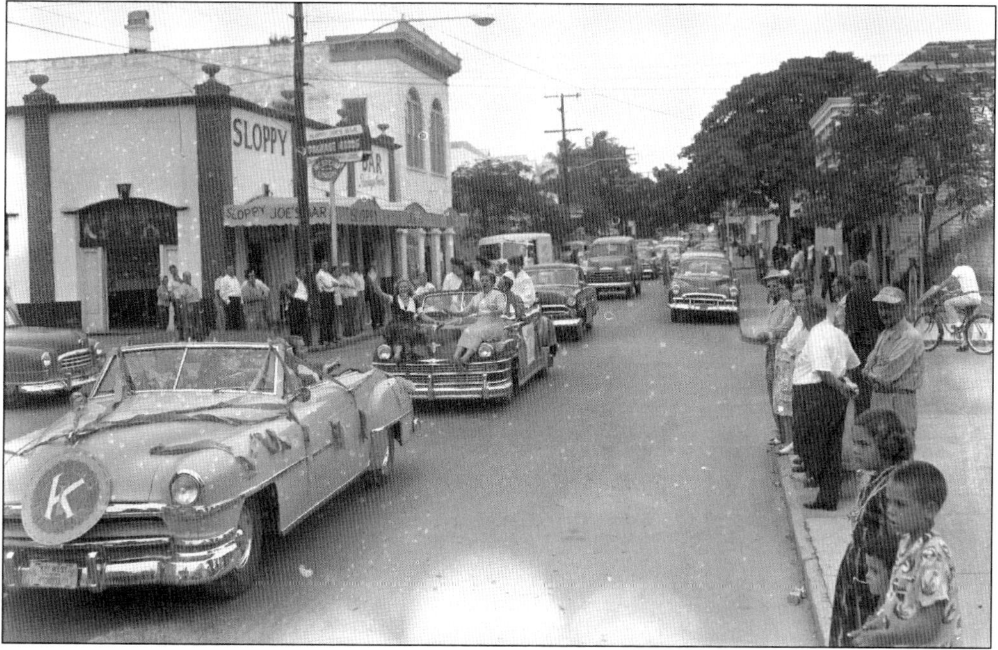

Some parades featured fancy costumes and carefully crafted floats, while others were more impromptu affairs. Here, cars sweep past Sloppy Joe's bar around 1960. The first automobile bears a Key Club insignia; two young women ride precariously on the hood of the second car. (Courtesy of Monroe County Library, Key West.)

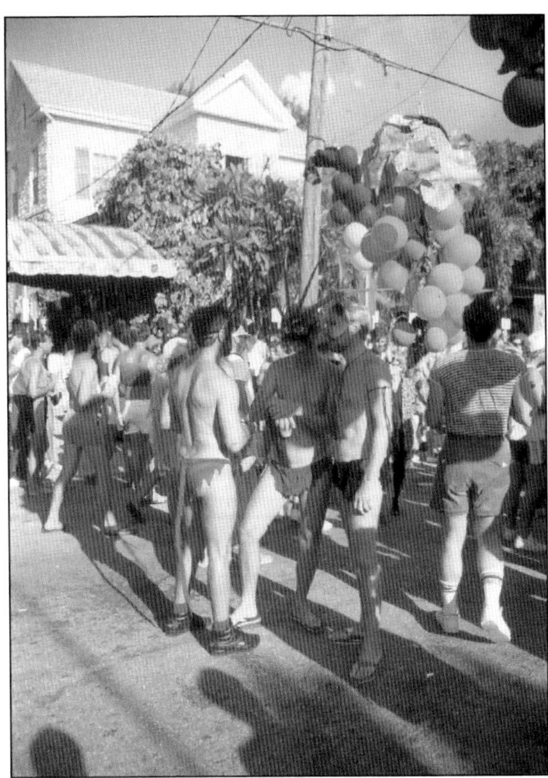

Scantily dressed men take time to chat during Fantasy Fest in 1988. Of all the parades that Duval Street has seen, few if any could outdo Fantasy Fest's wild abandon. During the 10-day extravaganza, a Conch King and Queen are elected, and money is raised for AIDS Help, a local organization that assists those with HIV. (Courtesy of Monroe County Library, Key West.)

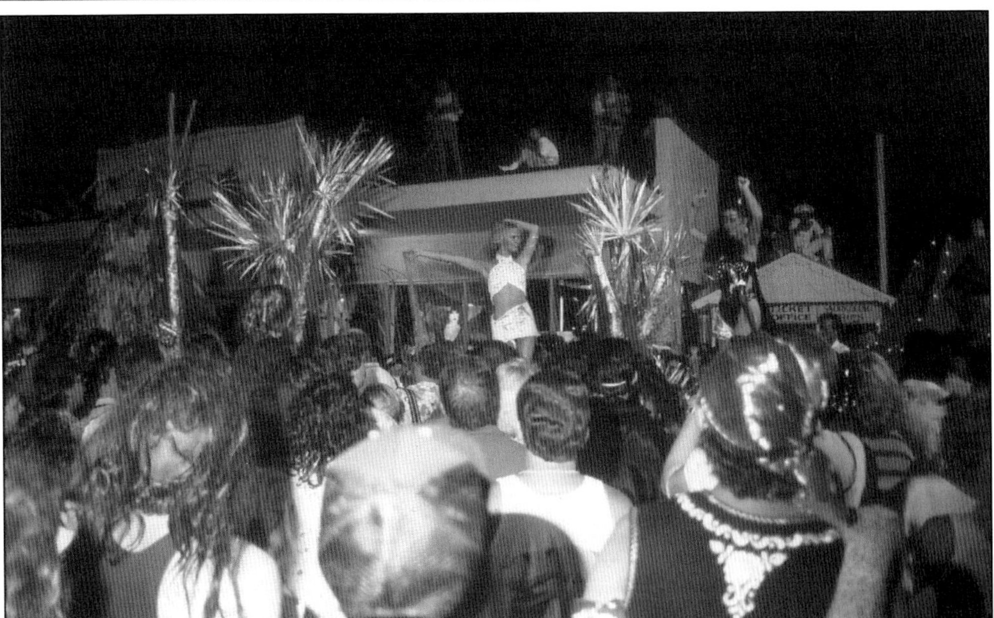

Two women dance for a crowd on Duval Street during the 1988 Fantasy Fest. Ever since Tony Falcone and Bill Conkle started the event in 1979, Fantasy Fest has turned a previously slow October into one of Key West's prime months for tourism. Fantasy Fest parades are another continuing chapter in this historic avenue that cuts clear across the island's Old Town. (Courtesy of Monroe County Library, Key West.)

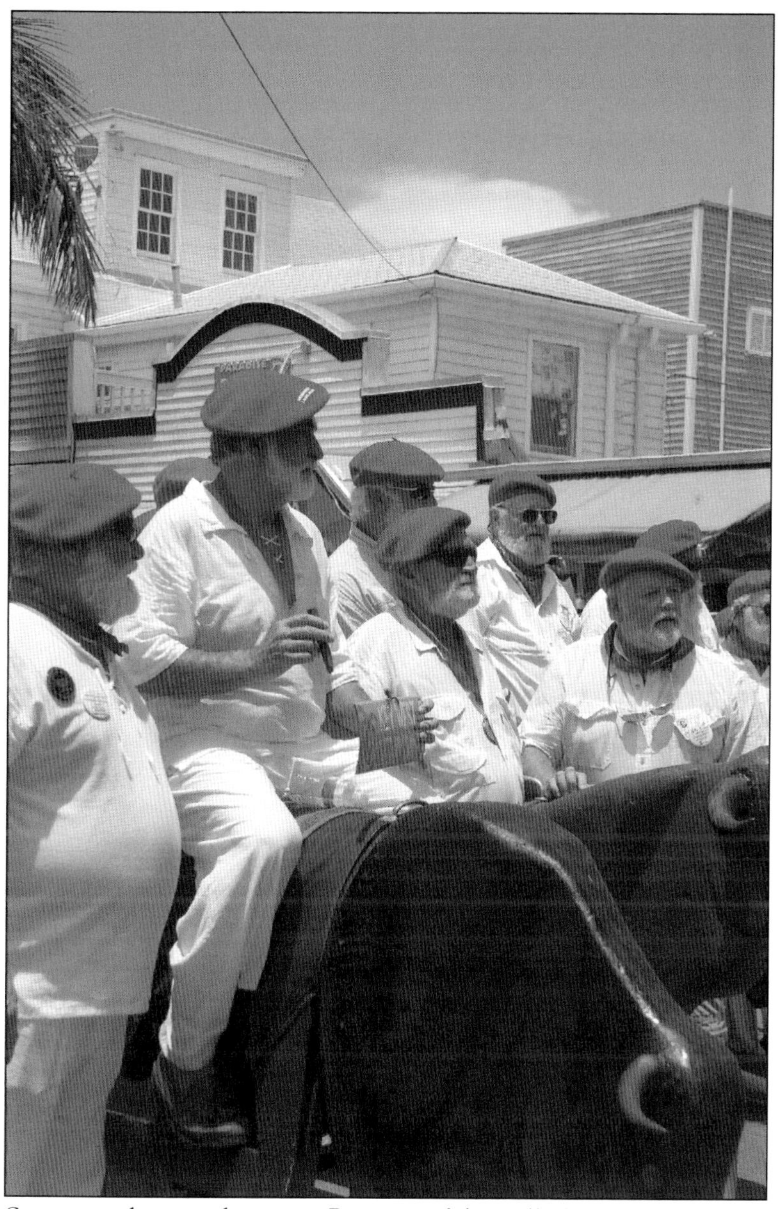

Pamplona, Spain, may have its dangerous Running of the Bulls, but Duval Street offers its own wonderfully wacky version, as shown in this photograph. Unlike in Pamplona (a city immortalized in Hemingway's *The Sun Also Rises*), the "bulls" moving down Duval Street are man-made, and there's no danger of being trampled underfoot. Instead, during the annual Hemingway Days, the bearded men participating in the Ernest Hemingway look-alike contest parade by at a tranquil pace, some with cigars in hand. Duval Street's Running of the Bulls whimsically pays homage to the writer's colorful life, from his time spent in Pamplona to his legendary sessions at Sloppy Joe's. This parade cannot help but remind residents and visitors of Duval Street's history as an oasis for artists, writers, musicians, and dreamers. The street has long acted as a stage upon which people can act out their hopes and fantasies. While Duval inevitably changes with each new generation, people's affection for this unique, island street never fades. (Courtesy of Erin Borrini, CC BY 2.0 license/Flickr.)

Bibliography

Bishop, Elizabeth and Robert Giroux, ed. *One Art: Letters*. New York, NY: Farrar, Straus & Giroux, 1995.

Born, George Walter. *Preserving Paradise: The Architectural Heritage and History of the Florida Keys*. Charleston, SC: The History Press, 2006.

Browne, Jefferson B. *Key West: The Old and the New*. St. Augustine, FL: The Record Company, 1912.

Burke, J. Wills. *The Streets of Key West: A History through Street Names*. Sarasota, FL: Pineapple Press, 2014.

Caemmerer, Alex. *The Houses of Key West*. Sarasota, FL: Pineapple Press, 1992.

Cox, Christopher R. *A Key West Companion*. New York, NY: St. Martin's Griffin, 1983.

Devlin, Albert J. and Nancy Marie Patterson Tischler. *The Selected Letters of Tennessee Williams*, Vol. 1: 1920–1945. New York, NY: New Directions, 2002.

Kennedy, Stetson. *Grits & Grunts: Folkloric Key West*. Sarasota, FL: Pineapple Press, 2008.

Merrick, George. "Pre-Flagler Influences on the Lower Florida East Coast." *Tequesta* 1, no. 1 (March 1941): 1-10.

Ogle, Maureen. *Key West: History of an Island of Dreams*. Gainesville, FL: University Press of Florida, 2006.

Poyo, Gerald E. *Exile and Revolution: Jose D. Poyo, Key West, and Cuban Independence*. Gainesville, FL: University Press of Florida, 2014.

Wells, Sharon. *Sloppy Joe's Bar: The First Fifty Years*. Key West, FL: Key West Saloon, 1983.

White, Louise V. and Nora K. Smiley. *History of Key West: Today and Yesterday*. St. Petersburg, FL: Great Outdoors Publishing, 1959.

Wilkinson, Jerry. Florida Keys History Museum. www.keyshistory.org. Accessed November 15, 2016.

Windhorn, Stan and Wright Langley. *Yesterday's Key West*. Miami, FL: E.A. Seemann Publishing, 1973.

About the Organization

The Historic Florida Keys Foundation, headquartered in the Old City Hall in Key West, promotes historic preservation in the Florida Keys through education, advocacy, collaboration, and stewardship. In 1972, the Florida legislature established the Historic Key West Preservation Board as a branch of state government, later renaming it the Historic Florida Keys Preservation Board to reflect the expansion of its mission to all of Monroe County. Over the decades, the foundation's efforts have assisted with the preservation of important heritage sites throughout the Florida Keys.

Since 1981, the foundation has presented awards to recognize excellence for preservation, restoration, and rehabilitation of important heritage buildings in the Florida Keys. The Historic Florida Keys Foundation also receives ongoing financial support from Monroe County in exchange for assisting their Historic Preservation program. The foundation leases three historic, state-owned properties: Old City Hall, the Armory, and the Oldest House, which is located on Duval Street. Directed by Dr. Diane Silvia, this private nonprofit organization is dedicated to expanding its historic programming and stewardship for years to come. To learn more about the foundation's awards and recent projects, visit www.historicfloridakeys.org.